Becoming Political

Becoming Political

Spinoza's Vital Republicanism and the Democratic Power of Judgment

CHRISTOPHER SKEAFF

University of Chicago Press
Chicago and London

The University of Chicago Press, Chicago 60637
The University of Chicago Press, Ltd., London

Published 2018
Printed in the United States of America

27 26 25 24 23 22 21 20 19 18   1 2 3 4 5

ISBN-13: 978-0-226-55547-8 (cloth)
ISBN-13: 978-0-226-55550-8 (e-book)
DOI: https://doi.org/10.7208/chicago/9780226555508.001.0001

Library of Congress Cataloging-in-Publication Data

Names: Skeaff, Christopher, author.
Title: Becoming political : Spinoza's vital republicanism and the democratic power of judgment / Christopher Skeaff.
Description: Chicago ; London : University of Chicago Press, 2018. | Includes bibliographical references and index.
Identifiers: LCCN 2017041004 | ISBN 9780226555478 (cloth : alk. paper) | ISBN 9780226555508 (e-book)
Subjects: LCSH: Spinoza, Benedictus de, 1632–1677. | Judgment—Political aspects.
Classification: LCC B3998 .S528 2018 | DDC 320.01—dc23
LC record available at https://lccn.loc.gov/2017041004

∞ This paper meets the requirements of ANSI/NISO Z39.48–1992 (Permanence of Paper).

Contents

Acknowledgments

I am pleased to acknowledge my debts to—and community with—numerous others who helped this project evolve from a tangle of impressions to a finished book. I owe my first and greatest intellectual debt to Miguel Vatter, who inspired me to pursue research on Spinoza and offered crucial orientation as I began that work. Several years later, in the early days of drafting a book manuscript, I had the good fortune to resume a dialogue with Miguel that gave new life to the project and enabled me to see it to fruition. I am deeply grateful for his insight and generosity at each stage. My time at Northwestern University opened my eyes to what theory can do, and in many ways afforded me an education into the problem of "becoming political." I am also grateful to have learned from Bonnie Honig, Sara Monoson, Lars Tønder, and Linda Zerilli, among the many other participants in Northwestern's wider critical and political theory community.

At the University of Michigan, where the book first took shape, I was sustained, enlightened, and encouraged by outstanding colleagues working across a range of disciplines. For thought-provoking comments and conversation, I thank Pamela Brandwein, Celeste Brusati, Lisa Disch, Hussein Fancy, Andreas Gailus, George Hoffmann, Robert Jansen, Miranda Johnson, Valerie Kivelson, Mika LaVaque-Manty, Anne Manuel, Sara McClelland, Lars Rensmann, Andrew Ross, Arlene Saxonhouse, Jennifer Solheim, Johannes von Moltke, Silke-Maria Weineck, Elizabeth Wingrove, and Mariah Zeisberg. The Michigan Society of Fellows and the Department of Political Science, my two academic homes at the U of M, provided first-rate institutional support. Warm thanks to Donald Lopez, Linda Turner, and all the MSF Fellows, especially the incoming junior cohort of 2009, for sharing ideas, advice, and good cheer. Profound thanks also to my political theory colleagues for adopting me as one of their own. I am particularly indebted to Lisa Disch, Mika LaVaque-Manty, and Elizabeth Wingrove. Lisa organized a manuscript workshop early on and helped me to fine-tune my book prospectus at a key moment. Mika consistently practiced what he preached, facilitating my personal and professional autonomy in countless ways. Elizabeth remained a tireless and empathic advocate as well as an extraordinarily attentive reader of my work.

I am much obliged to several other colleagues whose insightful comments enriched my thinking and writing. Special thanks to Samuel Chambers, Demetra Kasimis, Moira Killoran, William Clare Roberts, Hasana Sharp, Lars Tønder, David Lay Williams, and Hent de Vries for extended conversations about some portion or incarnation of this project. An additional thanks to four anonymous readers, two of whom offered helpful questions and suggested revisions on an early, partial submission of the manuscript, and two of whom provided perceptive and highly constructive commentary on the complete manuscript. Many thanks also to Edwin Curley for sharing with me working drafts of his second volume of *Spinoza's Collected Works.*

At the University of Chicago Press, my deepest thanks go to Elizabeth Branch Dyson for her unflagging enthusiasm and expert guidance at every step. Additional thanks to Benjamin Balskus, Rachel Kelly, Jo Ann Kiser, Dylan Montanari, and Mark Reschke, among others at the Press, for their help with the editing, production, and marketing processes.

An earlier version of chapter 1 was published as "Judgment beyond Jurisdiction: Spinoza's 'Freedom to Philosophize' and the Politics of Immunity," *Law, Culture and the Humanities* 12, no. 3 (2016): 766–86. Chapter 5 and the coda rework some ideas that originally appeared in "'Citizen Jurisprudence' and the People's Power in Spinoza," *Contemporary Political Theory* 12, no. 3 (2013): 146–65.

In the course of working on this book, I have benefited immensely from the camaraderie, curiosity, and care of remarkable friends. They include Lindsay Aagaard, Philip Baker, Jean-François Godbout, Andrew Kerner and Alison Roth-Kerner, Danielle and Mika LaVaque-Manty, Jake Matatyaou, Sara McClelland, Chris Nelson, John Roos and Katherine Weider-Roos, Lee Seymour, Blair Stransky, and Amy Vail. In addition to friendship of the finest caliber, Benjamin Healy provided clutch edits on the penultimate drafts of chapters 1 and 2. A very special thanks also to Demetra Kasimis for years of close reading, keen listening, commiseration, and comedy. Emily Terrell and Shelly Barnett offered the best child care a parent could wish for, especially one who is writing a book. I must also thank Ellen and George Galland, who offered the best child care a grandchild—or three—could wish for. One of the joys of returning to the Chicago area, where I completed the book, lay in finding new community, intellectual and otherwise. I thank those in the inaugural cohort of the Fundamentals of Psychoanalytic Thought program at the Chicago Institute for Psychoanalysis for their personal and professional generosity, and for nourishing my sense of possibility as I began another life chapter.

I wish to extend heartfelt thanks to my family, who has seen me through it all. A writing accountability routine with my sister, Karen Skeaff, helped me to complete the book and, happily, brought us into closer touch. I am forever grateful for her example and forever hopeful that I might approximate her writerly creativity. For their love and support from day one, and for sparking in me a passion for learning, I thank my parents, Susan and Douglas Skeaff. Finally, to Anna Galland and our children, Sadie, Elena, and Will, I give the greatest thanks—for their patience, affection, and life-affirming presence. This book is for them.

Abbreviations

Works by Spinoza

E	*Ethics* (*Ethica*)
Ep	*Letters* (*Epistola*)
KV	*Short Treatise on God, Man, and His Well-Being (Korte Verhandeling van God, de Mensch, en des Zelfs Welstand*)
TIE	*Treatise on the Emendation of the Intellect* (*Tractatus de Intellectus Emendatione*)
TP	*Political Treatise* (*Tractatus Politicus*)
TTP	*Theological-Political Treatise* (*Tractatus Theologico-Politicus*)

References to the *Ethics*

Roman numeral = part
ax = axiom
app = appendix
c = corollary
def = definition
def aff = definition of the affects
d = demonstration
ex = explanation
L = lemma
p = proposition
prol = prolegomenon
post = postulate
pref = preface
s = scholium

Notes on Citations

Quotations are from Edwin Curley, ed. and trans., *The Collected Works of Spinoza*, vols. 1–2.

References to the KV cite the part, chapter, and section numbers introduced by Sigwart and adopted by Curley (e.g., KV 1.3.7).

References to the TIE cite the paragraph numbers introduced by Bruder and adopted by Curley (e.g., TIE 1).

References to the TP and TTP cite the chapter and paragraph numbers introduced by Bruder and adopted by Curley (e.g., 4.2).

Introduction

Judging Democracy

Democracy today stands judged before a tribunal of professional opinion-makers. And the people are to blame. Deep-seated racism and chronic ignorance, anti-establishment fury and utopian enthusiasm, social media compulsion and distraction sickness, say the professionals, all variously conspire to subvert the aims of those advanced post-industrial states presently serving as democracy's global stewards. The basic charge is that an excess of democratic life—whether populism on one side or individualism on the other—imperils good democratic government.[1] By the same logic, a good democratic government properly so-called is one sufficiently limited or constitutional in its form and limiting in its function: able to neutralize the hyperactivity of democratic society and to provide security from a range of political and economic threats.[2]

The latest denunciations of hyperdemocracy are noteworthy less for their caricaturish portrayal of an ill-informed and hateful populace—or, conversely, for their flattery of elites—than for the received wisdom that they embody. In particular, they perpetuate a certain image of political judgment, according to which popular opinions about public matters should ideally resemble the technocratic rationality espoused by governing institutions. This is a compelling image. It accounts, in part, for the pressure that potential voters experience, especially during election season, to exhibit a capacity for calculating the costs and benefits of candidates' proposals for health care, the economy, national security, social security, education, immigration, and so on. How to balance the budget? How to even understand the economy? Which social programs should take priority, and which representatives best advance them? It is no wonder if people often feel as though they are preparing to hand over the essential work of politics to those who claim professional competence in that domain. The message is clear: expert judgment is an entitlement to govern, and the members of a democratic society play their part when they choose the most qualified rulers.

Today's concern-trolling critics of the *demos* can claim, with at least some plausibility, that they are summoning the perennial insights of the Western tradition for the age of Twitter.[3] After all, when viewed from the perch of canonical political philosophy, questions about the meaning of democracy and judgment are also ultimately questions about qualifications for ruling. Ancient philosophers such as Plato and Aristotle associate political judgment with either a superior theoretical knowledge of politics or a practical wisdom of applying to political life the right principles at the right time. Notwithstanding the significant differences between these and other premodern thinkers, a key commonality they share is that their concepts operate within the space of "natural law," that is, an order of universal moral precepts that transcends the historicity of politics. Natural law distinguishes right from wrong and justifies those "prudent" human actions that conform to its principles. It grounds the prudential judgment of those few wise men capable of accessing, and making palatable for the common people, unpopular truths about natural hierarchy and the duties required for collective well-being. However, with the shift to political and scientific modernity, the story goes, the transcendent principles of natural law are thrown into crisis, giving rise to a problem of judgment, elaborated in various ways by thinkers from Hobbes to Habermas as an issue of adjudicating value conflicts in the absence of shared or preestablished criteria.[4]

The trouble with this canonical story, as theorists such as Arendt, Rancière, Zerilli, and Urbinati have shown, is that it tends from the outset to prejudge democratic politics and judgment from the perspective of the supposed risk they pose to truth or "correct outcomes" (to adopt the more current expression).[5] In similar fashion, even when it is not outright denigrating the opinions of ordinary people, contemporary political theory typically grants the "people-judge" little more than a highly formalized role in determining the fundamental priorities and direction of the polity.[6] So, for instance, the formation and circulation of public opinion is said to be democratic if it meets certain procedural norms of argumentation, or if it fulfills a supervisory role in the maintenance and justification of state sovereignty. Prevailing theory tends, in this way, to impose on democratic judgment a prescripted role, thereby obscuring how certain claims, communities, and practices acquire a political status and salience in the first place—how, for example, "Black Lives Matter" comes to be seen and heard (or not) as a fundamental call for justice rather than as the particular claim of an interest group, or how "economic" facts regarding wealth inequality become matters of common concern.

In scholarship as in punditry, the democratic character of judgment remains mostly a presupposition, something inferred from a set of assumptions about who may engage in deliberative practices, what sorts of issues elicit their judgment, and how judging ought to proceed. But what if it belongs precisely to the activity of democratic judgment to question such assumptions and to compose, each time anew, the very subjects, objects, and modes of politics that both conventional wisdom and prevailing theories take as given?

A Democratic Power

This book recuperates from Spinoza's thought a radically democratic proposition: judgment is the element in which a people generate and regenerate a political constitution or form of life in common. In the freedom of judging, individuals foster a joint capacity for self-organization and a complex, evolving interconnection as they raise, reflect on, and resolve basic questions of who and what counts as political. Just as crucially, in the practice of judging—of circulating, shaping, and differentiating the sentiments and sensibilities of collective intelligence—they forge political tools of dissensus, or self-*alteration.* If, for Spinoza, judging counts as the activity par excellence in which a people are powerful, this is because it enables them to contest the project of ruling and to demonstrate the political possibility of being equally free to articulate the terms of their association. Admittedly, such a proposition diverges from a more familiar view of democracy that treats popular judgment at best as a vehicle of rule, a means of defining and refining the common will. In *Becoming Political,* I draw out the evidence for Spinoza's decoupling of democratic judgment from sovereignty and government and I consider the implications—both for an understanding of Spinoza's political thought and, more indirectly, for the conceptual landscape of contemporary political theory.

Let me begin with some initial data. Spinoza does not so much thematize judgment on its own as treat it in the course of broader discussions of epistemology, anthropology, and politics. Very schematically, Spinoza's explicit statements on judgment fall into two categories: in his epistemology, a rejection of the idea that judgment is an operation of free will, and, in his political theory, a vindication of free judgment. The link between his denying that humans possess a free power to exercise or suspend judgment and his affirming the freedom of judgment in political life resides in Spinoza's anthropology of affect, and, specifically, his exploration of the "determination" of judgment.

In an elaboration of his conception of *conatus*, the endeavor of each thing to persevere in its being, Spinoza writes:

> When this striving (*conatus*) is related only to the mind, it is called will; but when it is related to the mind and body together, it is called appetite. This appetite, therefore, is nothing but the very essence of man, from whose nature there necessarily follow those things that promote his preservation. And so man is determined to do those things. . . . From all this, then, it is clear that *we neither strive for, nor will, neither want, nor desire anything because we judge it to be good; on the contrary, we judge something to be good because we strive for it, will it, want it, and desire it.* (E III p9s, my emphasis)

Moving quickly to show that familiar terms like "will" and "appetite" derive their meaning from the *conatus*, Spinoza insists here that judgments have determinate causes and conditions. In the process, he reverses the commonsense interpretation of the relationship between action and judgment: rather than judgment setting my efforts in motion, it is my endeavor, already underway—my inclinations and investments—that provokes my judgment.[7]

This position leads Spinoza to entertain the idea of an indefinite variety of judgments at play in society. "Different men," he observes, "can be affected differently by one and the same object; and one and the same man can be affected differently at different times by one and the same object." And because everyone "judges from his own affect what is good and what is bad, what is better and what is worse, it follows that men can vary as much in judgment as in affect" (E III p51s). In his *Theological-Political Treatise*, Spinoza takes the political measure of this seemingly infinite diversity of affects and judgments. Given that "men vary greatly in their mentality (*ingenium*), because one is content with these opinions, another with those, and because what moves one person to religion moves another to laughter," Spinoza argues, "each person must be allowed freedom of judgment and the power to interpret the foundations of faith according to his own mentality (*ingenium*)" (TTP pref 28). The question is what "freedom of judgment" means here if not the Cartesian power of a mind to exercise or suspend judgment at will. In essence, Spinoza answers that freedom of judgment means freedom from having to submit one's powers of intelligence—one's "mentality," or "complexion" (*ingenium*)—to the powers and pleasures of another. Politically, such freedom entails a right to think and to express oneself according to one's own complexion, which is to say, according to the continuous variation of one's affective life.

Gaining a feel for the fuller texture of judgment in Spinoza's thought requires much more than attending to his explicit citations of the term. It requires attention to how judgment operates and evolves as a concept in relation to other concepts—above all, democracy, an idea that Spinoza positions "at the essence of the emergence of politics," as one commentator aptly observes.[8] For despite the fact that Spinoza provides no systematic theory or explicit doctrine of judgment, I submit that a certain problem or proposition regarding the democratic power of judgment animates his major texts. This problem remains largely implicit, and so it needs to be posed, charted, articulated. Each chapter of *Becoming Political* revolves around concepts that help to provide such an articulation by giving a sense—a context, orientation, specificity—to this animating concern. In the process, each chapter offers a different perspective on the political meaning of judgment as it bears on questions of immunity, community, constitution, state, and democracy. Rather than solely explicate Spinoza's texts, I offer interpretations that mobilize and develop his thought by opening it up to a series of concerns that are crucial to political theory and practice today, questions that in some cases Spinoza did not and perhaps could not address. The original reading of Spinoza that I offer in each of the chapters is only possible thanks to these "external" theoretical elements that I introduce. At the same time, I am interested in making Spinoza's thought newly available to contemporary critical and political theory—not so much as a fixed archive of doctrines that might simply be applied to current theoretical problems, but rather as an open system of conceptual resources that can help to question prevailing terms of debate and to reformulate the key problems at stake.

Vital Republicanism

Given that Spinoza has no express theory or ready-made account of the democratic power of judgment, I rely on an approach that, roughly speaking, analyzes the conditions and components of that power and synthesizes them into a whole. For these purposes, I take as my key paradigm the idea of a "vital republicanism," by which I mean an approach to political life that makes law the means for a people's self-organization and that makes the vitality or jurisgenerative power of their judgments the true basis for rule of law. Let me briefly comment on each side of this organizing idea, beginning with republicanism. Consistent with what Miguel Vatter calls the modern tradition of "revolutionary" republicanism, Spinoza's political rationalism, as I read it, is oriented toward a critique of rule or domination and an affirmation of freedom as equal empowerment.[9] Critical as he is of all forms of rule, however, Spinoza does not believe that it can be eradicated so much as checked through institutional means such as law, and challenged through the extra-institutional pressures of informal public spheres. Put differently, Spinoza advances a constitutionalism that operates to combat social and structural domination by setting the state against itself. As I argue in chapters 3–5, he offers a theory of the state as a necessary but not sufficient component for a free political life: necessary for establishing the order and security for communal life to be possible but not sufficient for the free development of that life. The other necessary components, as I have suggested, include an autonomous rule of law and the people's constituent power of judgment, or democracy. Ultimately, this vital republicanism aims at creating a state that is constitutionally open to its deconstitution and reconstitution—open, that is, to a critique and internal transformation driven by constituents whose judgments generate new political rights, powers, and norms of living.

The "vital" dimension of his republicanism refers most broadly to Spinoza's theoretical effort to situate political life within a comprehensive naturalism, viz. a metaphysical conception of nature (or God) as the immanent cause of itself and all things. Starting from an account of this dynamic and infinitely productive being, Spinoza develops a theory of the natural right and power of individuals as finite modes or expressions of Nature/God's regulated production. "By the right of nature," he explains, "I understand the laws of nature themselves, or the rules according to which all things happen, i.e., the very power of nature. So the natural right of the whole of nature, and as a result, of each individual, extends as far as its power does" (TP 2.4). Spinoza's power-based understanding of natural right—articulated in metaphysical terms as the "endeavor" or *conatus* of each thing to preserve its being—has sparked endless debate over its political meaning and implications. Does Spinoza mean simply that might is right? Is he reducing norms to facts?

Crucial for my purposes is the differentiated view of power that Spinoza's doctrine of *conatus* illuminates. In contrast to Hobbes, who regards *conatus* solely as the individual's striving to preserve his existence, Spinoza posits an additional striving on the part of human individuals to persevere in becoming.[10] By virtue of their participation in the infinite power of nature (or the divine power of God), he contends, humans strive to bring about the greatest of self-transformations—changing corporeally into another body of maximal aptitude and mentally into a mind of maximal consciousness. "In this life, then, we endeavor especially that the infant's body may change . . . into another, capable of a great many things and related to a mind very much conscious of itself, of God, and of things" (E V p39s). Through his conception of natural right as power and perfection, Spinoza sets out a prudential or providential strategy whereby individuals transform themselves by transforming the conditions of their activity. When it is read alongside his writings on free judgment, law, and juridical constitutions, one can discern in Spinoza's thought an inner link between this natural prudence or strategy of *conatus* and the political capacity to create norms or rules of living that facilitate individuals' common empowerment.[11] Borrowing language from Canguilhem, I characterize such normatively creative power as vital normativity, and I show how it finds exemplary expression in a people's constituent power of judging—and thereby regenerating—the sense and scope of their common or radically public right.

Employing vital republicanism as the book's organizing idea allows me to foreground in my reading of Spinoza the interrelation of life and law, that is, of the *bio*political and the *juridico*-political dimensions of judgment conceived as a democratic freedom and power-in-common. And as much as I take "vital republicanism" to illuminate important and largely underappreciated features of Spinoza's political thought, I also take it to show the promise of doing political theory with Spinoza today. Thus the notion of "vital republicanism" designates both an interpretive thesis about Spinoza's thought and a theoretical line of argument that I begin to develop in relation to strains of contemporary critical and political theory. These include the theorizations of biopower and biopolitics found in thinkers such as Esposito, Negri, and Agamben, as well the neorepublican political theory developed in recent years by Skinner, Pettit, and Laborde, among others.[12] Situated with and against the biopolitical literature, the republican features of Spinoza's thought throw new light on the emancipatory role that law might play in the formulation of an affirmative biopolitics, which is fast becoming the signature contribution of the Italian school. By the same token, Spinoza's analyses of the psychosocial dynamics and forms of affective power at stake in the organization of individual and communal life—in a word, his treatment of the biopolitical substance of society—draws attention to a crucial feature of political association that neorepublican theory tends to overlook. In these ways and others, the "vital" and the "republican" aspects of Spinoza's thought can be productively brought out by and brought to bear on current theorizing.

I understand Spinoza's vital republicanism as signaling a way to decouple the democratic power of judging from the many images, institutions, and justifications of rule that stand in judgment over the becoming of political life. Spinoza, to be sure, does not simply banish sovereignty or government from politics any more than he simply rejects religion. As I show throughout the book, rather than negate or frontally oppose the logics and logistics of rule, Spinoza attempts always to convert them into more emancipatory forms of communal thought and action. My discussion of the different components of his vital republicanism consequently acquires an aspectival quality as I track the agonism or tension between domination and freedom that is operative in his conceptions of judgment, community, law, religion, state, and democracy. For this purpose, I employ many paired concepts such as jurisdiction and jurisprudence, assimilation and alteration, rule by law and rule of law, hierocracy and theocracy, constituted and constituent power. My point in using such binaries is not ultimately to reduce them to a central opposition but rather to broaden the scope and pluralize the perspectives on the democratic power of judgment.

Charting the Course

Chapter 1, "Judgment beyond Jurisdiction," interprets Spinoza's "freedom of philosophizing" (*libertas philosophandi*) as a term that poses the problem of the relationship between politics and judgment. Situating the idea of *libertas philosophandi* in the polemics of the period, I show how his treatment of the concept stages a basic conflict between two ways of envisioning and employing judgment politically. The state's sovereign authority to determine matters of public utility is a paradigmatic form of what I call "jurisdiction" in contrast to "jurisprudence," exemplified by citizens' right to "philosophize" or judge publicly the utility of the state's laws. With this bifocal vision, Spinoza shifts the terms of engagement between politics and judgment away from an exclusive focus on sovereignty—*who wields the supreme authority to decide controversies?*—and toward an inclusive focus on sovereignty and empowerment—*how might a people become free and equal judges of their common affairs*? Moreover, in dialogue with Roberto Esposito, I argue that Spinoza's treatment of free judgment—and the treatment it has received by his critics past and present—illustrates and clarifies the political dynamics at play in the modern conceptualization of freedom as an immunity.

Chapter 2, "Judgment in Common," explores the ontological status of judgment in Spinoza, unpacking the idea that judgment is inalienably common. In the first instance, this idea means that judgment belongs to an intrication of open systems or ecologies (psychic, social, biological) of affect. To conceptualize judgment in this radically relational way, Spinoza employs the concept of *ingenium*, or "complexion," which signifies something like an individual's characteristic sentiments and affective disposition. I argue that Spinoza's notion of complexion presents a common that is always, so to speak, in judgment. On this view, the common in any community cannot be divorced from a multiplicity of ways of interpreting, differentiating, evaluating, and, as a condition for all of these operations, *desiring*. With specific attention to the psychosocial mechanism that Spinoza calls the "imitation of the affects,"

I explore how individual "complexion" functions as a principle of judgment that acquires a differential application in and through competing strategies or social logics of mimetic desire. Hence the formulation "judgment in common" comes to mean that division, and, more specifically, conflict, is an intrinsic feature of community. The question then becomes, what kind of conflict? My answer is that Spinoza's account of mimetic desire presents an incommensurability between modes of imagining or prefiguring how a common world is at once shared and divided.

Chapter 3, "Constitution of Judgment," considers how Spinoza's thought illuminates the problem of sustaining the revolutionary or transformative power of a people to give themselves a political constitution. I elaborate the features of a Spinozist "constitution of judgment," understood as both a constituent power at work in a people's judgments and a fundamental law generated by these judgments. This republican conception of a constitution, which I develop through a reading of what Spinoza calls "natural divine law," is not so much a species of positive law as it is a regulative principle or immanent norm of a people's empowerment. It is an idea of a constitution that expresses, as a necessary truth, the way that humans achieve the perfection of their essences, of their specific virtues and powers, as citizens of a free people. However, this idea of a constitution of power, or perfect constitution, is not necessary in the sense that it determines what individuals will in fact do, for it exists only by virtue of judgments that actualize or enact it in singular circumstances. From Spinoza's perspective, it is ultimately the conative force of each thing—a law of nature and not the legal power and authority of the state—that grants and guarantees the right to make such judgments. In this sense, I argue, Spinoza shows that the right to participate in judging what belongs to an empowered people springs from natural law and targets human law, facilitating the adaptation of human legal orders to changing historical circumstances (evolution) as well as the innovation or internal transformation of such orders along more expansive, cosmopolitan dimensions (revolution).

Chapter 4, "State of Judgment," examines the constructive meanings that Spinoza accords to state and religion as they combine in a conception of civil religion that he develops over the course of the *Theological-Political Treatise.* I consider, in particular, Spinoza's analysis of and unmistakable praise for the ancient Hebrew "theocracy," which is a feature of the *Treatise* that commentators have accorded little theoretical (as opposed to historical) significance. I argue that Spinoza's treatment of ancient Israel becomes in TTP 17 a case study of how, to use a contemporary idiom, a people acquired and preserved a state of nondomination. Building on this case, Spinoza fashions a novel conception of civil religion that assigns to the universal moral core of scripture a political role as the source of public happiness and solidarity. The optic of civil religion, I suggest, helps to disaggregate the politically salient meanings of religion in Spinoza, and, in turn, to approach the vexed issue of the modern state's conceptual debt to religion less as an "either/or" question of dependence or independence than as a "both-and" question of interdependence along different (institutional, cultural, justificatory) dimensions.

Chapter 5, "Democracy of Judgment," employs the Spinozist notion of "citizen jurisprudence" as a conceptual tool for theorizing the internal relationship between democracy and judgment. Developing the jurisprudential line of thought that runs through the previous chapters, I present citizen jurisprudence as both the figure (as juridical right) and effect (as political potentiality) of democracy conceived in an expansive sense: not solely as a state form but as an activity of equally free individuals determining the sense and the scope of common affairs. Whereas prevailing theories of democracy see the people's judgment as a means of indirect control over government, thus assuming that the *telos* of such judgment is to justify state coercion, the concept of citizen jurisprudence illuminates a more radically democratic and dissensual practice of enunciating the terms of equal empowerment.

The Coda chapter reflects back on the main interpretive and theoretical threads of the book, gathering them together under the sign of a "right to problems." The chapter also considers how the promise of Spinoza's vital republicanism might be carried forward in contemporary theorizing: namely, by pursuing the generative interplay or "elective affinity" between modern republican thought and contemporary (biopolitical) theories of communal life.

1

Judgment beyond Jurisdiction

> Spinoza said in the very title of one of his political treatises that his ultimate aim in it was not political but the *libertas philosophandi.*
>
> HANNAH ARENDT

So said Arendt in the course of a lecture on Kant's political philosophy.[1] She offered the remark in passing, less as an interpretive claim than as a self-evident illustration of the peculiar detachment, bordering on disdain, that philosophers maintain toward politics: most treat politics as a means to extrapolitical ends. On the face of it, Spinoza's *Theological-Political Treatise* exemplifies such an instrumentalist attitude, its title page announcing that "the freedom of philosophizing (*libertas philosophandi*) can be granted without harming either piety or the peace of the republic, and cannot be taken away without destroying both piety and the peace of the republic." Thus, while the treatise carries an ostensibly political charge—*libertas philosophandi*, Spinoza asserts, belongs to the very essence of republican life—its argument seems ultimately to be in service of a personal intellectual liberty, a right or faculty of the (philosophic?) individual that the well-governed state must permit and guarantee. Assuming this to be the case, Arendt portrays Spinoza's "freedom of philosophizing" as an incidentally rather than constitutively political freedom, more subjective property than associative practice—in short, "not political."

However inadvertently, Arendt's passing reference to Spinoza pinpoints a fundamental presupposition of his expositors, namely, that the "freedom of philosophizing"—which he characterizes broadly in the TTP as a freedom to form and express one's own opinions or judgments—should be understood from within a negative horizon of meaning. By this I mean, first, and most obviously, that Spinoza scholars routinely assimilate his *libertas philosophandi* to the model of negative liberty when they read it as a freedom to think and communicate without interference. Spinoza's idiosyncratic philosophical premises notwithstanding, his conclusions in the TTP about the necessary limits of coercive power over thought and speech, which, he insists, "can't be suppressed" and "must be granted" by the state, encourage commentators to find in his work an anticipation of more familiar defenses of personal liberty (20.42, 20.44). On this basis, some extol the "freedom of philosophizing" as evidence of Spinoza's credentials as a liberal thinker, perhaps even the original or originary liberal democrat,[2] whereas others diminish or disclaim Spinoza's vindication of this freedom as a momentary retreat from his immanent materialism.[3]

Additionally, I speak of a "negative horizon of meaning" in order to underscore a more metaphysically basic feature of the political modernity with which commentators, whether by design or default, tend to align Spinoza's *libertas philosophandi*. I am referring to the opposition between freedom conceived as a form of sovereign individuality, on the one hand, and the political dimension, or what Arendt calls the sphere of human plurality, on the other. The negativity at issue here subtends the canonical alternatives of negative liberty (absence of interference) and positive liberty (sovereign agency).[4] For each of these represents freedom as that which "makes the subject the proprietor of himself or herself . . . essentially 'proper' and no longer 'common'."[5] From this vantage, what unites disparate camps of Spinoza scholarship is an assumption that the "freedom of philosophizing" fits the mold of an *immunity*, understood as an exemption from the obligations and offices of the commonwealth, a freedom from being disposed to others and their demands. The received "immunitarian" interpretation of Spinoza's *libertas philosophandi*, I want to suggest, is not so much incorrect—he does, after all, depict free philosophizing in privative terms—as it is inadequate or partial. It moves within the theological-political terms that organize the primary argumentative thread in the TTP, but it elides a crucial sense in which Spinoza's text poses a challenge to those very terms. How, then, might this particular immunity be thought otherwise? And what would that entail politically?

By taking up these concerns in this chapter, I aim to pose anew the problem of the political status of Spinoza's "freedom of philosophizing." Considering that in Spinoza's day this term signified, above all, a type of academic freedom, one can immediately appreciate how innovative is his endeavor to defend *libertas philosophandi* publicly as a freedom for all to think and speak, or, in a word, to judge. The key interpretive question for present purposes is how precisely this immunity bears on politics. My answer is that Spinoza's approach to *libertas philosophandi* puts into relief two distinct modalities—I call them jurisdiction and jurisprudence—in which agents envision and enact judgment as a political immunity. The state's sovereign authority to determine matters of public utility stands as the paradigmatic form of jurisdiction, in contrast to the exemplary case of jurisprudence, citizens' right to "philosophize" or judge publicly the utility of the state's laws. With this bifocal vision, Spinoza effects another innovation, shifting the terms of engagement between politics and judgment away from an exclusive focus on sovereignty—who wields the supreme authority to decide controversies?—and toward an inclusive focus on sovereignty *and empowerment*—how might a people become free and equal judges of their common affairs?

Spinoza's *Libertas Philosophandi* and the Politics of Immunity

As much as I seek to reflect on the nature and political implications of a particular idea in the general economy of Spinoza's thought, my interpretation of *libertas philosophandi* also aims to contribute something new to a broader theoretical debate over the relationship between freedom and immunity in political modernity. Modern political life, one could say, is, above all, sheltered life. Several generations of critical theorists, from the Frankfurt School to French poststructuralists to current exponents of Italian biopolitical theory, offer versions of this diagnosis, with all its dialectical tension between security and vitality. The stock image of the overprotective parent conveys something of that tension. If I try too hard to shield my child from harm, I may well sequester her from experiences that stimulate her capacities to survive and thrive independently. I can end up arresting her development, augmenting rather than alleviating her vulnerability.[6]

Consider some political-theoretical variants of this "immunitary dialectic." Horkheimer and Adorno trace its apocalyptic effects in their *Dialectic of Enlightenment*, where humanity's endeavor to preserve itself through rational mastery over nature requires suppressing and ultimately destroying the fundamental nature of being human.[7] Derrida, for his part, speaks of an "autoimmunity," or suicidal tendency at the heart of democracy: on one hand, democracy's intrinsically boundless capacity for self-critique invites antidemocratic polemic; on the other hand, in the name of protecting democracy from its enemies and the misuse of its freedoms, democratic governments routinely suspend democratic rights.[8] And Agamben's *Homo Sacer* series offers one of the most influential renditions of the dialectic to date.[9] Here the immunitary apparatus of law, by capturing or including the "bare life" that it simultaneously excludes from the juridical-political order, serves as the very vehicle of sovereign domination.

Perhaps no other contemporary theorist explores the conceptual tensions and historical dynamics of immunity as comprehensively as Roberto Esposito. Esposito's "immunization paradigm" combines a theoretical argument about the semantic connection between ideas of immunity and community with a genealogical argument about the specifically modern character of immunization.[10] As Esposito notes, the terms "immunity" (*immunitas*) and "community" (*communitas*) both derive from *munus*, which renders as "gift," "duty," or "obligation." Whereas community expresses an affirmative relation to this root, as in an obligation to give a gift or to care for the other, immunity denotes an exemption from such obligations and their attendant risks. At its most elemental, says Esposito, immunity is "the power to preserve life."[11] This power assumes different historical guises: the salient political categories of modernity—sovereignty, property, and liberty—are but "the linguistic and institutional forms adopted by the immunitary logic in order to safeguard life from the risks that derive from its own collective configuration and conflagration."[12] Modernity thus turns on, or is an invention of, the demand to preserve life. "Modern" describes the moment when immunization begins to serve not only as a "means toward achieving the good—the flourishing of a historical culture with its particular conception of what constitutes excellence and living well—but as the highest good, as what life in society is fundamentally about."[13]

According to Esposito, modern immunization passes through two phases. In the first, ideas and institutions of juridical order mediate between the political and biological domains, organizing collective existence around the basic imperative to preserve life. The second phase begins toward the end of the eighteenth century with the proliferation of governmental technologies that target public health, demographics, and urban planning.[14] These developments mark the emergence of biopolitics, whereby the maintenance and development of life becomes an immediately political object and politics comes increasingly to be patterned on biology and medicine. Biopolitical immunization turns lethal when articulated in the discourses of nationalism and racism (which focus on the ethnically defined body, be it individual or collective), transforming into a politics aimed at "curing" life by selectively exterminating "degenerate" portions of it. If, for Esposito, the genocidal project of Nazism represents the catastrophic apex of this thanatopolitics, the defeat of Nazism in no way entails the disappearance of immunitary rationality. On the contrary, the immunitary project persists and, following the Cold War, intensifies to such an extent that the need for exemption and protection becomes "the linchpin around which both the real and imaginary practices of an entire civilization have been constructed."[15] Indeed, in current demands for protection—whether advanced in the language of epidemiology, immigration policy, or information technology—Esposito discerns an obsessive and excessive quality, a surplus of defense that generates more risk and more violence than it can possibly prevent.[16] The notion of "preventive war," war fought to avoid war, epitomizes the self-destructive bent of the contemporary condition.[17]

Esposito insists, nonetheless, that the category of immunity harbors possibilities for emancipatory politics. Immunity's negative trajectory is not its destiny. Esposito's conviction on this score contrasts with the overwhelmingly negative portrayal of immunity in the critical theoretical literature as "a quintessential manifestation of state power."[18] Ed Cohen distills the prevailing view: "Immunity suspends the binding of particular duties and responsibilities while maintaining the inviolability of the social bond. It negates the dissolution that threatens when supposedly constitutive obligations go unfulfilled by legally reattaching those exempted as immune. Thus immunity uses exceptions to the law to demonstrate that the law remains without exception."[19] Without denying its significance, Esposito maintains that this monologic of immunity is capable of being "converted" into the "singular and plural logic" of *communitas*.[20] He argues that a conversion of this sort entails recuperating in theory and practice the semantic node—the *munus*—that joins immunity to community, understood no longer as a locus of identity, belonging, or appropriation, but rather as plurality, difference, and alterity.[21] In this manner, immunity becomes a common immunity or co-immunity, a bond that opens the members of a community to the other, building communal strength through a diversification and pluralization of the whole.[22] When no longer simply separated and opposed, immunity and community take on a reciprocal relation, which, Esposito emphasizes, is what one finds in the biological forms of immunitary tolerance at work in pregnancy and organ transplants.[23]

Suggestive as Esposito's sketch of "common immunity" may be, the political dimensions of the concept remain underspecified. Esposito concedes the difficulty of translating the idea of common immunity from a set of ontological prefigurations and biological metaphors into political terms, though he seems to understand this difficulty primarily as one of transforming a "philosophical formula into actual practice."[24] Complicating the issue, however, are some basic ambiguities at the conceptual level itself—in particular, Esposito's equivocation on the juridical status of immunity. At times, as in his recent deconstruction of the idea of the person, Esposito suggests that inherited juridical categories should be abandoned altogether in pursuit of a post-immunitary philosophy of impersonal life.[25] At other times, rather than call for a displacement of law, Esposito gestures toward a new way of thinking the "reciprocal immanence" of juridical norms and potentialities of life.[26] In each instance, he refers to but does not fully develop the contributions of Spinoza and Spinozists such as Canguilhem and Deleuze.[27] So even though Esposito hints that "Spinozian juridical naturalism" takes immunity "beyond" the dialectic of protection and negation, he leaves unclear what immunity's conversion from privative to productive might entail politically and how something like "common immunity" relates to the dominative (bio)politics of immunization. One might ask, then, in light of Esposito's efforts: how, specifically, does Spinozism reach beyond modernity's immunitary dialectic?

My interpretive focus on Spinoza's "freedom of philosophizing" is, in part, an attempt to gain traction on this question. Spinoza's treatment of *libertas philosophandi*, I want to argue, can be read as a case study of the specific institutions and practices that convert immunity, "the power to preserve life" (Esposito), into tendentially dominative and emancipatory forms of judgment. If the sovereign form that I call jurisdiction exemplifies the dominative or negative logic of immunity, then, by contrast, the dissensual activity of jurisprudence, a citizen-driven reflection ("philosophizing") on collective affairs, demonstrates the emancipatory logic of a common immunity. To understand the relationship of jurisdiction to jurisprudence, particularly the sense in which the latter goes "beyond" the former, one ultimately needs to see how Spinoza connects *libertas philosophandi*, as a right to judge, to an idea of "surplus power." I explore this connection in the penultimate section of the chapter. Given that key features of my exposition, particularly the emphasis on common potentiality as a fund for creative resistance, bear a strong resemblance to Antonio Negri's influential reading of Spinoza, in the final section of the chapter I offer a brief reflection on the key differences and stakes of our respective interpretations.

Immunizing the Freedom of Philosophizing

In order to develop a feel for the innovation and intervention that Spinoza carries out with his account of the "freedom of philosophizing," I want to begin by situating the term in its intellectual and historical milieu. Ultimately, this contextualization helps to reveal how Spinoza's writings resist a tendency, prevalent in both his own day and the present, to vindicate freedom by immunizing it. As Esposito notes, echoing arguments found in Foucault, Arendt, and Marx, among others, the mainstream of modern political thought imagines freedom as "that which insures the individual against the interference of others through voluntary subordination to a more powerful order that guarantees it."[28] Spinoza has long been read—in continental theory, at least—as a counterpoint to this individualistic line of thinking. Even so, the full measure of his challenge to modernity's subjectivist image of freedom remains unthought so long as contemporary readers continue to reinscribe his conception of *libertas philosophandi* within a negative horizon of meaning—a point to which I will return below.

Two discourses are especially important for the contextualization of Spinoza's "freedom of philosophizing": first, the academic debates of mid-seventeenth-century Netherlands in which *libertas philosophandi* gained currency; and second, the long-standing dispute in the Dutch Republic over the relative authority of Church and State, particularly on the right of religious practice (*jus circa sacra*). Connecting the two discourses is a problem of judgment that Leibniz famously characterized as the defining issue of the period in Europe, namely, the question of the "judge of controversies." Who or what is to serve as the last judge in the interpretation of scriptural truth? In civil disputes? In conflicts between governors and governed? Who, in short, is the judge of controversies? This is the question, Leibniz proposed, upon which "the decision, conclusion, results, and effects of other controversies depend."[29] That Leibniz framed a diverse set of debates over sacred and secular matters alike as a second-order problem of authoritative judgment testifies not only to his personal ambitions to reconcile the post-Westphalian split between politics and religious morality on a higher metaphysical plane.[30] It also points to a broader tendency in the intellectual culture of mid to late seventeenth-century Europe to approach the controversial relationship between philosophy and theology in juridical-political terms as a question of jurisdiction.[31]

Decoupling the study of nature from the explication of God's purposes promised to open up unexplored avenues of scientific discovery. At the same time, this proposed separation sparked new quarrels over philosophy's possible subversion of theology. In the Dutch Republic, the key disagreement on this issue was between orthodox Calvinist theologians and advocates of Descartes' novel metaphysics and method. Whereas the former defended Aristotelianism as the only philosophy consistent with revealed religion, denouncing Cartesianism for what they saw as its implicit skepticism, atheism, and pretensions to liberate philosophy from its traditional role as *ancilla theologiae*, the latter defended the Cartesian investigation of nature as independent of theology and consistent with the essential teachings of the Bible.[32] The polemic between these groups initially became a political matter insofar as it raised questions about the power structures of the universities, which fell under the jurisdiction of the government.[33] In one key instance, the States of Holland (a parliamentary body) was forced to declare an "Order relating to the entanglement of theology and philosophy and to the abuse of the freedom of philosophizing to the detriment of Scripture."[34] The law stipulated that the spheres of philosophy and theology were not to interfere with one another. Where overlap and contention might arise, philosophers were to avoid interpreting Scripture "according to their principles" and instead defer to theologians.[35] Defining the freedom of philosophizing as the freedom to engage solely in inquiry regarding the natural properties and causes of things, the States' edict codified a signal feature of the Cartesians' platform while temporarily mollifying their theologian critics.[36]

By the time of the States' edict on philosophizing (1656), however, the question of the relationship between theology and philosophy had stirred a much broader controversy over public order. A new cohort of "radical Cartesians," working largely outside of the academy (and often publishing in the vernacular), had begun to apply the spirit if not the letter of Descartes' system to hotly contested questions of biblical hermeneutics and the relative authority of church and state in public life.[37] These freethinkers were reacting to what they saw as the Calvinist ministry's undue influence over both the civil magistracy and the larger public—an influence acquired, in part, through the strategy of claiming ever more topics and issues, from the details of personal lifestyle to those of cosmology, for the purview of theology. Against such "theologization," the republican-minded coterie of amateur Cartesians attempted to radicalize the mainstream Cartesians' immunization strategy, seeking protection not only for the philosophical reasoning of professional scholars but for individual reasoning as such. They saw the academic "separation" of theology and philosophy as insufficient for this purpose.

As far as these radical Cartesians were concerned, the authority of the clergy needed to be controlled by the power of the state if individual freedom was to be guaranteed. Academic Cartesians had remained studiously agnostic on questions of politics and religion when defending the freedom of philosophizing. Their radical counterparts, however, were at pains to forge an indissociable connection between the toleration of individual thought and the state's absolute right over religious practice (*jus circa sacra*). Exemplary, in this regard, was the 1665 tract *De Jure Ecclesiasticorum*, published under the pseudonym Lucius Antistius Constans. Among its central claims, *De Jure Ecclesiasticorum* proposed that reason, not divine will, is the supreme organizing principle of the state; that reason demonstrates that individuals must transfer their "right and power" (*jus et potestas*) to a supreme civil authority; and that clergy are merely functionaries, designated at the behest of the civil sovereign to administer external rites of religion (*jus circa sacra*).[38]

Although the argument for the state's *jus circa sacra* was by no means a new one, radical Cartesian thinkers found in Hobbes a new theoretical guarantee or justification. Constans's tract is particularly interesting in this regard, because it reveals the radical Cartesians' quandary in using Hobbes's theory of sovereignty to safeguard individual freedom of thought. Hobbes had unified religious and political authority in the "Publique Reason" of the sovereign, to whom all subjects owed their unconditional obedience. Nevertheless, Hobbes had conceded the impossibility of commanding the "internall and invisible" aspects of faith and belief: "A private man has alwaies the liberty, (because thought is free,) to beleeve, or not beleeve in his heart. . . . But when it comes to confession of that faith, the Private Reason must submit to the Publique."[39] In *De Jure Ecclesiasticorum*, Constans mapped Hobbes's distinction between internal and external religion rather crudely onto a division between the mental and the physical.[40] This permitted Constans to vindicate freedom of thought in a strict sense. All external religion was of the order of the controllable, and it was also all that mattered for the peace and security of the state.[41] One's freedom to believe and to doubt remained an inviolable right, proper to the individual. At the same time, Constans's schema afforded no place in public life for the judgment of citizens. For any such expression proceeded through speech or writing and therefore the physical medium—precisely the sphere over which the sovereign held exclusive jurisdiction.[42]

With Spinoza, however, the idea of the freedom of philosophizing reemerged from the interiority of individual conscience, where radical Cartesians like Constans had enclosed it in arguing for the indivisibility of sovereignty. Moreover, in marked contrast with the narrowly academic justifications for *libertas philosophandi* furnished by professional philosophers, Spinoza broke new ground by defending the freedom of philosophizing publicly as a public freedom.[43] The question is how precisely to understand the political character of this freedom. In what sense does Spinoza's *libertas philosophandi* operate "beyond" sovereign jurisdiction?

Most of the Anglophone literature on Spinoza answers this question in a manner that casts him as "an eccentric Hobbesian."[44] Spinoza is said to extend Hobbes's notion of individual judgment or "private reason" from the inner mental sanctum to the outer forum, and from an immunity granted primarily for religious conviction to a broad protection of any "conscientious judgment," including all manner of philosophical opinion.[45] Thus, on the standard view, Spinoza's defense of the freedom of philosophizing combines a "separation thesis" (philosophy/theology) with a "single authority thesis" (state > church) in support of a "principle of toleration" (politics/philosophy).[46] In other words, Spinoza's separation between theology and philosophy presupposes a *unification* of theology and politics in the figure of a sovereign who wields exclusive jurisdiction over both civil and religious law. The right of the sovereign, and hence the integrity and stability of the state, hinges in turn on the state's ability to secure a certain autonomy or *separation* of philosophizing from politics, a right of subjects to think and speak freely—that is, without interference—so long as they act in accordance with the law.

Without yet saying anything more specific about the nature of these key separations—theology from philosophy and philosophy from politics—what I want to highlight here is the immunitary cast that judgment takes in this scenario. On one hand, political judgment assumes the sovereign form of a judge of controversies (a Spinozist counterpart to Hobbes's "Publique Reason"). On the other hand, the freedom of philosophizing, understood as conscientious judgment, occupies the negative space of sovereign jurisdiction, positioned beyond the coercive power of the state but within the right and power of each individual to form and express his opinion. If *libertas philosophandi* translates here into a quintessentially intellectual freedom, it is at best an instrumentally political one; that is, a subjective right or civil liberty guaranteed by the sovereign power of the state. This standard reading of Spinoza's "freedom of philosophizing" finds a great deal of corroboration in the TTP, as I shall detail below. But it fails to capture the full measure of the challenge that Spinoza poses in his development of the concept. More than just a freedom from sovereign jurisdiction, or an immunity defined in opposition to the political dimension, Spinoza's "freedom of philosophizing" comes to signify a constitutively political freedom that resists rather than reiterates the immunitary logic of jurisdiction.

Jurisdiction and Jurisprudence

On my reading, Spinoza's treatment of the freedom of philosophizing juxtaposes two basic senses of judgment as a political immunity. Envisioned and employed in a theological-political key, judgment takes the authoritative form of jurisdiction: one sovereign agency maintains the right and power to make legal decisions and judgments—to speak the law—whereas private citizens possess a freedom of philosophizing insofar as their judgments on particular matters (e.g., the nature of their faith) are recognized by the sovereign to be immune from the dictates of law. In this schema, *libertas philosophandi* refers to a freedom of judging that presupposes obedience to law more broadly. To put it another way, the freedom at stake in philosophizing is that of interpreting how best to assume responsibility as a subject of law. The more prominent argumentative thread in the TTP operates in this register. Here Spinoza defends the freedom of philosophizing by taking its critics on their own terms, viz., the dominant discourses of faith (theology) and of the state (political theory). He thereby defines and defends *libertas philosophandi* on the grounds of what faith and political order permit and prohibit. Spinoza's general formulation of the freedom of philosophizing asserts that "in a free republic everyone is permitted to think what he wishes and to say what he thinks" (TTP 20 title). Schematically, his chief concern in the theological chapters (1–15) is with freedom of thought or belief (thinking what one wishes); in the political chapters (16–20) his concern broadens to include freedom of expression (saying what one thinks). The separation between these freedoms is only analytical. Spinoza goes on to insist that, in reality, the freedom of thinking and speaking are effectively inseparable. By the conclusion of the TTP, he tends to combine them simply to speak simply of "freedom of judgment." Likewise, Spinoza shows the domains of piety and peace to be practically indistinguishable in that they comprise a single public sphere, or civil order. This detail helps to account for the composite expression that appears in the treatise's title page, which asserts that one is to find therein a theological-political vindication of the freedom of philosophizing.

However, in Spinoza's telling, *libertas philosophandi* also comes to be envisioned and enacted in a political-philosophical key. In this case, freedom of philosophizing-cum-judging takes what I shall call a jurisprudential form. Consistent with the initial meanings of "prudence," jurisprudence consists of a certain savoir-faire that ordinary individuals exercise when judging how to preserve and enhance their "natural right," that is, their ability to think and act in the world. Spinoza sometimes refers to this type of judgment as *cautio*, and he treats it as synonymous with "freedom of human nature," which, he adds, "is not obedience" (TP 4.5). What this small but significant qualification underscores is that the grammar of jurisprudence is not essentially moral; it does not speak, as jurisdiction does, of permission and prohibition. As a consequence, the key political-philosophical question animating Spinozist jurisprudence is a query about how best to participate in common potentiality. Indeed, far from simply presupposing obedience, jurisprudence necessarily calls it into question. If jurisdiction speaks the law, jurisprudence always in some manner speaks against it.

JUDGING IN A THEOLOGICAL-POLITICAL KEY: JURISDICTION

To see how Spinoza's discussion of *libertas philosophandi* summons an immunitary apparatus of sovereign jurisdiction, it helps to examine more closely the "separations" at stake in his analysis. The first concerns the relationship between philosophy and faith (or theology).[47] According to Spinoza, what separates these two domains in theory and what reconciles them in practice is a question of orthopraxy.[48] "The goal of philosophy," he writes, "is nothing but truth," whereas "the goal of faith . . . is nothing but obedience and piety" (TTP 14.38). So understood, faith "grants everyone the greatest freedom to philosophize, so that without wickedness, he can think whatever he wishes about anything" (14.39). Here Spinoza does not align theology, the word of God, with the text of Scripture per se but with the moral law contained therein: the command to obey God wholeheartedly by loving one's neighbor as oneself, that is, by practicing justice and charity (pref 26, 14.9). It follows that theology bears not on speculative questions but rather on matters of conduct that correspond to certain speculative requirements.[49]

Requirements of what sort? Spinoza's answer runs as follows: "Faith requires, not so much true doctrines, as pious doctrines, i.e., doctrines which move the heart to obedience, even if many of them do not have even a shadow of truth. This is true provided the person who accepts them does not know they are false. If he did, he would necessarily be a rebel. For how could someone who is eager to love justice and obey God worship something he knows to be foreign to the divine nature?" (TTP 14.20–21). Faith's speculative requirements can all be subsumed into one core tenet—"love thy neighbor"—which is also a call to interpret religion for oneself, an exigency to adapt the moral law to one's singular beliefs so that one can assume responsibility for pursuing the right action.[50] Spinoza takes it as axiomatic that "opinions govern men in different ways: those which move one person to devotion move another to laughter and contempt" (14.22). The interpretive freedom that faith grants—or better, necessitates—is thus the ability to discover one's own reasons for adhering to the moral core of Scripture.[51] In this respect, the freedom of philosophizing, far from posing a threat to faith, is essential to preserving the latter. Hence Spinoza can write that everyone is "bound to accommodate" the core tenets of faith "to his own power of understanding, and to interpret them for himself . . . so that he may obey God wholeheartedly" (14.32). *Libertas philosophandi* signifies here a freedom from orthodoxy in the practice of piety. And the piety of each person's faith must be judged "from his works alone" (pref 28).

Who shall be the judge of such works? The answer to this question leads Spinoza to thematize the second key separation in the TTP, the distinction, so to speak, between "politics" and "philosophy."[52] The civil sovereign wields exclusive jurisdiction over religious affairs: "Religious worship and the exercise of piety must be accommodated to the peace and utility of the republic, and hence, must be determined only by the supreme powers, who must also be its interpreters" (19.2). Otherwise put, the state must serve as the last judge of piety, interpreting how the rule of charity applies to particular cases. But

Spinoza hastens to add, "I'm speaking specifically about the exercise of piety and about the external practice of religion, not about piety itself and the internal worship of God" (19.3). In this fashion, he reconciles sovereign jurisdiction, on the one hand, with the interpretive freedom (or "philosophizing") that faith requires of individuals, on the other. The two complement each other as the "external" and "internal" cultivation of piety, respectively. Already in chapter 7, Spinoza identifies this inner aspect of piety with an inalienable freedom of thought: "each person has the supreme right to think freely (*summum jus libere sentiendi*), even about religion, and it is inconceivable that anyone can abandon his claim to this right" (7.91). The concluding chapter of the TTP spells out the implications for the "public" or external aspect of thinking freely, the practice of "saying what one thinks." Here the sovereign's jurisdiction over all matters of public utility, which encompasses the practice of justice and charity, makes possible the separation of theology from philosophy and thereby guarantees "to everyone the same freedom of philosophizing as we've shown that faith does" (20.23).

Spinoza's theological-political defense of *libertas philosophandi* reveals how the discourses of faith and the state connect in a project of immunization. In a first step, he demonstrates that faith grants a dispensation from orthodoxy, a freedom of philosophizing, understood as an ability (*potentia*) to "think as one wishes" and so to interpret the foundations of faith according to one's own reason. As noted, this interpretive freedom is conditional upon the performance of piety. In parallel fashion, the second step of Spinoza's argument demonstrates that one's *libertas philosophandi,* now viewed as the freedom to "say what one thinks," remains conditional upon one's subscription to law as manifest in one's actions or "good works." Interpretation of the fundamentals of faith (the first formulation of *libertas philosophandi*) and saying what one thinks about any matters whatsoever (the second formulation) are not so much independent activities as moments in the same negative dialectic that binds individuals to sovereignty by safeguarding their opinions from interference.

JUDGING IN A POLITICAL-PHILOSOPHICAL KEY: JURISPRUDENCE

Aside from appearing as the outward manifestation of individuals' inner piety, Spinoza's *libertas philosophandi* constitutes another form of judging, one that a people at large exercise in relation to their government. This other judgment, which I am calling jurisprudence, consists of a right to judge the utility of one's rights. Jurisprudence is not, I would add, wholly "other" to *libertas philosophandi* understood as conscientious judgment. Indeed, the latter to some extent prefigures the former. One can see this in Spinoza's discussion of faith's speculative requirements, where he refers to a "necessary rebellion" that results from the imposition of belief.[53] Recall that in that context the exigency to judge is a function of the underdetermined status of a moral law (the rule of charity), each individual being required to adapt the necessity of obedience to the particularity of his own beliefs and "complexion" (*ingenium*). The individual needs the freedom to subscribe to those beliefs that "move [his] heart to obedience" and thereby inspire him to good works of charity toward his neighbor. If, on the contrary, the individual is required to follow dogma that he does not believe to be true, Spinoza argues, he will "necessarily be a rebel," unable to worship God wholeheartedly (TTP 14.20). Echoing an originally Lutheran idea, Spinoza declares that "no one can be compelled by force or by laws to become blessed"; instead, "what is required is pious and brotherly advice, good education, and above all, one's own free judgment" (7.90).

Jurisprudence truly comes into its own when the judgments of a people give voice to a decidedly different but equally necessary rebellion. Call it the "rebellion of reason against obedience when the laws are against reason."[54] For Spinoza, the exercise of judging critically the *dictum* of the state's law is necessary in the twofold sense that it is inevitable (it cannot be suppressed) and indispensable (it is essential for a free political life). Indeed, he goes so far as to say that anyone who partakes of such rebellion is acting as one of the "best citizens" of a free republic (TTP 20.15). In order to grasp this peculiar necessity of jurisprudence, it helps to consider judgment through a different optic, shifting from the theological-political problematic of obedience to a political-philosophical problematic of potentiality or empowerment. The text of the TTP itself marks such a shift: at the outset of chapter 16, Spinoza asserts that he must offer a theory of natural right, "the foundation of the republic," so as to probe the limits of free philosophizing in political life (16.1). In his elaboration, "the right of nature extends as far as its power (*potentia*) does. . . . But the universal power of the whole of nature is nothing but the power of all individuals together. From this it follows that . . . the right of each thing extends as far as its determinate power does" (16.3–4). What Spinoza calls, in these pages, the "supreme law of nature" is not in any sense a moral law that permits or prohibits; it is an immanent law of the *conatus* whereby each thing strives to preserve and enhance its power to act, "to do everything it can" (16.3).

One could say that Spinoza's "law of nature" offers individuals a dispensation from obedience because this law is nothing more or less than the dispensation of potentiality. It is in relation to the latter that individuals are "bound" to judge their "good" (*utile*), that is, the effects of power on their ability to think and to act (TP 4.5). And it is in relation to this natural plane of potentiality that Spinoza offers a different rationale for political society. Considered simply in terms of their *utile*, "men had necessarily to conspire together" as a condition for preserving and enhancing their ability to act in the world, to live securely and to live well (TTP 16.13, trans. modified). It is therefore part of natural right to seek some measure of security and order ("there is no one who does not desire to live in safety free from fear, as far as is possible"), leading individuals to organize themselves so that the theoretically "unrestricted" character of natural right, which permits everyone "to do just as he pleases," comes to be regulated by common rules. For as Spinoza puts it in his *Political Treatise*, "as long as human natural right is determined by the power of each one taken separately, it is null [and] consists more in opinion than in fact, since there's no secure way to maintain it." Thus natural right calls for community, which in turn requires an agency of sovereign jurisdiction to assure everyone in the exercise of their rights. "The right of nature proper to the human species can hardly be conceived except where men have common rights and are jointly able to claim for themselves lands they can inhabit and cultivate, are able to protect themselves, fend off any force, and live according to the common opinion of all" (TP 2.15, trans. modified). But even while necessary for the establishment of a civil condition, the immunitary apparatus of sovereignty proves insufficient for the common development of freedom—or, to be more precise, freedom envisioned and enacted as a common development of singular potentialities.

For Spinoza, the circulation of reason alone can defend the vitality of natural right (TP 5.5). He presses this point by arguing both that freedom of judgment cannot be relinquished and that it is an indispensable political virtue. Spinoza's case for the twofold necessity of free judgment comprises, in turn, his argument for democracy. In a democratic state, "no one so transfers his natural right to another to the point of having no occasion to deliberate in the future. Instead he transfers it to the majority of the whole society, of which he makes one part. In this way everyone remains equal, as they were in a state of nature" (TTP 16.36, trans. modified). Spinoza depicts democracy as "approach[ing] most nearly the freedom nature concedes to everyone," which is, on the one hand, a right to judge what is good or bad according to one's own rather than another's way of thinking (*ingenium*) (ibid.). This is a freedom from any obligation to submit one's powers of intelligence to another. On the other hand, the freedom nature "concedes" is always a determinate force, a natural exigency or endeavor (*conatus*) to judge what is most conducive to one's potentiality. In this respect, democracy best expresses the true reason for political society, the very "end" or essential endeavor of the republic, which, Spinoza recapitulates in the TTP's conclusion, is "not to change men from rational beings into beasts or automata, but to enable their minds and bodies to perform all their functions safely, to enable them to use their reason freely, and not to clash with one another in hatred, anger or deception, or deal inequitably with one another. So the end of the republic is really freedom" (20.12).

Spinoza's conclusion that freedom is the "end" of political life invites an important objection to my reading, however. After providing a theory of natural right that steers the juridical logic of immunity away from the merely privative and toward the productive—that is, after conceptualizing right (*jus*) as co-extensive with potentiality—it would seem that, by positing freedom as an abstract ideal at the end of his treatise, he winds up re-inscribing individual judgment in the negative horizon of immunization. Spinoza's vindication of *libertas philosophandi* seemingly culminates in a plea for both state and subjects to affirm a fundamental norm of toleration as the limiting rule for their action. The best state, he argues, will restrict its jurisdiction to the realm of action and allow for the free circulation of citizen judgment; for their part, citizens should argue but obey (TTP 20.14–15).[55] Note that, in this schema, right no longer appears as a synonym for effective power (*potentia*) but is now a merely formal category.[56] Similarly, Spinoza reverts to a legalistic conception of power understood as the means of the state. This becomes apparent in the way that he qualifies his defense of judgment: everyone retains the right to judge, "provided just that he only speaks or teaches, and defends his view by reason alone, not with deception, anger, hatred, or an intention to introduce something into the republic on the authority of his own decision" (20.14). In effect, Spinoza's proviso confines jurisprudence to a "proper use" that is liable to be defined by the sovereign authority as a justification for its violence. For the supposedly irrational judgments that the state cannot abide are simply those that, in its determination, are "seditious," namely, opinions "which, as soon as they are assumed, destroy the agreement by which each person surrendered his right to act according to his own decision" (20.20).

The legalism objection raises and responds to the question of the relationship between jurisdiction and jurisprudence: the right or power of everyone to judge goes "beyond" sovereign jurisdiction only as an inclusive exclusion, or negative immunity. Construed as such, immunity appears as "somewhat of a trickster," in that it "operates by defining lawful exceptions to the law precisely in order to maintain that the law applies universally and *therefore without exception.* In other words, since the law declares that its exceptions always already derive from it, such exceptions do not trouble its jurisdiction."[57] One can readily see such immunitary logic at work in Spinoza's TTP, where the question of the limits of free judgment in the state calls for a determination on whether such judgment upholds or undermines the reason for the pact. For Spinoza, that decision on sedition, on the dissolution of the social bond, remains the prerogative of sovereign power—even in the best case of a "moderate" government that concedes to everyone the freedom of judgment (TTP 20.8). The jurisprudence of citizen-subjects would thus seem to be, in the final instance, incorporated in the sovereign power of jurisdiction, a manifestation of state power.

On closer inspection, however, Spinoza's TTP offers its own response to the legalism objection and, as a consequence, a way of thinking the relationship of jurisdiction to jurisprudence otherwise. To be sure, Spinoza remains emphatic that the state must possess an asymmetric right to determine the limits of free judgment. But that approach to the limits of free judgment—as a decision on whether it upholds or undermines the reason for the pact—already presupposes the state's aim of establishing a legal order, which is why Spinoza describes the pact in question as the transfer that establishes individuals' equal subjection to law. Consider again Spinoza's discussion of the exemplary citizen who argues publicly that a given law is unreasonable. This citizen makes no attempt to claim a coercive right, that is, to impose his particular judgment as common law, which is the exclusive province of the sovereign. Moreover, all of the opinions that Spinoza adduces as seditious are those that it would be contradictory for an individual to want to obtain for everyone else as subjects of law: "that the supreme power isn't its own master, or that no one is under an obligation to keep his promises, or that each person ought to live according to his own decision" (TTP 20.21).[58] In short, this line of reasoning moves entirely within the theological-political problematic of obedience. Recall, though, that when Spinoza's analysis proceeds in the register of natural right and potentiality, the ultimate reason for political society—indeed the ultimate reason for any agreement—is the perceived "utility" for all parties. From this naturalistic perspective, one's obligations as a subject of law are not the definitive criteria by which to judge one's agency. On the contrary, no agreement is binding unless it is deemed useful, or conducive to one's empowerment.

Understood in a political-philosophical key, the TTP's "ideal" of free judgment emerges in and as the exercise of judgment.[59] In a largely neglected passage, immediately after rehearsing stock examples of seditious opinions, Spinoza adds: "*Other opinions . . . aren't seditious—except perhaps in a republic somehow corrupted*, e.g., where superstitious and ambitious men, who can't endure people who think in a manner worthy of a free man, achieve such a great reputation that ordinary people value their authority more than that of the supreme powers" (TTP 20.21, my emphasis). With these words, Spinoza reminds his readers that he has all along been discussing the scope of freedom of judgment in the "best" or "free republic," which, by definition, "grants everyone this freedom," as opposed to a polity that is "somehow corrupted" and which tends to coerce or usurp such freedom (20.8, 20.12). So rather than determine the boundaries of citizen judgment in view of some prior norm of good government or ideal freedom, Spinoza makes the radical extension of free judgment itself the measure of the state's vitality. Instead of the state standing in sovereign judgment over the extension and comprehension of its subjects' powers of thought and speech, the quality of any regime comes to be measured by the criterion of free judgment itself: "The less we grant men this freedom of judgment, the more we depart from the most natural condition, and the more violent the government" (20.38).

The Right to Judge as Common Immunity

I am now in a position to offer a fuller answer to the question of the relationship between jurisprudence and jurisdiction—and more specifically, the question of how the former constitutes a "judgment beyond jurisdiction." This "beyond" relates to the excessive nature of judgment, its status as a "surplus power" that Spinoza calls, simply, affect. It helps here to recall his assertion that the natural right of judging is something that "no one can surrender . . . even if he wants to" (TTP 20.3). Though at first glance this claim seems merely to rehearse familiar arguments about the inalienability of individual thought or conscience, the crucial difference is that Spinoza understands the "inalienability" of judgment as a function of the improper potentiality of affect. As Hasana Sharp explains, Spinoza's conception of affect refers most basically "to a universal power to affect and be affected, to the fact that finite beings enhance and diminish one another's power necessarily, by virtue of their inescapable interdependency."[60] So rather than ground the natural right to judge in a subjectivist metaphysics, where the individual is proprietor of himself, Spinoza situates this right in a relational ontology of power, where the right of each thing is but one element in an infinite chain of causal determinations—or, affections—that are beyond the control of any individual agent or agency.[61] From Spinoza's political-philosophical perspective, then, the right to judge is inalienable insofar as it is necessarily common.

My suggestion is that the politics of immunity in Spinoza's TTP take shape as divergent approaches to this affective "surplus" of judgment. What

I have described as Spinoza's more prominent thread of argumentation, his theological-political defense of *libertas philosophandi*, builds a rule of government—or even, of governmentality—on the recognition that judgment is a phenomenon that cannot be controlled. Judgment escapes the direct command of the state because it escapes the direct command ("will") of subjects themselves (TTP 20.8–9). As Spinoza puts it in the *Ethics*, "men have nothing less in their power than their tongue" (E III p2s).[62] Despite their theoretically absolute power, sovereigns cannot prevent individuals from judging everything according to their own temperament (*ingenia*), which is itself disposed in a multiplicity of ways by ambient networks of affect. To command over judgment one would need to prevent individuals from being affected "with this or that affect," which, as Spinoza notes periodically in the TTP, would be tantamount to destroying individuals qua individuals (TTP 20.6). Given the irreducible multitude of judgments in society, a simple decree prescribing or proscribing certain opinions will be ineffective. Moreover, it will be imprudent policy because most individuals, most of the time, believe that they *can* decide at will what to think and say. The experience of judgment, in this sense, epitomizes the common fiction that individuals tend to maintain about freedom (as lack of constraint), a fiction born of the coincidence between consciousness of one's action and ignorance of the causes by which one is moved to act (E III p2s). Spinoza insists that any overt attempt to deprive individuals of this imagined freedom tends to generate resentment among the populace and trigger a vicious cycle of revolt and repression. In particular, the morally scrupulous feel emboldened, even obligated to incite rebellion and, if necessary, to die for their principles (TTP 20.36). The suppression of such dissidents inspires others to revere and emulate them. Those in favor of such ideological repression see it as enacted for their benefit, with the consequence that the sovereign power becomes unable to change the law without great difficulty (20.31). Consequently, he writes, "nothing is safer for the republic than that piety and religion should include only the practice of charity and justice, and that the right of the supreme powers concerning both sacred and secular matters should relate only to actions. For the rest, everyone should be granted the right to think what he wants and to say what he thinks" (20.46).

The Spinozist state governs less by laws that command obedience and prohibit sedition than by interventions in the affective lives of subjects that induce their obedience and inhibit sedition (cf. TP 10.8). For even though, strictly speaking, the right to judge cannot be controlled, it remains subject to subtler and more indirect techniques of governing. Spinoza pays particular attention to this art of governing in chapter 17 of the TTP, where he asserts that "hearts are to some extent under the control of the supreme power, which can bring it about in many ways that most men believe, love, and hate whatever it wants them to . . ." (TTP 17.9). He takes care to note that this form of governance can never become absolute: such power over minds is sometimes reinforced and other times usurped by other agents and agencies in society—for example, churches, universities, or charismatic leaders. Still, his key point is that the state is a dynamic form that must continue to make itself the dominant authority by converting the surplus power of judgment—an affective power that circulates between individuals as it constitutes them—into an immunity for which it serves as guarantor. This process amounts to a neutralizing appropriation, a conversion of the power between individuals into a power over them. Individual judgment remains here a negative immunity: free insofar as it negates the negation of jurisdiction. The lawful way to do this, of course, is by expressing an opinion, a "conscientious judgment," that remains one's "own" and yet consistent with the basic requirements of the social contract, including the sovereign's jurisdiction over public affairs. Alternatively, a subject can respond to the *dictum* of the common law by acting arbitrarily, "according to the decision of his own mind," which effectively is to repeat the sovereign's logic of immunity and further justifies the violence of the state (20.13, 20.17).

Beyond its role as the *arcanum* of the state, however, Spinoza thinks the surplus power of judgment affirmatively as a common source of fortification that enables resistance to domination. In this affirmative or active sense, judgment operates as a constituent power of critique. Spinoza opens such a possibility when he indicates that judgment constitutes a "virtue" or power in its own right, not so much immediately but gradually through the common circulation of opinions. In society, the communication of irreducibly diverse affects—which vary according to the singular circumstances and dispositions of the bodies (and, in parallel, ideas) interacting—makes for a correspondingly diverse field of opinions. Since "each one judges from his own affect what is good and what is bad, what is better and what worse, it follows that men can vary as much in judgment as in affect" (E III p51s). Or, in more colloquial terms: "men's minds vary as much as their palates do" (TTP 20.4). For Spinoza, the common circulation of diverse opinions serves as the condition for individuals' mental fortitude because it allows them to discover what is "useful" (*utile*). Useful is that which disposes the body to affect and be affected in increasingly many ways, and which concurrently disposes the mind to become increasingly perceptive (E IVp38, E IIp14). In this connection, Spinoza underscores the enabling and ennobling effects—the peculiar "utility"—of public deliberation: "When the few decide everything, simply on the basis of their own affects, freedom and the common good are lost. For human wits are too sluggish (*humana ingenia hebetiora*) to penetrate everything right away. But by asking advice, listening, and arguing, they're sharpened (*acuuntur*). When people try all means, in the end they find ways to the things they want which everyone approves, and no one had ever thought of before" (TP 9.14). Spinoza conjures a particularly vivid image here. Individuals' *ingenia*, their "wits," or affective dispositions, remain *hebetiora*, too dull, sluggish, or inactive until they engage with those of others. Such a deliberate and deliberative engagement generates new ideas and, perhaps more significantly, stimulates and sharpens participants' powers of intelligence. Spinoza's verb, *acuere*, which, aside from "to sharpen," renders as "to stir emotionally" and "to tune," conveys an image of consensus process properly understood—that is, an activity that generates commonality not in spite of but through and across singular differences.

In this light, Spinoza's insistence that the best citizens use reason alone to criticize the state functions as more than just a plea to act in accordance with some suprasensual norm of rational communication.[63] (And so the effects of this "norm" need not redound solely to the benefit of state power.) His rationalist "proviso" serves also and more fundamentally as a defense of the reason for political society, namely, the "utility" of joining forces with others so as *to preserve the vitality or development of power* (*potentia*). The formulation offered in the *Ethics*, "To man, therefore, nothing is more useful than man (*homine igitur nihil homine utilius*)," extols the supreme virtue of individuals harmonizing in such a way "that the minds and bodies of all would compose, as it were, one mind and one body" and that "all, together, should seek for themselves the common advantage (*utile*) of all." For "men who, from the guidance of reason, seek their own advantage want nothing for themselves that they do not desire for other men" (E IVp18s). The commonality that Spinoza invokes in these contexts is more premise than promise, more project than property. What rational individuals desire for themselves and others is greater power to think and act. This is, in essence, the "highest good" that Spinoza characterizes as the knowledge and love of nature/God, a good that "is common to all, and can be enjoyed by all equally" because it is not some one thing but the "virtue" or power of intelligence (E IVp36, E IVp24). The right to become *sui juris*, maximally possessed of one's own potentialities, is virtually inclusive of all others' rights.

Jurisprudence, then, emerges as a reflection on the "utility" of one's rights as held in common, an activity that composes a new common sense and a new sense of common potentiality. Put in more expressly juridical terms, the activity of jurisprudence is one of constituting a common or radically public right. As I have indicated throughout, this modality of judgment does not stipulate rights and rules in the legislative manner of the sovereign, determining the permissions and prohibitions of legal subjects. Nonetheless, in reflecting on *utile*, jurisprudence furnishes other rules of living together, norms that articulate which conditions might enable (or arrest) the development of common power. Hence the fundamentally critical aspect of this right to judge: citizens who demonstrate that a given law runs against "sound reason," that is, citizens reflecting critically on the *utile* of positive law, participate in the creation of a dissensual common sense. They inscribe a new idea of the common within and against the given distribution of rights and roles in society. The immanent norm of *utile*, of equal empowerment, becomes in this respect a weapon for opposing all that constricts citizens' agency, for challenging all images and institutions of political community—whether or not they are duly constituted or justified on grounds of peace, order, and security, etcetera—that operate in some way as sources of stultification and mortification. Thus, jurisprudence operates "beyond" jurisdiction in an affirmative manner by generating a common immunity to domination, including and especially that of the state. And crucially, jurisprudence converts rather than reiterates the negative logic of immunity by affirming another immunity in common: a right or immunity that builds resistance through (affective) contagion rather than negation, and a commonality that forms through processes of alteration rather than assimilation.

Agonism or Accumulation?

Aside from throwing light on the political meaning of Spinoza's *libertas philosophandi*, the figure of "jurisprudence," as I have sketched it, outlines an answer to this chapter's initial question about Spinozism as an egress from the immunitary dialectic of political modernity. On this theme, I took as my immediate provocation some of Roberto Esposito's recent formulations of an affirmative biopolitics. But, arguably, the project of employing Spinoza's thought to illuminate an alter-modernity or counter-tradition has been most forcefully and consistently pursued by another Italian thinker: Antonio Negri. So my approach in this chapter raises a question about how my reading of Spinoza might stand as an alternative to the alternative Spinoza found in Negri's writings. Moreover, my substantive emphasis on the creative resistance of a radically democratic or constituent power places my interpretation close to Negri's reading of Spinoza's *potentia* as production of the common (in both senses of the genitive). In Negri's account, the "common is a surplus, a potency that mankind has constructed, and that it can go on constructing in the gesture that frees it from command and exploitation."[64] Here one sees the signature of Negri's Spinozism: the surplus or asymmetry between an immanent, constitutive, insurgent potentiality (*potentia*) and the parasitical operations of a transcendent, constituted, sovereign power (*potestas*). By way of conclusion, I want to briefly juxtapose our respective positions on this one point, namely, the meaning of surplus power in Spinoza.

For his part, Negri understands this surplus through a paradigm of production and accumulation. This is evident in his recent claim that, "in Spinoza, the productive forces produce the relations of production," a formulation that harks back to the *potentia* versus *potestas* dynamic at the heart of Negri's exposition of Spinoza in the *Savage Anomaly*, and to Negri's subsequent synthesis of Spinoza's ontology with Marx's conception of living labor in *Insurgencies*.[65] The same formulation also points to the biopolitical twist he and Michael Hardt have given to the idea of constituent power, which appears in their *Empire* trilogy as "biopolitical production" (of forms of life, knowledge, social relations, and affects) that necessarily exceeds and resists global apparatuses of subjection and control.[66] In each instance, the basic schema is that of an "absolute antagonism" between multitudinous power (forces of production), on the one hand, and sovereign power (relations of production), on the other.[67] The former produce the latter in the sense that every incarnation of sovereign power is in reality nothing other than a corrupt form of immanent potentiality. Adamant that "the political thought of Spinoza is to be found in his ontology," Negri holds that "in Spinoza the political is . . . a potency exceeding all measure . . . an accumulation not of substantial (individual) segments but of modal (singular) potencies."[68] However, as critics note, Negri's insistence on the ontological and absolute character of this surplus potency tends to absolve it from any essential relation to the governmental forms of capture, control, and regulation that are said to be its (illusory?) products.[69] As a consequence, a persistent problem for Negri is how to account for the endurance of state or constituted powers in specifically political and historical terms rather than exclusively ontological or economic ones.[70] State power appears in his writings mostly as the passive accumulation of common potentiality, a temporary blockage or fetter on constituent processes.

In contrast to Negri's production/accumulation paradigm, I have approached surplus power in Spinoza through a paradigm of *agonism* so as to put into relief competing strategies or politics of immunity. Jurisdiction and jurisprudence thus represent two interrelated but distinct ways of interpreting and employing the affective surplus of judgment. Jurisdiction combines a sovereign power of decision with a pastoral power of governing subjects in a tolerant or nonrepressive fashion. Here the state endeavors to neutralize and integrate the expansive force of its constituents' *conatus*, their natural striving to judge and pursue what is conducive to their empowerment, by interpreting it as if it were a desire to secure "conscientious judgment" as the inviolable property of each individual. In this fashion, the state actively resists its disintegration, inviting subjects to affirm their freedom of judgment in a specific and selective way as a form of free responsibility, that is, as a form of obedience. Through and in the activity of jurisprudence, however, citizens resist the state's integral ordering of political life, redeploying the common "utility" of affective surplus power via judgments that generate a kind of auto-immunitary resistance—a common immunity—to the state's excess of protection. As I shall elaborate in the chapters that follow, this common immunity takes the political form of a new constitution, a new sense and scope of common affairs. Thus, the conflictual encounters between jurisdiction and jurisprudence emerge as struggles over the creation of new legal relations and not just new relations of production. Viewed in this manner, juridical norms and potentialities of life find an internal and affirmative relationship beyond the strictures of a base/superstructure schema.

2

Judgment in Common

In her 1990 book, *Governing the Commons*, Elinor Ostrom offered a rejoinder to Garrett Hardin's influential argument that shared resources ("commons") inexorably suffer "tragedy," or depletion at the hands of self-interested individuals acting contrary to the common good.[1] Refuting his claim on its own rational-choice and game-theoretic terms, Ostrom proceeded to challenge a further presumption, made by several of Hardin's exponents, that the only means of avoiding such tragedy consisted of either centralized state control ("Leviathan") or private property rights.[2] Ostrom showed, on the contrary, that cooperative management of social and ecological commons was both a theoretical possibility and an empirical reality in localities throughout the world, from mountain meadows in Switzerland to water projects in the Philippines. Her argument pierced the aura of inevitability that Hardin's followers had lent their policy solutions, which, she contended, were often little more than "metaphorical" (one could say ideological) applications of a particular image of social interaction treated as the paradigm for sociality as such.[3]

Ostrom's critical recuperation of "the commons"—a term that recalls, among other things, struggles over land use in precapitalist England—finds a certain parallel today in various streams of activism and research that employ the category to specify the new forms of "enclosure" entailed in the neoliberal project of privatizing public goods and implementing capitalist market relations across a range of domains, from urban planning and environmental policy to education and popular culture.[4] These latest appeals to "the commons" launch a challenge not only at the level of "solutions," questioning the case-by-case merits of neoliberal policy programs and intellectual positions on pressing social problems. More fundamentally, they contest the form and function of the "problems" as presented by neoliberalism: the social ontology of "competitive individualism" that such programs and positions conjure into being when, say, students are invited to see themselves as consumers in an education system increasingly divorced from larger structures of public accountability, or when the precarity that neoliberalism manufactures in labor markets compels workers to bear "entrepreneurial" and existential responsibility for the structural dislocations of capitalism.[5] Commons will appear as tragic, or not at all, if one begins from the image of sociality promoted by neoliberal rationality.

Cognate with, although not strictly identical to, the contemporary reprise of the idea of the commons is a broadly post-Marxist reinterpretation of "the common in communism."[6] Hardt and Negri, arguably the most prominent theorists of "the common" in recent years, define it as both the presupposition and result of the biopolitical production peculiar to post-Fordist capitalism.[7] For them, the common refers, on one hand, to shared capacities, dispositions, affects—in short, to a creative potentiality much like the generic capacity for language.[8] On the other hand, they conceive of the common as the actualization of such creativity in specific ideas, information, images, knowledges, codes, social relationships, and affects.[9] Hardt and Negri take pains to stress the communicative rather than communitarian essence of this concept: whereas "*community* is often used to refer to a moral unity that stands above the population," the common "is based on the *communication* among singularities and emerges through the collaborative social processes of production."[10] In their view, the notion of the common carries great critical and constructive potential insofar as it can liberate leftist thinking from a seemingly intractable deadlock between private and public powers of ownership, wherein state regulation, be it socialist or Keynesian, represents the only solution to the ills of capital, and the only viable response to the ills of state control appears to be deregulation and privatization.[11] Accordingly, Hardt and Negri believe that the traditional pairing of public and private, along with inherited republican terms such as "common good" and "public interest," obfuscate what the new communism reveals, namely, that the defining conflict of the times is between "the common and property as such"—between forms of coproduction and partaking that do not intrinsically lend themselves to a logic of scarcity and exclusive uses (the sharing of ideas or aesthetic experiences, for instance) on one side; and on the other side, the relentless drive, embodied by consumer technology companies such as Amazon, Apple, Facebook, Google, and Microsoft, to corral such collaboration into the forms of property and profit.[12] Neither tragic nor enclosable, Hardt and Negri's insurgent "common" names an inexhaustible source of human creativity.

If Ostrom wanted to demonstrate that "commons" can and do exist as abiding features of actual, historical communities, then the authors of the *Empire* series, for their part, want to vindicate the metaphysical necessity of "the common" as the immanent teleology of actual, conflict-ridden, and seemingly "tragic" communities. Hardt and Negri's efforts can seem, in this respect, to amount to a sort of ontological overkill. When arrayed against exclusive and exclusionary *dispositifs* of property, their idea of the common threatens to become exclusive in its own way, precluding from its ultimate horizon radical forms of incommensurability and social discord. Along these lines, Jodi Dean argues that, despite their differences, thinkers like Hardt, Negri, Agamben, and Casarino build into their conceptions of the common an image of (a remnant of) communication free from internal discord, "as if referents and systems of meaning didn't clash with one another, as if knowledges did not emerge in and through conflict," as if, in other words, conflict bears no *necessary* relation to commonality.[13] Dean offers a sympathetic critique. She thinks that the category of the common(s) can facilitate both a deeper grasp of the mechanisms of depoliticization peculiar to the ideological formation she calls communicative capitalism and a broader vision of alternative forms of sociality. But, in Dean's view, leftists do better to affirm antagonism as an ineliminable feature of social relations so as to organize it in one direction or another. Her amendment, then, is at once ontological and strategic: "Division is common. We have to seize it."[14]

I take a slightly modified version of Dean's formulation as this chapter's provocation, although it is my ambition neither simply to "apply" Spinoza's thought to the current debates over the common(s) nor directly to adjudicate them. Rather, the aim here is to pursue in and with Spinoza the conceptual hypothesis that "judgment is common." I suggested in the last chapter that much of Spinoza's novelty concerning the relationship between politics and judgment stems from his immanent naturalism, that is, from the manner in which he inscribes a theological-political discourse on sovereignty within a relational ontology of power that he calls Nature (or God, or substance). Playing on the meaning of "immanence" (to dwell in, remain in), one could say that, from a Spinozist perspective, *judgment remains in common*—necessarily, inalienably, impersonally so. I want to unpack that idea in the following pages by considering in a more sustained fashion the ontological status of judgment in Spinoza's writings. What might it mean to conceive of judgment as a feature of the common?

By way of response, this chapter argues the following points. First, Spinozistically speaking, to say that judgment exists and persists in common means that it is immanent to a field of "transindividual" relations that constitute individuals and communities in their historical specificity.[15] Judgment belongs to an intrication of open systems or ecologies (psychic, social, biological) of affect.[16] The concept that Spinoza employs to conceptualize judgment in this radically relational way is *ingenium*, or "complexion," which combines commonality (from the Latin *plexus*: braiding, interweaving, network) and singularity (with all the connotations of novelty, genius, etc.) to signify something like an individual's characteristic sentiments and affective disposition. Moreover, and this is the second point, Spinoza's notion of complexion presents a common that is necessarily in judgment—divided as well as shared. On this view, the common in any community cannot be dissociated from a multiplicity of ways of interpreting, differentiating, evaluating, and, as a condition for all of these operations, *desiring*. With specific attention to the psychosocial mechanism that Spinoza calls the "imitation of the affects," I explore how individual "complexion" functions as a principle of judgment that acquires a differential application in and through competing strategies or social logics of mimetic desire.[17] Here the formulation "judgment in common" comes to mean that division, and, more specifically, conflict is an intrinsic feature of community. The question then becomes, what kind of conflict? The third and final point of the chapter is that Spinoza's account of mimetic desire presents an incommensurability between modes of imagining or prefiguring how a common world is at once shared and divided.

Complexion and the Ecologies of Affect

Spinoza employs the term *ingenium* to situate individual judgment in a concatenation of psychic and social relations, situated in turn within the open totality of relations he calls God/Nature. Much like the idea of affect, *ingenium* is not a term that Spinoza confines to one or another corner of his philosophy; rather, *ingenium* plays an important role in each of his major works, synthesizing the formal, geometric mode of his analysis with his forays into the experiential registers of language, passion, and history.[18] While the Latin *ingenium* permits of various translations, including "temperament," "talent," "nature," and "mentality," the word "complexion" perhaps best conveys the peculiar semantic charge Spinoza assigns to it, as a complicated interweaving of physical and mental determinations.[19] Here *ingenium* comes to signify a complex of provisionally congealed affects that are constitutive of an individual's characteristic judgments and comportment.[20]

Spinoza uses the term "complexion" to capture the distinctive individuality of human beings as much as communities in their historical specificity—without, however, reducing one to the other, so that individuals would be simply passive reflections of their society or society nothing but an aggregation of self-contained individuals. Rather, he understands both collective individuality and human individuality to emerge in and through a concurrence of the same basic elements—desires, bodies, thoughts, affects—and by way of the same processes of forming and reforming habit.[21] So, for instance, Spinoza explains the fabled obstinacy of the ancient Hebrew nation not in terms of some innate disposition but, first, in terms of their experience of Egyptian oppression and, second, in terms of the specific laws and mores that come to structure their lives once they acquire a state of their own (TTP 2.46, 17.94). Conversely, even though he presents Moses as having captivated, to the greatest degree, the hearts and minds of his people and as having thereby acquired the most integral of states, Spinoza underscores how the "complexions" of individual Israelites never simply reproduced that of the Mosaic regime (20.5). Indeed, Spinoza designates as "superstition" the fantasy of perfectly subordinating the diverse complexions at play in society to the complexion of a sovereign agency, such that subjects desire, think, and act at the specific pleasures of their ruler. And he stresses the practical futility of superstition with repeated appeals to the irreducible variety of human complexions amid the fluctuations of lived experience.

The individual "nature" to which Spinoza's idea of *ingenium* refers is an effect of second nature. Or to put the point another way, Spinoza's *ingenium* suggests that nature and culture are not finally distinguishable. Human beings and social formations are equally "parts" of Nature in that they belong to a single plane of immanence in continuous becoming—a causal nexus of effects becoming causes becoming effects *ad infinitum,* not as parts of a serial structure but as elements in an expansive weave of finite modal relations and durations. Here "modes," or singular things, persevere as dynamic, open systems whose existences are necessarily bound up with that of other modes. What Spinoza calls God/Nature can be read, accordingly, as the immanent structural necessity that each thing refer to something else.[22] His move to immerse finite individuals in the infinitude of nature is thus less an operation of reducing them, in the final instance, to mere effects of necessary causal laws than of seeking to understand them according to their constitutive relations. And when it comes to the specific challenge of understanding *human* individuals in this way, Spinoza is convinced that one needs to begin with a study of affect (E III pref).[23]

For the purposes of this chapter, a brief foray into Spinoza's theory of affective life helps to contextualize and prepare the claim, which I develop later, that "complexion" operates as a source or principle of judgment. To begin with, it bears emphasizing that in contrast to a view found both in Descartes and contemporary theories of emotion, Spinoza does not treat affect simply as a bodily response triggered by some external event. Nor does he limit the category of affect to the emotional (or "irrational") life of humans or animals: affects consist of passions *and* actions (E III def3). In the broad scheme of Spinoza's naturalism, affects name modulations in the potency or striving (*conatus*) that all finite beings experience by virtue of their necessary interrelation. One can examine these modulations from the side of bodies or from the side of minds, for corporeal and mental processes are two aspects of the same global tendency. Mind and body act and undergo together, but neither acts on the other. "By affect," Spinoza writes, "I understand affections of the body by which the body's power of acting is increased or diminished, aided or restrained, and at the same time, the ideas of these affections" (E III def3). So any amplification of power or activity belongs simultaneously to body and mind, just as any contraction in power, any passivity, corresponds to body and mind in equal measure. Cognitive and conative states, thoughts and emotions, are effectively inseparable, as is evident, for example, in the affect that Spinoza calls (borrowing from Maimonides) the "intellectual love of God" (E V p32–33).[24] Or, as he puts it in the third part of the *Ethics*, "decisions of the mind . . . vary as the dispositions of the body varies," and everyone, "from his own affect, judges a thing good or bad, useful or useless" (III 2s, III 39s). In sum, for Spinoza, affects register the many continual changes in an individual's psychophysical constitution, and these changes are generative of one's image of self and world.

Spinoza provides two accounts of how affects are produced. The first operates in a deductive mode, abstracting from individual idiosyncrasies in order to explain the spectrum of "human actions and appetites" on the basis of three primary affects: desire, joy, and sadness. Desire, joy, and sadness name the basic orientations taken by one's essential striving and by the concrete modifications to one's power of acting.[25] Whereas desire (or appetite) is another name for the striving to persevere in one's being (E III p9s), joy designates any amplification of this fundamental *conatus*, and sadness any depletion (III p11).[26] All other affects can be understood as permutations of these three. Proceeding in this way, Spinoza expounds on the nature and various qualities of the affects; he considers their compatibilities and incompatibilities, as well as the power they can exert over the human mind; and he delineates certain practical measures meant to mitigate the harmful features of the affects and to fortify their salutary aspects.

Spinoza initially appeals to causal mechanisms that relate the affects directly to objects. Love and hate, for instance, appear respectively as "joy with the accompanying idea of an external cause" and "sadness with the accompanying idea of an external cause" (E III 13s). Ideas of love and hate constitute objects defined not by any inherent qualities but solely in relation to the complexion of a particular individual who is affected by love and hate at a given moment. (By the same token, the affects constitute a "subject" defined provisionally by determinate—but in no way predetermined—objects of desire, joy, sadness, and their derivations.) Aside from this basic mechanism of "objectification," Spinoza further explains the generation of affects from particular associations that trigger, say, habitual affects of joy or sadness (III p14–17), which, if one adds a temporal dimension and the "image of a doubtful thing," become hope or fear (III p18; cf. TTP pref 1–2). And beyond objectifying and associational mechanisms, Spinoza details a mechanism of the affects whereby an individual comes to love those who love what she loves, hate what she hates, etcetera (III p19–24). All of these affective mechanisms qualify as relations to objects given that Spinoza accords no special importance to the human elements at play: the "objects" of affects in all these instances can, of course, be other humans (e.g., relatives, competitors, allies, enemies), but they can also be animals, inanimate objects, or vague notions of success.[27] The overall effect of Spinoza's analysis, when proceeding in its deductive mode, is to suggest that many and diverse humans, when subject to the same affective pressures, will behave to some degree in the same manner.[28] His treatment of the affects would thus seem to demonstrate that individuality, or complexion (*ingenium*), is nothing but a particular determination of necessary laws. In this spirit, Spinoza employs a geometric idiom to summarize the accomplishments of *Ethics,* Part III: "I have explained and shown through their first causes the main affects and fluctuations of mind (*fluctuatio animi*) which arise from the composition of the three primitive affects" (III p59s, trans. modified).

However, Spinoza switches immediately into a more poetic register, reflecting, "from what has been said it is clear that we are driven about in many ways by external causes, and that, like waves on the sea, driven by contrary winds, we toss about, not knowing our outcome and fate" (E III p59s). Here Spinoza's likening of psychic fluctuation (*fluctuatio animi*) to the turbulent waves of a sea, while affirming the necessity of dimly understood causal mechanisms—analogous perhaps to the laws of fluid dynamics or wind-wave and weather modeling—simultaneously points to the limitations of geometric demonstration, which cannot account for the indefinite variety of affects and the incalculable forms of emotional turmoil that individuals actually experience.[29] Spinoza concedes as much in the lines immediately following the wave image: "I believe it is clear to anyone that the various affects can be compounded with one another in so many ways, and that so many variations can arise from this composition that they cannot be defined by any number" (III p59s). Only a few propositions earlier, he argues that affects differ not only according to their objects, but also according to each individual, who, in the concrete form of her desire, differs essentially from others, and even from herself over time (III p57, p51). And as Spinoza demonstrates to great effect when discussing the affective texture of religious and political forms of life, those features of the affects that concern humans in their irreducible differences prove to be of the utmost consequence.[30] Causal mechanisms can assign a necessary place to such differences but cannot ultimately give them a precise figure.[31] That is what "complexion" provides.

In this respect, one can read the appearance of the term "complexion" in part three of the *Ethics* as marking an important tonal and analytical shift. Consider Proposition 31 along with its corollary and scholium. The proposition reads, "If we imagine that someone loves, desires or hates something we ourselves love, desire, or hate, we shall thereby love, desire or hate it with greater constancy." In the corollary, Spinoza adds, "it follows that each and every one strives, so far as he can, that everyone should love what he loves, and hate what he hates." And in the scholium immediately following, he reformulates this point, replacing the specific reference to love and hate with a broader assertion: "each and every one, by his nature, wants the others to live according to his complexion" (III p31s, trans. modified). The question is what conceptual work "complexion" (*ingenium*) is doing here, if any. At first glance, it appears to be operating merely as a blanket term, encompassing a range of affects, including but not limited to those already mentioned—love, hate, and desire. In this capacity, "complexion" would not introduce any qualitative change in the argument Spinoza has advanced in the proposition and corollary so much as constitute a broadening of the argument's scope: "complexion" could stand in for any of the possible combinations of affect that might concretely define an individual's characteristic striving.

But Spinoza's introduction of "complexion" in the scholium to E III p31, beyond serving this descriptive purpose, also testifies to a qualitative change in his argument. As Pierre-François Moreau suggests, one can discern this shift in the subtle grammatical difference between the proposition, where Spinoza employs the first-person plural, "we," and the corollary and scholium, where Spinoza speaks rather of "each and every one" (*unumquemque*). When using the first-person plural, Spinoza adopts the perspective of a geometrical order that grasps human nature through a causal matrix of affect, starting from the three primary affects, which it applies universally. When speaking of "each and every one," by contrast, Spinoza points to the precise affective disposition that constitutes individuals in their singularity, albeit from the same basic, or common elements. Moreau elaborates. For a given individual, "one specific passion may be dominant; this passion is associated, for biographical reasons or because of his environment, with another; this passion finally acquires certain characteristics owing to the structure of his body. For another individual, the same elements organize themselves otherwise, in a very different tone. Only experience can teach us this existential given. . . . We thus need a concept to designate this irreducibly passionate node . . . and it is that which is designated by the term *ingenium*."[32] Thus, in Spinoza's texts, "complexion" (*ingenium*) functions not only to index the irreducible diversity of human desires and affective dispositions, a diversity that cannot be deduced *a priori* because it emerges only historically in the social relations and encounters that give concrete, if contingent form to the affects. "Complexion" also serves positively to *conceptualize* processes of human and collective individuation. Or to put my point in slightly different terms, if "complexion" reveals the limits of Spinoza's deductive mode of understanding human actions and appetites through a causal matrix of three primary affects, "complexion" simultaneously leads one to consider the utility of a second account of affects by which Spinoza explains the formation of sociality and individuality.

Complexion and the Appetite for Emulation

Spinoza's second account of the genesis of human affects centers on what he calls the "imitation of the affects" (*affectuum imitatio*) (E III p27s). The basic process that he presents at E III p27 and in the few propositions that elaborate on the idea of *affectuum imitatio* is one of social formations emerging and fragmenting on the basis of an affective contagion that touches everyone in some form or another, at some moment or another. "If we imagine a thing like us," Spinoza writes, "toward which we have had no affect, to be affected with some other affect, we are thereby affected with a like affect" (E III p27). Here Spinoza does not frame the production of affects in relation to an object, as he did in his first account. He alludes rather to affects that derive from mimetic desire, that is, from an imagined element of similarity—"some likeness" (*aliquid simile*)—with something or somebody who one believes is affected in a particular way and who consequently becomes the model for one's own affects. In the present section, I offer a first pass at elaborating this psychosocial mechanism. The next section will complicate this initial picture and show that the dynamics of mimetic desire find very different applications, in Spinoza's view. Ultimately, I want to argue that Spinoza's concept of complexion names the precise principle or source of judgment that enables humans to make sense of both plurality and singularity, that is, of the fact that individuals exist in and through relationships with others who are different in a nontrivial sense. It helps first to lay out the principal features of Spinoza's account of affective imitation—in very schematic terms, emulation, fluctuation, and assimilation.

EMULATION

Spinoza's analysis of mimetic desire reveals in the formation of each individual's singular complexion a universally shared appetite for emulation.[33] This means, in part, that I strive spontaneously to emulate others, taking them as models for my own inclinations and aversions. Nowadays, one is more likely to encounter claims about affective imitation and contagion in discourses of neurobiology, particularly research on "mirror neurons" and the automatic imitation of affective states that transpires between bodies. While much or most of this research would suggest that spontaneous mirroring can be understood without reference to processes of socialization or habit formation, Spinoza, for his part, understands the "spontaneity" of affective imitation as a function of mimetic relationships that are inextricably psychic, social, and biological. From Spinoza's perspective, an individual acquires self-awareness—consciousness of his essential being or fundamental striving—through the affective variations of everyday life, through habitual experience with joys and sadnesses, and thus through processes of socialization whereby he takes others, in a nonconscious way, as models for his desire. In this manner, one emulates or identifies with others imagined as similar. "We strive to do whatever we imagine men to look on with joy, and on the other hand, we shall be averse to doing what we imagine men are averse to" (III p29).[34] In this sort of mimetic identification, when an individual is striving to act so as to please others, he reciprocally experiences joy in imagining another trying to please him. Spinoza calls this joy "praise," in contrast to "blame," or the sadness with which one is averse to the other's actions (III p29s). It is clear, however, that Spinoza does not understand these as natural moral sentiments. One is born and educated into a pre-established web of mores, he argues, such that the affect of "sadness follows absolutely all those acts which from custom are called *wrong*, and joy, those which are called *right*." Spinoza emphasizes that family serves as a key site for the internalization of social norms: "Parents—by blaming the former acts, and often scolding their children on account of them, and on the other hand, by recommending and praising the latter acts—have brought it about that affects of sadness were joined to the one kind of act, and those of joy to the other" (E III def aff 27). Hence the most "spontaneous" set of moral intuitions one holds are, at root, functions of habit, memory, and "second nature." Specific others (my parents, for example) and, by extension, a host of indefinite others—the anonymous collective, or social imaginary—are immediately implicated in the structure of my desire, which, strictly speaking, is neither my own nor the property of anyone.

In the passages on affective imitation (E III p27–31), Spinoza offers no definitions or descriptions of the "men" he cites, no criteria by which human individuals recognize others as "similar."[35] This is no oversight. His point is to highlight the mediating role of imagination in the mimetic processes of emulation: these are relational processes that constitute and reconstitute individuals and not merely "intersubjective" relationships between preconstituted selves. Thus the "men" that serve as the models for my actions and appetites are what Spinoza calls images or "universal notions," namely, abstractions distilled from a jumble of images that affect my body at a given moment and that surpass my powers of perceiving essential differences between things. As Spinoza notes, a universal notion like "man" is, in fact, always partial, a projection of each individual's particular history of experience: "For example, those who have more often regarded men's stature with wonder will understand by the word *man* an animal of erect stature. But those who have been accustomed to consider something else will form another common image of men—e.g., that man is an animal capable of laughter, or a featherless biped, or a rational animal" (E II p40s1).

The contemporary Italian author Elena Ferrante gives expression to this sort of intrication of others in one's own strivings when she writes of the *frantumaglia*—a Neapolitan word for the scraps or fragments of memory—that is constitutive of one's sense of self and world. When asked in an interview to elaborate on this idea, she responds:

> Where do I start? In my childhood, my adolescence. Some of the poor Neapolitan neighborhoods were crowded, yes, and rowdy. To gather oneself, so to speak, was physically impossible. . . . The idea that every "I" is largely made up of others and by the others wasn't theoretical; it was a reality. To be alive meant to collide continually with the existence of others and to be collided with, the results being at times good-natured, at others aggressive, then again good-natured. . . . Of course, today I have small quiet places where I can gather myself—but I still feel that the idea is slightly ridiculous. . . . I can't even think without the voices of others, much less write. And I'm not talking only about relatives, female friends, enemies. I'm talking about others, men and women who today exist only in images: in television or newspaper images, sometimes

> heartrending, sometimes offensive in their opulence. And I'm talking about the past, about what we generally call tradition; *I'm talking about all those others* who were once in the world and *who have acted or who now act through us.*[36]

Ferrante vividly depicts an affectively dense and dynamic weave of relations lurking behind the idea of (her) "self," or what Spinoza calls complexion. Read in the context of Spinoza's approach to emulation, one could say with Ferrante: others "act through us" insofar as one learns about one's desires, and acquires one's self-image, by imitating a tangle of real and imagined others.

Inseparable from the spontaneous emulation of others, in Spinoza's telling, is a striving *to be emulated* (E III p31c) and therefore to see in others confirmation of one's own desires, thoughts, feelings, or, in short, one's own complexion (III p31s). Having others whom I perceive to be similar to me adopt what I take to be my own manner of thinking, feeling, and acting is a way of vindicating my fundamental striving. Spinoza illustrates by citing Ovid: "He has a heart of iron who loves what another concedes. Let us hope while we fear and fear while we hope, we lovers" (*Speremus pariter, pariter metuamus amantes; Ferreus est, si quis, quod sinit alter, amat*) (III 31c).[37] Following Spinoza's Ovid, then, I believe my mistress is worthy of my love so long as I can see or imagine other, similar suitors, similarly loving her. Spinoza leaves implicit at this point what the drama of the poem continues to explore, viz. that a man's love for his mistress will flag in the absence of the external validation provided by rival suitors who similarly love her.

FLUCTUATION

While Spinoza's initial focus with affective imitation is on the confirmation and intensification of affects, his text soon makes way for the idea that affective ambivalence, dissonance, and psychic fluctuation are equally endemic in the mimetic processes under discussion. "If we imagine that someone loves, desires or hates something we ourselves love, desire, or hate we shall thereby love, desire or hate it with greater constancy. But if we imagine that he is averse to what we love, or the opposite, then we shall undergo fluctuation of the mind" (E III p31, trans. modified). One sees in this passage how Spinoza's two accounts of affective production (based, respectively, on object relations and similitude) generate a triangular relation between myself, an object that affects me in some way, and an "other" who serves as a model for my own affects.[38] Thus the first sentence in the passage above depicts a scenario in which the mechanism of imitation reinforces an affect that an individual (call him Jens) associates with an object, strengthening his patriotism, say, by reminding him that other Dutchmen are similarly celebrating the triumph of the Oranje over Brazil in the World Cup. The second sentence indicates how the triangular relation becomes conflictual: if Jens sees his colleague Bram, also a Dutchman, scoffing at the parochial enthusiasm of the crowd and dismissing the idea of (national) sports as bread and circuses, then Jens necessarily will be affected—or infected, so to speak—by Bram's aversion, even as Jens continues to experience a love for his country and its sports heroes, with the consequence that Jens will undergo a "fluctuation of mind." According to Spinoza's logic, the psychic turbulence that Jens experiences, in this case, would not simply result from his seeing a colleague (and compatriot) contradict rather than confirm his feelings. More profoundly, the fluctuation consists of an affective conflict that he has internalized by virtue of imitating another whose affects are at odds with what Jens believes to be his own.

ASSIMILATION

According to Spinoza's psychology of similitude, then, whereby individuation takes place in and through mimetic relationships of affect that traverse "selves" and "others," it is as if each individual desires for others to have always already possessed the same thoughts and feelings, or, in a word, the very same complexion as he does. Given the emotional and cognitive dissonance that one encounters when this appears not to be the case—because, for example, I recognize that you and I love the same thing in different ways, or desire incompatible goods, or imagine in different ways the thing we both love—everybody strives, as far as he can, to bring about the assimilation of others' complexions to his own. This striving, in other words, is a genuine existential endeavor and not just an idle fantasy—an endeavor to change social reality so that it conforms to one's assimilationist fantasy. Spinoza poses this as a key problem not only in his *Ethics* but also, as one might expect, in his political works (e.g., TTP 17.15, TP 1.5). In the TTP, it appears most starkly as an impasse centered on the social reality of diverse "complexions" and the antisocial trajectory of mimetic desire. Spinoza writes that "men vary greatly in their complexion (*ingenium*), . . . one is content with these opinions, another with those, and . . . what moves one person to religion moves another to laughter" (TTP pref 28). "No one doubts," he ventures, "that the common complexion (*ingenium*) of men is extremely variable. . . . Opinions govern men in different ways: those which move one person to devotion, move another to laughter and contempt" (14.22, trans. modified). On the one hand, everyone knows by experience of the existence of an irreducible variety of complexions in society. On the other hand, Spinoza asserts, everyone wants "everything to be done according to his complexion." (TTP 17.15, trans. modified; cf. 7.1, 14.1). Why so? With his mimetic account of affects, Spinoza shows that this assimilationist drive, or antisocial tendency, emerges from a form of sociality—conjunctural and spontaneous as it may be—and not from some aggressive instinct or mutual diffidence between self-possessed individuals.

Strategies of Mimetic Desire

For Spinoza, human beings have judgment "in common" in the very broad sense that, as participants in nature's potentiality, they are all striving, or desiring, and *consequently* judging what is to their advantage (*utile*) (E IIIp9s). Judgment follows desire, the life force that traverses each and all but belongs to no one. As I showed in the previous section, judgment is common in another sense as well, one more peculiar to the imitative mechanisms that Spinoza documents: everyone takes others as the models for her own characteristic judgments (complexion), while simultaneously desiring that others adopt her complexion. Everyone strives to emulate and to be emulated. Mimetic desire of this sort, Spinoza believes, typically gives rise to ambivalent and ultimately antisocial forms of sociality premised upon an imagined fusion with others around a shared object of desire, love, hate, and so on. But that is not the end of the story.

What remains particularly striking about Spinoza's elaboration of these dynamics, when compared with both canonical philosophy and theorists of group psychology such as Freud and Le Bon, is that Spinoza proceeds neither to pathologize the phenomenon of affective contagion nor to associate sociality primarily with passivity. Rather than external impositions on the intellectual powers of an autonomous mind, affects appear in Spinoza's optic as constituent elements of the mind's ecology, which, as noted above, bears an internal relation to biological and social ecologies. It follows, on his logic, that the production of affects always involves, in some measure, a type of reasoning that extends beyond the domain of thought to that of social relations, giving rise in its own way to new and other forms of commonality. Hence Spinoza uses the term "common notions" to describe the "foundations of our reasoning" in the increasingly perspicuous grasp of the agreements, differences, and oppositions between bodies—a point to which I will return in chapter 5 (E II p40s1).

If, in Spinoza's presentation, all judgments follow the natural or ontological law of desire, it is also the case that judgments apply that law in a dynamic and differential fashion, more and less passively or actively, passionately or rationally. In this section, I want to propose how this process of articulation works by taking up again the appetite for emulation that Spinoza places at the heart of his psychology of similitude. Consider, as a starting point, the following scholium:

> The appetite by which a man is said to act, and that by which he is said to be acted on, are one and the same. For example, we have shown that human nature is so constituted that each of us wants the others to live according to his complexion (see III p31s). And, indeed, in a man who is not led by reason this appetite is the passion called ambition, which does not differ much from pride. On the other hand, in a man who lives according to the dictate of reason it is the action, or virtue, called piety (see IV p37s1 and p37 alternate dem.). (E V p4s)[39]

Here Spinoza recalls the rule of mimetic desire, together with its passionate and rational declensions—affects of ambition and piety that pertain at once to alternative forms of individuality and sociality (as defined in earlier parts of the *Ethics*). The affective polarity in the above passage corresponds, I suggest, to distinct strategies or social logics by which mimetic desire acquires its precise collective and subjective figures. Spinoza's fuller treatment of "ambition" presents a spontaneous form of sociality and judging that turns on a logic of exclusionary assimilation, whereby one's relationship to others is premised upon their identification with and subordination to one's self. By contrast, Spinoza's elaboration of "piety" portrays a more reflective mode of sociality and judging that follows a logic of common alteration. Here, one's relationship to others is premised upon an openness to, and a development or transformation with, others *as others*. Complexion remains the key concept, for it represents the principle of judgment by which mimetic desire acquires its determinate social and subjective articulation. The idea of complexion allows Spinoza to demonstrate how individuals partake of heterogeneous strategies of mimetic desire in their efforts to make sense of themselves, others, and the "objects" they hold in common. My claim in what follows is that these alternative strategies prefigure divergent commonalities, that is, incommensurable ways of envisaging how a common world is simultaneously shared and divided.

The bulk of Spinoza's elaboration of the psychology of similitude concerns "ambition," the passionate declension of mimetic desire. Spinoza initially defines ambition as the "striving to do something (and to omit doing something) solely to please men," but he also characterizes it as the "striving to bring it about that everyone should approve his love and hate" (E III p29s; III p31s). One can understand these respective definitions as two sides of a coin, in line with the undecidability signaled by the idea of an "appetite for emulation" (a striving to emulate and to be emulated). To the extent that the affect of ambition prevails in the mimetic relation between individuals, they remain trapped in a no-win situation. If I fail to bring it about that others desire the same thing that I do, I am led nonetheless to imitate desires that are not my own, and so I internalize this conflict. But if I succeed in bringing it about that others desire the same things I do, I have likely convinced them to desire some exclusive good, and so I have only succeeded in making others my rival.[40] The etymology of "emulator" from the Latin *aemulator*, meaning "zealous imitator" or "imitative rival" (an English connotation from the 1650s), helps to buttress this point. For the "loss" that one experiences in either of the ways that ambition plays out turns on the assumption that others are rivals, and as such, obstacles to one's pursuits. Spinoza's citation of Ovid (in E III p31c), mentioned above, underlines how everyone hopes—and simultaneously fears—that others desire what and as he or she does. As Spinoza later reformulates the point, those who love under the influence of ambition "are not of one mind in their love—while they rejoice to sing the praises of the thing they love, they fear to be believed" (IV p37s1).

Spinoza also advances a more radical point about ambition. It is not just that ambition may lead an individual into conflict with others when they happen to desire the same scarce good. It is that an individual in the grip of ambition *necessarily* conceives of his own power, desire, and the good in exclusionary terms. Others, by definition, *can only ever* be obstacles to his pursuits. Here an individual either proceeds as if he is locked in a zero-sum conflict with others, or he joins with others on the condition that they are stripped of their alterity and subordinated to his self-conception. (In reality, a mind that is dominated by the affect of ambition vacillates between both of these imaginings.)

Spinoza's text shows that this antisocial tendency grows out of a dialectic between ambition and glory. In naturalistic terms, glory denotes a "joy accompanied by the idea of an internal cause" when the joy arises "from the fact that the man believes that he is praised or blamed" (E III p30s). Insofar as this joy depends on the imagined praise of others, glory qualifies as a species of love.[41] But to the degree that such love includes an image of oneself as an "internal cause" of joy, glory is a form of self-love. And ambition, Spinoza suggests, can ultimately be understood as "an excessive desire for glory" (III def aff 44). To appreciate what this means, it is worth noting, first, that while affects, for Spinoza, are not necessarily excessive—*hilaritas*, for example, names a balanced form of pleasure, affecting all parts of the body equally—they are ordinarily so. "Generally," he writes, "affects are excessive, and occupy the mind in the consideration of one object so much that it cannot think of others. And though men are liable to a great many affects, so that one rarely finds them to be always agitated by one and the same affect, still there are those in whom one affect is stubbornly fixed" (E IV p44s). Affective fixation tends toward what Spinoza calls "wonder" (*admiratio*), which is not an affect in itself so much as the limit-form of passivity, an acute preoccupation of the mind's powers by an object imagined as absolutely singular, without connection to other things, or "alone in the mind" (III p52s; III def aff 4).[42] An individual strives excessively, ambitiously, or, to use more contemporary language, narcissistically for glory to the extent that his desire to please others, and simultaneously to have them confirm and conform to his own affects, is dominated by an aspiration to experience himself as exclusively powerful, and thus to assimilate all others' desires to his own.[43]

Such an aspiration for mastery or absolute distinction shares the same logic of exclusionary assimilation that characterizes the "singular imagination" of *admiratio*—indeed, Spinoza defines "veneration" as wonder (*admiratio*) at someone's personal qualities, skills, or virtues because they are considered far superior. When engulfed by ambitious desire, an individual fancies himself as un-common, or extra-ordinary, and acts not only to be emulated but *venerated*—"held to be Godly," in the anthropomorphic sense (E III pref).[44] For when "the mind considers itself and its power of acting, it rejoices, and does so the more, the more distinctly it imagines itself and its power of acting," Spinoza writes (III p53). Such joy is encouraged the more an individual imagines others praise him (III p53c) and the more he imagines his own affects and actions as *sui generis.* "So everyone will have the greatest gladness from considering himself, when he considers something in himself which he denies concerning others. . . . And on the other hand, if he imagines that his own actions are weaker, compared to others' actions, he will be saddened . . . and will strive to put aside this sadness, either by wrongly interpreting his equals' actions or by magnifying his own as much as he can." (III p55s) Thus ambition and glory carry individuals naturally, necessarily toward "hate and envy" (III p55s).

In the *Theological-Political Treatise*, the assimilative impetus of ambition assumes its clearest subjective figure in the "theologian." Much like Machiavelli's *grandi*, who personify the desire to dominate, the "theologians" populating Spinoza's TTP are so characterized for their endeavor to assimilate others' interpretations (of self and world) to their own. They are possessed by an ambition to command the complexions of others (TTP 7.1, 14.1). The TTP does not, however, account for the affective causes of such "theological hatred," beyond gesturing toward the general conditions for superstition—in a word, fear. One could say that the *Ethics*' treatment of mimetic desire permits such an account of why and how "theologians"—and others similarly infected by ambition—make every effort to have others love or hate the same thing as them. As noted, ambition originates in an appetite for emulation, which, far from constituting a vice or a madness that would pertain to a few bad apples (the TTP is perhaps more ambiguous on this score), affects everyone in some measure.[45] At a primordial level, everyone desires to have his characteristic passions and actions reinforced and reflected back to him by others who seemingly bear the same complexion. This originary desire is not itself violent but often becomes so, as the rivalrous reciprocity of ambition escalates and intensifies. And in this respect, what the TTP does manage particularly well to convey is that the psychic and social turbulence to which all people are subject at one point or another leads them to seek relief in temporizing solutions (joy and sadness are given a past and future as part of a whole semiotic structure) and through the persecution and sacrifice of nonconformists "to the hatred and cruelty of their opponents" (pref 11). Such scapegoating serves the unifying purpose of providing individuals who would otherwise be inclined to view each other as rivals with "an object they can really share, in the sense that they can all rush against that victim in order to destroy it or drive it away."[46] The TTP demonstrates that the more and less violent enforcement of orthodoxy works, in this fashion, to achieve for the community of believers, fearful of the threat that the other poses to their desires, a momentary equilibrium.

What, then, of the rational declension of the appetite for emulation? How can this appetite find expression less as a passion that fuels hatred than as an action or virtue aimed at benefiting others? I would suggest, first, that in the transindividual sphere of similitude, Spinoza has reason proceed not so much by frontally opposing the exclusionary logic of ambition—nor, despite some readings, by demoting the idea of sociality to the status of a necessary evil—but rather by converting mimetic desire from its assimilationist forms into forms of mutuality, alliance, and the common development of singular powers. Reason puts to another use, or actualizes in a different manner, the demand that others act according to one's own complexion. The strategy or path that reason takes entails working through rather than pretending to master or escape from the currents of mimetic desire, with the difference that now the complexion that one wants others to adopt is defined by a certain generosity, like allies or friends who, "bear[ing] with each according to his complexion," grant each other the presumption that they are of independent mind (E IV app 13; III p59s; IV p37s1).

In contrast to the mutual rivalry that characterizes the mimetic dynamics of ambition, reason stands for reciprocity of a different order: the mutual implication of self and other, of individual and collective or federated powers. True to geometrical plan, the fourth part of the *Ethics* offers a causal demonstration of such reciprocity. Here reason shows that, insofar as individuals strive necessarily to preserve and enhance their power of acting, they endeavor necessarily to form alliances with others who desire, reciprocally, to develop their own singular powers of mind and body in common (E IV p19–31, 35–36). Accordingly, instead of a mimetic escalation of conflictual desire centering on the joint pursuit of scarce or exclusive goods (or, at least, goods imagined as such), reason implies a reciprocal amplification of powers the more each pursues "understanding"—the supremely useful good that "is common to all, and can be enjoyed by all equally"—and becomes conscious of herself as the cause of others' joy (IV p36). Guided by reason, an individual still strives for others to adopt her *ingenium*, but this means that she desires that others come into their own powers of reasoning. The mimetic dynamic here is thus pedagogical in orientation, as each endeavors with others to persevere in the greatest of self-transformations (IV app 9, V p39s).[47]

In addition to portraying reason as a causal structure of mutual implications, Spinoza presents reason and its "dictates" in a more purposive light, as a way that humans "wish" or "search for" (*quaerere*) the useful (*utile*) in the abilities of fellow humans (IV p18s).[48] It is in this light that one should understand Spinoza's appeal to "an idea of man, as a model of human nature" (*naturae humanae exemplar*), that is, a representation of the "free man" whom individuals might look to in the course of undertaking the practical and precarious endeavor of becoming rational, or active (IV pref).[49] This exemplary figure represents the perfection of human nature and the optimal realization of its powers. One could see the "free man" as the rational counterpart to the jumbled images of "men" that serve as models for human affects and actions so long as individuals remain submerged in the mimetic turbulence of ambitious desire. Similarly, in E IV p18s, Spinoza momentarily sets aside what he calls his "cumbersome geometric order" to represent, in a decidedly cosmopolitan image, the perfect agreement of singular and plural human powers—a federation of each and all, united, as it were, in "one mind and one body."

All that said, "it rarely happens" that humans live in such a perfect synergy of powers, according to the guidance of reason: Spinoza takes this to be an effectual truth of social existence. Human life is "so constituted" that individuals are "usually envious and burdensome to one another." Nevertheless, "they find from experience that by helping one another they can provide themselves much more easily with the things they require, and that only by joining forces" can they effectively avoid external dangers. They find that they "derive from [their] fellow men many more advantages than disadvantages" (IV p35s). Although this sounds like a much more tepid acknowledgment of the supreme *utile* that humans constitute for one another when they live by reason—"man is a God to man," Spinoza writes in the sentences immediately preceding—it is his way of saying that people are never wholly bereft of reason, which ordinarily holds the status of an aspiration. As Spinoza puts the matter in the TTP,

> no one can doubt how much more advantageous it is to man to live according to the laws and certain dictates of our reason. . . . There's no one who does not desire to live securely, and as far as possible, without fear. But this simply cannot happen so long as everyone is permitted to do whatever he likes, and reason is granted no more right than hatred and anger. . . . Also (as we showed in Ch. 5), if we consider that without mutual aid men must live most wretchedly and without any cultivation of reason, we shall see very clearly that to live, not only securely, but very well, men had to agree in having one purpose. . . . So they had to make a very firm resolution and contract to direct everything only according to the dictate of reason. No one dares to be openly contrary to that, for fear of seeming mindless. They had to agree to rein in their appetites, insofar as those appetites urge something harmful to someone else, to do nothing to anyone which they would not want done to themselves, and finally, to defend another person's right as if it were their own. (16.12–14)

Spinoza's string of negatives here—"no one can doubt," "there's no one who does not desire," etcetera—makes an appeal to certain truths of experience whereby everyone recognizes, at least in some minimal way, the superior utility of ordering communal life according to rational principles. One need not be a paragon of reason, like the "free man" of Ethics IV, to grasp these truths. At the same time, Spinoza highlights here the sheer necessity and compulsion people feel to escape from structural insecurity, hostilities, and pervasive anxiety. Everyone strives to avoid psychosocial turmoil even as they are complicit in its production. Spinoza thus locates "in each man a passionate aspiration for the benefits of reason."[50] As I shall discuss in subsequent chapters, a key political question that follows, for Spinoza, is how to preserve and expand that aspiration amid the spontaneous dynamics of mimetic desire (to say nothing of the more cultivated or institutionalized forms of ambition and the desire for mastery), which churn up affects such as envy, anger, love, and hate that so occupy subjects' minds as to leave "no room for reason" (TTP 16.22).

Let me sum up my argument in this section. Mimetic desire finds expression in divergent commonalities, or ways of prefiguring how a common world is simultaneously shared and divided. Communities of ambition form around objects imagined to be common: here individuals commune in some dominant affect, for example, love or hate, with the identitarian presumption or assimilative aspiration that others will—indeed, must—be like them. Communities formed "reasonably," by contrast, no longer predicate solidarity on some one thing, but rather on the good that is constituted by virtue of combining with others in an alliance of reciprocal empowerment. In this case, the shared object of desire is nothing other than the good of being a member of that society, that is, the good of being treated as a free and equal constituent of the community, equally capable of judging the useful (*utile*) according to one's own complexion. To desire for others what I desire for myself is, in this case, to see that they autonomously develop their own abilities and that they know ever more adequately what is of use to them (E IV p37s1–2, E IV p45s, E IV p35). If this "pious" form of sociality can be viewed as something of a virtuous circle, in contrast to the vicious circle of ambitious desire, that it is because it depicts a communal learning process—another form of affective contagion or mimesis—whereby individuals increasingly gain an understanding of the reciprocal immanence, rather than exteriority, of self and other.[51] Here, as Balibar writes, it is a matter of individuals coming to "know each other as different individuals who have much in common. . . . Men know that their fellow Men are irreducible to one another, each having . . . a specific *ingenium*, while being mutually *convenientes*."[52]

It follows that the difference between these commonalities is irresolvable. Rather than a disagreement over an object to be possessed, a status to be won, or, in short, a struggle over the same order of good, the discord between "ambition" and "piety" has the character of an incommensurability. And yet, as Balibar convincingly argues, Spinoza's parallel demonstrations of the passionate and rational declensions of mimetic desire do not depict wholly separate communities or isolated processes.[53] They depict variable postures that individuals—including one and the same individual—assume at different moments by virtue of the affects they express in their judgments and their comportment. One whose attitudes and actions are determined (even if not wholly defined) by the passion of ambition is borne along a path that tends toward mastery, whereas one whose attitudes and actions are guided by reason of piety pursues a path that tends toward mutuality. Here the "ambitious" and the "pious" are not so much sociological descriptions that map onto philosophers, theologians, masses, magistrates, etcetera, as they are differential and dynamic forms of individuality.

Commonalities in Conflict, Constitution in Common

Considered in the context of Spinoza's ecologies of affect, the notion of "judgment in common" ultimately refers to divergent trajectories taken by a mimetic desire that is constitutive of selves and social formations alike. The undulating, often turbulent, sea of affective relations that traverse and enmesh but also singularize human individuals, dividing them from each other and from themselves, simultaneously makes for a conflictual polarity between commonalities governed by a logic of exclusionary assimilation, on one hand, and those that develop through a logic of common alteration, on the other. Although they give expression to starkly divergent affective orientations—in one case, a desire to assimilate others to oneself, and, in another, the desire to transform oneself with others—these respective strategies or social logics are born of a shared necessity: each and every one, as far as she can, must persevere in being according to her characteristic judgment, or complexion (*ingenium*). With a look ahead to the chapters that follow, I want to close here by considering some political implications of Spinoza's conflictual ontology of judgment.

The first major repercussion is that any body politic or political constitution will be internally divided on the question of the common—of its meaning, its extension, its feeling, or taking these all together, its *complexion*. Consequently, politics, in its different modalities, operates for Spinoza much as it does for Machiavelli, namely, as the interpretation, organization, and "conversion" of an ineradicable social discord. It is worth noting that this basic trait of Spinoza's thought falls out of view in what are, arguably, the most prominent Spinozisms of late: those of Jonathan Israel (who places Spinoza at the origins of a modern "democratic republicanism") and of Hardt/Negri (who recruit Spinoza for a postmodern communism), which tend in their own fashion to evacuate Spinoza's political thought of the idea of *necessary* conflict.[54] Where for Israel's Spinoza, the facticity of social conflict finds an ideal resolution in the "common good," a notion that Israel presumes normative without further critique, in Hardt and Negri's Spinozism, conflict ultimately gives way to the ontological truth of social relations, that is, The Common.

To speak of an internally divided political constitution is not simply to invoke the idea of the state as arbiter of the divisions plaguing society. For as I have noted, Spinoza's treatment of mimetic desire presents a social conflict with the character of an incommensurability—a conflict for which there exists no mediating term, no "common good" capable of being "furthered, defended and presided over by the state."[55] Certainly, Spinoza defends the necessity of state power for making and enforcing through its order of coercive law "a common rule of life," with authoritative definitions of just and unjust, good and bad (E IV p37s2). But he is equally insistent that the laws of nature continue to act in the civil condition. People thus continue to judge according to their complexions, which means that the "sphere of similitude" continues to operate in a relatively autonomous fashion, the more and less spontaneous forms of mimetic desire generating social formations possessed of their own opinions on what is true and false, good and bad, right and wrong. These are opinions that refer, before and beyond the jurisdictions of state or religious law, to the norm of the useful (*utile*).

Thus Spinoza's vision of "judgment in common" implies that the state is always acting on actions and appetites—on diverse complexions—in anything but a neutral or impartial way. It too must adopt a certain strategy in relation to dynamics of mimetic desire. In the interest of its own perseverance, the state cannot merely follow the spontaneous vacillations of ambitious desire, nor can it "permit each to live according to his own complexion," as Spinoza professes to do in his dealings with others (Ep 30).[56] It must adopt and project something like the strategy of reason, allowing constituents to live as if by their own inclinations while educating them into the habits of civil solidarity and the benefits of public happiness, as I will discuss in chapter 4. And even if the state can simulate reason by securing civil liberties for its subjects, it cannot supplant the reason that survives and at times thrives in the sphere of similitude, forming new relations, generating new rights and abilities, and constituting new norms of living in common.

Put another way, in Spinoza's common, rights are not simply state-afforded protections wielded by originally disconnected individuals against each other and community as such. Rather, rights are co-extensive with the powers accruing to individuals by their alliances, collusions, or, in the most general terms, their participation in one or another common form of life. By the same token, on this view, the energies that an individual contributes and the obligations she owes to a given community can but need not require a diminution in her freedom or a sacrifice of her individuality. Theoretically speaking, then, the radically relational, albeit conflictual, environment of Spinoza's common entails that one must distinguish, without simply divorcing, the idea of a political constitution from the idea of a state. And with this point, we might circle back to the contemporary efforts to reprise of the common(s) in the face of neoliberal privatization, which, it should be emphasized, proceeds under the global technocratic aegis of a "new constitutionalism" beyond the state. How might Spinoza's thought aid in conceptualizing a constitutionalism of the common, a constitutionalism capable of advancing political thinking beyond the deadlock of state control and neoliberal "governance"?

3

Constitution of Judgment

What is our one demand?

ADBUSTERS POSTER FOR OCCUPY WALL STREET

The best rule of living . . . is the one a man or a commonwealth pursues insofar as it is most *sui juris*.

SPINOZA

Tahrir, Syntagma, Puerta del Sol, Zuccotti, Taksim, Maidan: all name "insurgent squares," instances of that form of political action now known widely as occupation. Taking the liberty of gathering and remaining in public spaces, reconfiguring them through common initiative, ordinary people across the globe have in recent years challenged the routine *pre*occupation or restrictive capture of public spheres by powers of state and capital. Some contested an authoritarian denial of civil liberties and political rights (Egypt); others, the oligarchic corruption of democracy (America). But more than simply protest, occupiers and their counterpublics sought to demonstrate the possibility of another occupation, as it were—another employment of common space, time, and energies.[1] Hence the proliferation of general assemblies, the organization of communal libraries and kitchens, the formation of working groups of all sorts (facilitation, alternative banking, outreach, security, sanitation, etc.), and efforts to occupy the "social media vector" with stories, video, analyses and more.[2] This street-level vindication of a new commons clashed symbolically and materially with the dominant forms of enclosure under the current global trade regime, just as the nonviolence of the occupy encampments interrupted the reflexive association of "occupation" with conquest and colonialism.[3]

Many onlookers criticized the insurgent claim "to occupy" as hopelessly vague or politically vacuous. Particularly in the case of Occupy Wall Street (OWS), with its deferral of concrete policy proposals, pundits and commentators insistently demanded more specific demands.[4] Participants and more sympathetic observers defended the simplicity and generality of this "one demand," to use Adbusters' original framing for OWS, as necessary features of a radical project. For one thing, they argued that the systemic enormity of the injustices at issue made specific policy proposals less urgent than contesting the predominant values and governing structures of society. They contended, further, that the demand to occupy served as a call to revive a political activity that is in some way prior to, or more foundational than, the exercises in governance, administration, and professional politicking often taken for politics as such. Viewed in this light, the occupation strategy, far from being politically vacuous, laid claim to an activity aimed at creating sites for assembly, discussion, experimentation—for the re-emergence of another politics and other political actors.

Consider, for example, the language of the anti-austerity movement in Greece. The first vote of the People's Assembly of Syntagma Square, May 27, 2011, began "For a long time decisions have been made for us, without consulting us" and proceeded to call on "all of society to fill the public squares to take their lives into their own hands," to "shape our claims and demands together."[5] Rather than an appeal for particular concessions from the government or the so-called Troika (the European Union, International Monetary Fund, and European Central Bank), one can hear in this initial demand to shape demands both a judgment as to the illegitimacy of existing institutions and the assertion of a people's power to give themselves a new political "constitution" or form of life in common.

If the global return of the street can be read, in this way, as a sequence of "constitutional" conflicts between peoples and the governing bodies that purport to represent them and if it can be read, moreover, as a multiplicity of attempts by these same peoples to reclaim their constituent power, then the language of occupation helps to specify a crucial, if underappreciated, aspect of such an endeavor: the importance of sustaining this self-organizational capacity over time.[6] Phenomenologically, an occupation differs from a demonstration in the determination to endure indefinitely. Occupation is more course than moment of action. So when the people occupying Syntagma Square or Zuccotti Park invoked a constituent power typically associated with extraordinary moments of transformative rupture, while undertaking a lower-case politics built around time-consuming processes of deliberation and consensus, they complicated the dichotomy between revolution and order that remains deeply engrained in inherited political language. Stated otherwise, the recent occupy phenomenon posed anew the problem of revolutionary constitution—the problem, that is, of situating radical political transformation within the rhythms and precincts of everyday life.[7]

I call this problem an underappreciated aspect of constituent power because, in both popular and scholarly imaginations, the "revolutions of 2011" (to say nothing of the related uprisings before and since) have more obviously reinforced the conceptual oppositions of spontaneity and organization, politics and law, and other related binaries that are thought to require reconciliation, overcoming, or a choice of one term over the other. Take these remarks by David Graeber, a key proponent of OWS:

> The idea of occupying a public space . . . allowed a common ground between liberals and others working in the tradition of civil disobedience who wished to democratize the system, and anarchists and other antiauthoritarians who wished to create spaces entirely outside the system's control. Both could agree that the action was legitimate based on a moral order prior to the law: since those practicing civil disobedience felt they were answering to universal principles of justice on which the law was itself founded, and anarchists felt the law lacked all legitimacy.[8]

In Graeber's estimation, the strategy of occupation enabled participants of various stripes to jointly articulate a broadly perceived legitimacy deficit in "the system" without having to resolve more divisive questions about the nature and ultimate aims of their joint action. Graeber suggests, nevertheless, that the main alternatives in play—the positive visions of what the demand to occupy was a demand *for*—consisted essentially of liberal constitutionalism, on the one hand, and anarchistic or direct democracy, on the other. In effect, he reads the project of occupation back into the familiar either/or between system and antisystem, reform and revolution.

My ambition in this chapter is to draw from Spinoza's vital republicanism a new way of conceptualizing the problem of revolutionary constitution. At first blush, Spinoza's thought may seem ill-suited for such a purpose, given that he was writing at a time prior to recognizably modern conceptions of constitution and revolution. But here as elsewhere, I would suggest that the relative distance of Spinoza's writings to a familiar problematic, far from disqualifying them, actually contributes to their critical purchase. At a time when constitutionalism has largely been reduced to a legalistic discourse of technocratic governance, or neoliberal "constitutionalization," Spinoza's thought can offer some conceptual tools for reimagining constitutionalism as a radically republican, which is to say, political endeavor.[9]

Recall that by Spinoza's "vital republicanism," I mean an approach to political life that makes law the means for a people's self-organization and that makes the vitality of their judgments the basis for a true rule of law.[10] In this spirit, the activity that I introduced in chapter 1 as jurisprudence exemplifies the idea that a people actively resist social and state domination by giving their political body a new "constitution," that is, by generating a new sense and scope of common affairs. There I proposed, without yet developing the claim, that a political constitution helps to preserve the vitality or development of a people's power. Here, then, I want to consider in a more sustained way the juridical dimensions of that republican endeavor, elaborating a Spinozist conception of law as constitutionally open to and facilitating of a people's "revolutionary" capacities for ongoing self-transformation. In so doing, I take the hortatory question of Occupy—*What is our one demand?*—as a provocation to inquiry. If the demand in question is for a right to act as a constituent power, how might Spinoza's thought elucidate the nature and significance of that claim?

The "constitution of judgment" cited in this chapter's title refers both to a constituting activity at work in a people's judgments and to a "supreme law" (re)generated by these judgments. This republican conception of a constitution, which I develop through a reading of what Spinoza calls "natural divine law," is not so much a species of positive law as it is a regulative principle or immanent norm of a people's empowerment. For it is an idea of a constitution that expresses, as a necessary truth, the way that humans achieve the perfection of their essences, of their specific virtues and powers, as citizens of a free people. And yet this idea of a constitution of power, or perfect constitution, is not necessary in the sense that it determines what individuals will in fact do; indeed, it only exists by virtue of judgments that actualize or enact it in singular circumstances.[11] From Spinoza's perspective, it is ultimately the conative force of each thing—a law of nature and not the legal power and authority of the state—that grants and guarantees the right to make such judgments. Hence one could say that the right to participate in judging what belongs to an empowered people springs from natural law and targets human law, facilitating the adaptation of human legal orders to changing historical circumstances (evolution) as well as the innovation or internal transformation of such orders along more expansive, cosmopolitan dimensions (revolution).[12] In Spinoza, natural and political-constitutional laws maintain a complex and dynamic relation with the statutory laws that make up the state's positive legal order. The primary interpretive task of this chapter is to examine how rights and powers of judgment mediate that relation.

I begin in the next section by considering how the phenomenon of occupation manifests itself in Spinoza's texts: in the figure of "prejudice." More than simply a question of the threat that religious sectarians pose for civil order, Spinoza takes prejudice to name the effect of a structural domination in which law is implicated. The problem here is that the idea and institution of law are habitually assimilated into the forms of ruling needed to ensure the order required for law to have any application in the first place. To the degree that it serves as but another means for the state to impose an integral order on political life, law effectively prejudges common affairs and preoccupies common capacities for autonomous thought and action. This Spinozist take on prejudice assumes in its own fashion the principled distinction, characteristic of modern republican constitutionalism and recently revived in the work of neorepublican theorists such as Philip Pettit, between the rule (*imperium*) of the state and rule of law conceived as a relatively autonomous sphere aimed at limiting state power.[13]

That law need not be subsumed under state rule, that law might retain a distinct foundation and function as a "rule of living," is a position Spinoza defends in his treatment of "natural divine law," my principal focus in the chapter's third section. Drawing on Georges Canguilhem's understanding of vital normativity as the ability of living things to furnish the norms of their own flourishing, I argue that Spinoza's natural divine law exemplifies a mode of immanent norm creation that presupposes the free (*sui juris*) judging capacity I have been calling jurisprudence. In the fourth section, I argue that the normativity of Spinoza's natural divine law undergirds his unique brand of constitutionalism—in particular, his appropriation of the republican maxim *salus populi suprema lex* as a statement about a people's constituent power and right of judging the terms of their association. By way of comparison with Hobbes, I underline how, for Spinoza, the legitimacy of the positive legal order turns on the relative amplification (rather than captivation) of citizen judgment as an essential freedom or specific virtue of communal life.

Ultimately, the Spinozist answer to the problem of revolutionary constitution, of preserving indefinitely common space and time and energies for political transformation, is to vindicate a rule of law that facilitates vital spheres of opinion circulation. As I show in the fifth section, these unofficial public spheres, in their turn, make possible the radical self-alteration of a people by judgments that advene to the established legal system as if from an anarchic state of nature beyond the functions and finality of the state's governmental organs.

Preoccupation with Order

According to prevailing liberal doctrine, rule of law neutralizes the effects of prejudices stemming from individuals' natural endowments (particularly racial and sexual differences) and cultural predicates (particularly religious differences). The storied transition from an essentially bellicose or insecure state of nature to an essentially peaceful civil order allegorizes the exclusion of these first- and second-order distinctions from the form of law. Prejudice, in other words, presents a problem of interpersonal and infrapolitical violence that law must ban lest the organs of the state be drawn into the fray. Legal and political theorists who subscribe to this narrative imagine that law's neutralizing exclusion of radical difference—and, by extension, the potential for hostility based on perceptions of superiority and inferiority—allows individuals to recognize each other in their full humanity as autonomous persons.[14] Given a historical cast, the "transition" from natural to civil state can be imagined as the supersession of tradition by Enlightenment, mediated politically by state absolutism and its revolutionary overthrow in favor of constitutional democracy.[15] Against this received theoretical and historiographical backdrop, Spinoza appears in most recent scholarship as a threshold figure, embracing a Hobbesian Erastianism to combat clerical domination while mounting an unprecedented defense of individual liberty of thought and expression against all manner of prejudice.

Ultimately, I mean to complicate this framing of the nature and problem of prejudice. It is important to note, nonetheless, that it finds a great deal of corroboration in his *Theological-Political Treatise.* In the preface to the *Treatise*, Spinoza argues that the proximate cause of sectarian strife in the United Provinces was the degeneration of religion into little more than the fawning reverence of clerics-turned-orators, "each possessed by a longing, not to teach the people, but to carry them away with admiration for himself, to censure publicly those who disagree, and to teach only those new and unfamiliar doctrines which the common people most admire" (TTP pref 15). The corruption of the Church into a theater of enthusiasm and denunciation, he explains, meant the collapse of faith into stultifying prejudices that "turn men from rational beings into brutes (*brutos*), since they completely prevent everyone from freely using his judgment and from distinguishing the true from the false" (pref 16). As he develops his argument over the course of the TTP, Spinoza sometimes names commoners as the key purveyors of prejudice, whereas at other times he singles out theologians as the chief culprits—a vacillation likely owing to the fact that, in Spinoza's analysis, each group serves as the enabling condition for the other.

While preachers and commoners alike display a penchant for tortured interpretations of Scripture—"almost everyone seeks to pass off his own inventions as the word of God"—their real abuse, Spinoza insists, lies in the effort to assimilate others' interpretations to their own. They are possessed by an ambition to compel belief (TTP 7.1, 14.1). He elaborates:

> We don't want to accuse the sectaries of impiety just because they accommodate the words of Scripture to their own opinions. For as Scripture was once accommodated to the grasp of the common people, so everyone is permitted

> to accommodate it to his own opinions, if he sees that in that way he can obey God more wholeheartedly in matters of justice and charity. We do censure them, though, for being unwilling to grant this same freedom to others, and for persecuting, as God's enemies, everyone who does not think as they do, even though they are very honest and obedient to true virtue. . . . Nothing more wicked or harmful to the republic can be imagined. (14.3–4, trans. modified)

This passage contains *in nuce* Spinoza's main depiction of the force of prejudice as an effect of interpersonal domination. On the basis of the immanent critique and reconstruction of Scripture offered in the preceding theological portion of the *Treatise*, Spinoza portrays religious sectarians here as figures of extreme depravity, tormenting honest persons who consistently practice acts of justice and charity ("good works") but happen nonetheless to maintain different interpretations of faith.[16] Likewise, Spinoza's positive assertion that "everyone is permitted" to interpret the moral tenets of Scripture according to his or her own lights presumes the particular conceptions of faith (obedience to the law of justice and charity) and of the state (as the sole legitimate judge and guarantor of such obedience) that he establishes in the theological and political portions of the TTP, respectively.

From what I have called the jurisdictional viewpoint of the state, sectarianism constantly threatens to become hegemonic struggle, as doctrinal disputes escalate into outright antagonism between social factions eager to enlist the force of law for their specific ends. Spinoza affirms, in this respect, that prejudice presents the state with an endless source of "seditions" (TTP pref 11). The precise danger here is not so much that some individuals or groups will transgress the established law while seeking to obtain particular advantages. As Walter Benjamin will later stress, the danger lies rather in the cooptation of the state's means, its monopolized violence, for a use "outside" of the law.[17] Sedition baldly confronts the holders of supreme power with a violence that is ultimately constitutive of the legal order and that sustains the hegemony of the existing regime. As Filippo del Lucchese observes, "in the concept of sedition there is a drive to seize the space of the political itself, a need to exclude one's adversary outright and impose new and different norms for social relations."[18] And indeed, the seditions to which Spinoza alludes in the opening pages of the *Theological-Political Treatise* project images (*species*) of religiosity (*religio*) and justice (*jus*), trafficking in a violence that posits a right and power to transform existing relations of law (pref 11).[19] Sectarian prejudice of this sort undermines radically the civil condition of order, peace, and social stability that the state's "legitimate" violence secures.

Certainly, in Spinoza's early modern political-theoretical context, where state and natural law are newly decoupled, and where the former has developed its unique "reason" for existence and rules for operating, apart from transcendent ends, any such challenge to the sovereign craft of procuring order could spell crisis. For if medieval and ancient political thought had in large part treated the "state" as little more than a vehicle of a predetermined order of "natural laws," or universal principles of morality, early modern political thought fashions the state as the sovereign agency that must establish the very conditions for legality and sociality in a destabilized and chaotic "state of nature." The modern state's arts and arcana of ruling furnish the order required for law to have any application whatever. Hobbes's "Publique Reason" offers a particularly compelling solution to the problem of establishing a stable political order, as I noted in chapter 1. It bears repeating that this sovereign figure provides more than just an overwhelming power that terrifies subjects into obedience. Hobbes's sovereign also serves as the sole lawgiver and judge of controversies in a world where nature has supplied no "general Rule of Good, and Evill Actions," and thus no other assurance that individuals will relinquish the desire to be judge in their own case. Despite his other departures from Hobbes, Spinoza agrees that any juridical order depends on a sovereign entity to make, apply, and enforce public laws (TTP 16.25, 16.38, 20.13).

Just as Spinoza is harshly critical of the force of prejudice at the interpersonal and infrapolitical level, he strongly rebukes those regimes, such as the Ottoman Empire, that transmute prejudice into a suprapolitical violence capable of terrorizing populations into submission. In this vein, Spinoza singles out a form of monarchic rule that endeavors to inoculate itself from subversion by deploying a religious "ceremony and pomp" (*cultu et apparatu*) so all-embracing as to "occupy with prejudices" (*praejudiciis occupant*) the judgment of each and every subject, leaving "no room in the mind for sound reason." He observes that the Ottoman rulers' occupation strategy, a draconian imposition of religious uniformity, has succeeded so well that Turks consider it a "sacrilege even to discuss religion" (TTP pref 9). Summarizing, Spinoza reveals that the pre-emptive seizure and colonization of common judgment figures prominently among the dark arts of government. Here prejudice, which, in the appendix to the *Ethics,* Part I, describes the opacity of humans' immediate perceptions of themselves and their environment, reappears in the employ of the state machine as an *arcanum imperium.*[20] The despot's systematization of prejudice into superstition, a governmental apparatus aimed at reproducing the ignorance and fear required for its own preservation, disposes the many to occupy themselves in service of the one:

"The greatest secret of monarchic rule, and its main interest (*regiminis monarchici summum sit arcanum*) is to keep men deceived, and to cloak in the specious name of religion the fear by which they must be restrained, so that they will fight for their servitude as they would for their survival (*salus*), and will think it not shameful, but a most honorable achievement to expend their life and their blood for the ostentation of one man." Spinoza hastens to emphasize the fundamental incongruity of such statecraft with the conditions of life in a republic, where it is "completely repugnant to common freedom to occupy with prejudice or in any way constrain the free judgment of each and every one" (pref 10, trans. modified).

By invoking the specter of monarchic domination, he cautions against governmental measures that serve only or primarily to radicalize the exclusionary desires animating the seditions more immediately at hand in the Dutch Republic: civil authorities must not attempt to command sectarian prejudice simply by imposing a Commanding Prejudice. Nor should they seek to impose *any* matters of opinion through legislative and other direct means. The sovereign powers, Spinoza insists, can only appear violent when they try explicitly to proscribe or prescribe opinion, inviting rather than preventing sedition (TTP 20.1). Accordingly, Spinoza's oft-cited theological-political solution to the problem of establishing civil order is for the state to arraign deeds, not words (pref 11). The state alone should interpret and uphold religion publicly as the exercise of charity and justice, limiting its jurisdiction in both sacred and secular matters to actions while granting to everyone the liberty of opinion (20.46, 18.26). In this way, he argues, doctrinal controversies will not so easily mutate into seditions, and seditions will appear for what they are, stripped of their religious and juridical pretenses (*specie*).

One needs to bear in mind, however, the contingent and partial nature of Spinoza's proposed "solution" to sectarian prejudice and, above all, its function as a statist strategy of integrating and transforming the violence between subjects into a lawful power over them. Spinoza neither obscures nor simply justifies the fact that the reproduction of the established legal order rests on the employment of "violence against violence for the ultimate control of violence."[21] Rather, he examines the mechanisms by which such state violence comes to be legitimated, or how state law achieves hegemony through appeal to a force that eschews simple coercion. Beyond exercising "direct command," he observes that sovereign power, adequately conceived, encompasses any means of inducing obedience, including and especially subtler modes of enlisting subjects' hearts and minds into its dominion (TTP 17). Hence the *arcanum* of "preoccupation," which Spinoza seems at first to associate exclusively with monarchy, in reality pertains to any instance of public rule or sovereignty, from the "most violent" regimes that deny their subjects any freedom of judgment ("to say to and teach what [one] thinks") to those "moderate" regimes that grant this freedom universally (20.9).

The character and the scope of "prejudice" extend beyond the interpersonal violence and arbitrary power of schismatics and despots to encompass a structural domination exerted by the state, no matter the specific constitutional arrangement of governmental offices. Spinoza highlights, in this respect, the "multiple means" (*multis modos*) available to any regime of disposing the majority of subjects to act at the pleasure of the sovereign power, such that they come to "believe, love, and hate whatever it wants them to" (TTP 17.9). As he puts it in the TTP's concluding chapter, the "judgment of a man can be preoccupied in many ways, and to an almost incredible degree, so that, though not directly under the command of another, it hangs so much on the words of this other that we can rightly say that to that extent it is subject to his control" (20.4, trans. modified). Although this mode of domination proceeds indirectly, it remains domination nonetheless—a way of subordinating some to the desires and powers of others. At stake here is an elementary capture and imposed employment of the vital sphere—of "life" in its impersonal or prebiographical dimensions as *conatus*—whereby subjected bodies and minds move toward the objects of given norms, doing and thinking what is necessary to sustain sovereign power.

On my reading, then, Spinoza's texts present "prejudice" as a problem of order in a twofold sense. First, interpersonal prejudice poses a problem for the state in its endeavor to establish and maintain a peaceful social order, or civil condition. As I noted in chapter 1, Spinoza's radical Cartesian acquaintances had focused rather single-mindedly on this theme, appropriating Hobbes's theory of the state in order to argue, among other things, that the social contract prohibited all subjects—but, most importantly, clerics—from arrogating to themselves the right to judge civil authority. Second, and more important for the purposes of this chapter, prejudice emerges in Spinoza's discourse as a problem that the state creates for the common development of the freedom to judge. Even when the state does not directly deny this freedom to certain of its members on, say, religious-doctrinal grounds, in its efforts to administer order, the state instills habits of obedience that dispose subjects more toward passivity than toward active, autonomous, and independent modes of citizen judgment. Further, the state's authoritative judgments about which issues qualify as urgent matters of political life, along with its rules and procedures dictating who is qualified to address public matters (members of a representative body, for example), have the continual effect of restrictively capturing in advance, or prejudging, the sense and scope of common affairs.

The primacy Spinoza assigns to freedom over order appears most clearly in the parallels between the concluding section of his *Theological-Political Treatise* and the conclusion to the theoretical portion of his *Political Treatise.* The "ultimate end" of the republic, Spinoza writes in the first of these texts, "is not to dominate," or to submit individuals "to the right of another" (*alterius juris*) (TTP 20.11). Expanding on this assertion, he declares that the essential endeavor of the republic is not to "change men from rational beings into beasts or automata" but, on the contrary, "to enable their minds and bodies to perform their functions safely, to enable them to use their reason freely, and not to clash with one another in hatred, anger or deception, or deal inequitably with one another" (20.12; cf. pref 16). In the *Political Treatise,* Spinoza offers a similar formulation when exploring the question of how best to organize a state. One can easily determine the answer, he argues, "from the end of the civil condition, which is nothing other than peace and security of life," or a state in which "men pass their lives harmoniously" (TP 5.2). In a crucial elaboration, Spinoza adds, "when we say, then, that the best state is one where men pass their lives harmoniously, I mean that they pass a *human* life, one defined not merely by the circulation of the blood, and other features common to all animals, but mostly by reason, the true virtue and life of the mind" (TP 5.5, Curley's emphasis).[22] A civil order that depends on the routinized inertia of subjects "who are led like sheep" undermines the very possibility of political community, and thus merits the name "solitude" (*solitudo*) more than "commonwealth" (*civitas*) (TP 5.4, trans. modified; cf. 6.4).

Spinoza's critical target in these passages from the TTP and TP is not so much animality per se but rather processes of brutalization.[23] Indeed, from the viewpoint of Spinoza's scalar naturalism, wherein all individual beings—and not just humans—are "animated," or possessed of intelligence adequate to their specific capacities, brutalization refers to processes and psychophysical conditions that could pertain to animals as much humans. The human who finds herself in the condition of Buridan's ass is, in some respects, just as impaired as any animal in that state (E IIp49s).[24] Both have suffered a reduction to a homeostatic, vegetative functioning of the sort Spinoza describes in the *Political Treatise,* with his depiction of a life defined merely by the "circulation of blood." Spinoza's allusions to governmental processes of brutalization, in short, point to the effects of "preoccupation" when taken to the limit.

Against this bleak scenario, Spinoza posits the desire and capacity of humans to "cultivate life" and to "live for themselves," not just surviving as a governed population but thriving as a self-organizing people (TP 5.6,

E Vp39s). Despite or because of the fact that prejudice in the structural sense follows from every state's necessarily hierarchical maintenance of order, Spinoza thinks that freedom demands a political constitution that allows for resistance—a common immunity—to the imposed employment of *conatus.* More than that, his texts indicate that the idea of law, in particular, must facilitate another mobilization of common endeavor so that a people might occupy themselves otherwise—in the project of living autonomous, truly "human" lives as a constituent power and not merely as the domesticated subjects of a constituted power. The question is why it must. What is the nature of this demand? The answer I develop in the remaining sections centers on the claim that Spinoza's critique of prejudice and corresponding theory of law is oriented by a republican idea of juridical independence (*sui juris*), an idea that he has reconfigured along naturalistic and, so to speak, biopolitical lines as an immanent norm.

Fostering the Normative Power of Life

What has come to be known as Spinoza's signature apposition, "God, or Nature" (*Deus sive natura*), encapsulates his critical reconstruction of inherited theology and recuperation of God as the "universal laws of nature" regulating the existence and operation of all things (E IV pref, TTP 3.8, 4.3, 6.9). Jewish and Christian theological traditions had considered God a sovereign ruler and providential lawgiver, and had distinguished two main conceptions of divine law that corresponded to two levels of God's foresight and care for the world. At a general level, divine law named the original decree by which God had created the universe and sustained it in existence; at a more specific level, God's law denoted the commands that dispensed the ranks, roles, and responsibilities of humans in relation to each other and to Him. Already in Spinoza's *Short Treatise on God, Man, and His Well-Being,* one finds the motif of providence transposed into a naturalistic key. God's "providence," he writes, "is nothing but that striving we find both in the whole of nature and in particular things, tending to maintain and preserve their being" (KV 1.5.1). In this context, Spinoza takes general or "universal providence" to mean "that through which each thing is produced and maintained insofar as it is a part of the whole of nature." "Particular providence," by contrast, designates "the striving which each thing has for the preservation of its being insofar as it is considered not as a part of nature, but as a whole." For instance, whereas a man's limbs are "provided and cared for" insofar as they are parts of man, a living whole, each limb also endeavors in its own right to "preserve and maintain its own well-being" (1.5.2). Prefigured in this early text are numerous issues Spinoza will address in his mature works through his *conatus* doctrine, such as the metaphysical question of how finite things have their essence in an infinite being, as well as the physical and psychical problem of affective imbalance, whereby certain parts of an individual's body or mind come to be disproportionately fixated on a pain or pleasure, to the detriment and even death of the individual as whole.[25] For the purposes of this chapter, the crucial question concerns the juridico-political or constitutional meanings of divine providence when recast in the naturalistic terms of the Spinozist *conatus*.[26] What implications might Spinoza's account of divine providence hold for the conceptualization of judgment and constituent power?

According to the prevailing Christian theologies of Spinoza's day, God dispensed not only purposes for all of creation but also prizes for virtue and punishments for sin. An individual's obedience to divine law merited salvation, temporal or eternal, while his transgression earned suffering. At least that was the expectation. For whether one's fidelity to divine law in the moral sense actually resulted in a just reward depended on divine law in the larger sense of God's overall plan for existence. One had to believe that the two divine laws, and the two levels of His providence, coincided in the right ways. Donald Rutherford argues that the dual conception of divine law that Spinoza elaborates in the TTP responds to these traditional worries about the appropriate intersection of natural and moral orders. Spinoza's "solution to the problem of providence," he submits, follows the Stoic path of locating ultimate virtue and happiness in the comprehension of natural necessity.[27] Rutherford's claim turns on an apolitical interpretation of the narrower and specifically "ethical" conception of divine law that Spinoza, in the fourth chapter of the *Tractatus*, calls a "rule of living": here, Rutherford explains, divine law signifies a rule that individual reason prescribes as a means for acceding to the highest knowledge of and attunement with divine law in the more general sense of nature's causal order (TTP 4.9).

Scholarly discussions usually proceed, in this vein, as attempts to show how Spinoza preserves a specific place for moral principles in the larger scheme of a naturalism devoid of normative intent and content.[28] What can it mean, for Spinoza, that humans "prescribe" the divine law to themselves, as he writes in the TTP, and how can they be accountable to its demands?[29] In seeking answers to these questions, commentators take "rule of living" to be prescriptive in the manner of a dictate, command, or ordinance, and then they attempt to reconstruct from Spinoza's texts an account of "normativity" understood as the "sense in which an agent is bound by these laws."[30] Construed in this fashion, the meaning of normativity falls within the horizon of disciplinary normalization, or normation: the rectification of individuals' beliefs and behavior by means of arbitrary or discretionary rules that impose a normative intention.[31] Consistent with the Latin etymology of "norm," the operative metaphor in this case is the carpenter's square (*norma*). "Normal" is what stands at a right angle, in conformity with the square's rule or pattern.[32] Most of the Spinoza literature approaches normativity on this model as the production of aligned thought and action. And as suggested in the title of one recent essay, "Following a *Recta Ratio Vivendi*: The Practical Utility of Spinoza's Dictates of Reason," a chief concern for specialists is to reconstruct from his writing an account of the forms of political and ethical life that result from rule-following conduct, particularly cognitive training.[33]

Against the grain of this scholarship, but without denying that Spinoza concerns himself with questions regarding the social production of morality and obedience, I want to emphasize how Spinoza's recasting of divine law and providence furnishes a conception of normativity that conforms neither to the model of prescriptive dictate nor descriptive norm. In splitting apart (in order then to reconcile) prescription and description, ordained rules and natural regularities, ethical and political rules of living, one risks missing what is distinctive and distinctively "revolutionary" about Spinoza's treatment of law, namely, that in thinking the "reciprocal immanence" of juridical and natural laws, he recasts the very concept of norms.[34] Rather than refer primarily to the dependence created by some normative order, Spinozist normativity, I suggest, refers more profoundly to a natural juridical independence (the *sui juris* status of one who acts in his own right, to use the language of Roman law) that entails a capacity for creating norms: a specific "virtue," power, or prudence that "is not obedience but freedom of human nature" (E IV def 8, TP 4.5).[35] Normativity, in this sense, means something other than conformity with a generic norm of ethical perfection or activity. It means rather the power to transform the norms or conditions of one's activity. To see normativity in this light, however, one needs to appreciate how Spinoza poses and addresses the "problem of providence" in an unconventional way through his doctrine of the *conatus*, the prudence proper to each thing.[36]

As a singular expression of divine or natural power (*potentia*), *conatus* names each thing's endeavor not only to persist in its given state and thus to escape destruction, but, more broadly, to express and augment its essential power indefinitely (E III p6–8). That the *conatus* encompasses more than inertial movement is evident from Spinoza's definition in *Ethics* IV of "virtue and power," which refers back to one of his *conatus* propositions in order to describe a human striving for causal efficacy, or activity: "By virtue and power I understand the same thing, i.e. (by IIIP7)"—the proposition that identifies *conatus* with the actual essence of each thing—"virtue, insofar as it is related to man, is the very essence, or nature of man, insofar as he has the power of bringing about certain things, which can be understood through the laws of his nature alone" (IV def 8). Immediately following this remark, Spinoza adds an axiom: "There is no singular thing in nature than which there is not another more powerful and stronger. Whatever one is given, there is another more powerful by which the first can be destroyed" (IV ax1). As Laurent Bove notes, Spinoza's definition here of virtue/power and the subsequent axiom successively posit each thing's "intrinsic infinitude," understood as a power of autonomy, and its "extrinsic finitude," understood as a fundamental condition of hetero-affection.[37] It is by virtue of an immanent and infinite cause that each thing, in its essence, remains "intrinsically infinite," or within God. But in its determinate, durational existence, as one thing related to a multiplicity of others, all of which express in different modes the *conatus* that God has given them equally, each thing is acted upon by others in ways that can enhance but often oppose its endeavor to persevere in being. Or again, in Spinoza's words, "even if each thing is determined by another singular thing to exist in a certain way, still the force by which each one perseveres in existing follows from the eternal necessity of God's nature" (E II p45s).

What the language of virtue points to in this context is precisely a notion of *conatus* as particular providence, now reconceived in terms of empowerment, or becoming-active. True enough, Spinoza's immanent naturalism upends the received notion that God intervenes in the struggles and alliances of finite beings, in their determinate existence, to favor some over others. "Philosophers," he writes, "know that God directs nature as its universal laws require," taking account not only of humans, for instance, "but of the whole of nature" (TTP 6.34). What is more, "daily experience" itself offers "infinitely many examples show[ing] that that conveniences and inconveniences happen indiscriminately to the pious and the impious alike" (E I app). It is clear, nonetheless, from Spinoza's early texts onward that such deflationary moves combine with an affirmative argument that God *only* provides for particular things in their essence. "God . . . is a cause of, and provider for, only particular things," Spinoza writes in the *Short Treatise*. "So if particular things have to agree with another nature, they will not be able to agree with their own, and consequently will not able to be what they truly are" (KV 1.6.7).

In this respect, the "free man" whom Spinoza invokes in *Ethics* IV to model the successful strategy of agreeing with or "acting by the law" of one's own nature (IV def 8) is also a way of specifying the virtue, power, or care for one's life that individuals must foster in order, so to speak, to meet God's favor. The vocabulary of virtue reflects Spinoza scalar, as opposed to dichotomous, understanding of the freedom and power that finite individuals—

never entirely self-caused, or "active," but always minimally so—are capable of achieving (IV 3–4). "The more each one strives, and is able, to seek his own advantage (*utile*) i.e., to preserve his being, the more he is endowed with virtue; conversely, insofar as each one neglects his own advantage (*utile*), i.e., neglects to preserve his being, he lacks power." God, in a manner of speaking, helps those who help themselves in the most deliberate fashion—those who act, live, and preserve their being on the basis of reason (IV p24). Spinoza alludes to this particular providence in the TTP when he speaks of "God's internal aid," or "whatever human nature can furnish for persevering in its being from its own power alone," as opposed to "God's external aid" (and one could say "general providence"), namely, "whatever in addition turns out to his advantage from the power of external causes" (TTP 3.9).[38]

In the *Political Treatise*, Spinoza puts the question of particular providence, or prudence, into the languages of natural right and Roman law, articulating the necessity of preserving oneself in light of the power or virtue of being *sui juris.* "The only way the Commonwealth is bound by [rules]," he argues, "is the way a man in the state of nature is bound to take care not to kill himself: to be able to be *sui juris*, or not to be an enemy to himself, he must take care not to kill himself. This care (*cautio*), of course, is not obedience, but freedom of human nature" (TP 4.5). On a quick read, this passage might suggest something like an imperative to preserve oneself, to do what one must to escape destruction. But the issue is more complicated. Spinoza's refusal to qualify as obedience the "care" (*cautio*) or prudence one employs regarding one's life underlines that the imperative to preserve one's life is not a directive to which one chooses to subscribe or not. This "freedom of human nature" must not be confused with contingency; freedom is rather "a virtue, or perfection" that assumes the necessity of acting, as far one can, to preserve oneself (2.7, 2.11). There are, however, more and less efficacious ways of doing so. That is why, according to Spinoza, in the state of nature, neither an individual nor a commonwealth can be said to sin in the sense of morally transgressing but only in the sense of failing itself, or falling short of its essential powers (TP 2.18, 4.4). Thus the question of *cautio* here is one of vigilance and vitality, of persisting thanks to some strength of one's own, rather than fortuitously avoiding death in accordance with "external" order of chance (E II p29s).[39] Exercising a basic prudence about how "not to kill oneself"—internal resilience in the face of changing circumstances—is continuous with, and the threshold for, becoming maximally free, powerful, or *sui juris* (TP 2.11, 3.7). In the TP, Spinoza expressly identifies the activity of an individual (human or collective) "insofar as it is most *sui juris*" with what he calls "the best rule of living" (*optima vivendi ratio*) (TP 5.1, trans. modified).

Being *sui juris* appears, in this way, as a norm of ethical and political activity. And, as I shall suggest, the capacity for creating ethico-political norms, or rules of living, defines the activity of those who are *sui juris.*

Chapter 4 of the *Theological-Political Treatise*, titled "Of the Divine Law," contains Spinoza's most sustained examination of the idea of a "rule of living" in particular and of the idea of law in general. Spinoza selects as his starting point the broadest possible definition of law: "taken without qualification," law denotes a means by which "each individual, or all or some members of the same species, act in one and the same certain and determinate way" (TTP 4.1). Given this definition of law as regularity of action, one can then distinguish between laws that follow "necessarily from the very nature or definition of a thing" and laws that depend on human opinion (*placitum*). For Spinoza, rationally deduced laws of physics, such as Descartes' third law of motion, or psychological laws regarding the associative operations of human imagination, exemplify laws belonging to the first category, which one could classify as "eternal truths" (4.24). By contrast, the category of law that depends on human opinion "is more properly called a principle of right (*jus*)" that "men prescribe for themselves and others, for the sake of living more safely and conveniently, or for some other causes" (4.1, trans. modified). Though Spinoza's exposition proceeds primarily from the perspective of humanly ordained law, he insists on the metaphysical priority of law understood as an expression of natural necessity. An adequate grasp of the former presupposes the type of causal explanation achieved through knowledge of the latter. One might well wonder, then, what is at stake in distinguishing eternal truths from principles of right. Why foreground the discretionary element of the latter?

Spinoza holds that insofar as human beings are a part of nature they constitute part of the power of nature. Thus the creation of "rules of living" is an instance of how nature's power is made determinate through the power of the human mind. The final "binding force" (*sanctio*) of these laws depends on the opinion or pleasure of men (*ex hominum placito*)—on immediate, or, so to speak, prerational bodily and mental dispositions rather on than the sort of deductive reasoning that comprehends natural laws and distinguishes truth from falsity. One cannot ascribe any eternal truth and necessity to the juridical artifacts of humankind—for instance, the "extrinsic notions" of what counts as just and unjust, sin and merit in political society (E IVp37s2)—even if human powers of mind and body are necessarily rooted in the infinite causal chain of nature's regulated production (TTP 4.3). Here Spinoza anticipates features of the natural right theory that he develops in later chapters of the TTP and in the TP, such as the inseparability of law's validity from its facticity. Law cannot exist apart from subjects who are actually disposed to obey it—disposed, that is, to perceive in the idea and act of adhering to law more good than bad, more pleasure or less pain. Therefore, any agreement or decision or contract, including and above all the social pact, has no force except by virtue of its utility, which Spinoza explains in terms of a "universal law . . . firmly inscribed in human nature" whereby individuals pursue what they judge to be the greater good or lesser evil (16.20; cf. TP 2.18). Rules of living depend most proximately on a human freedom of opinion, which, despite having its own complex of causes in the natural condition, is more usefully understood as the key basis for these rules. For "we ought to define and explain things through their proximate causes," Spinoza argues on grounds of utility. Short of comprehensive knowledge of the real order and connection of things, "for practical purposes it is better, indeed necessary, to consider things as possible" (TTP 4.4).

Technical definitions aside, Spinoza observes, the ordinary experience of law indicates that law is simply a command that carries with it the possibility of either compliance or noncompliance. From the perspective of common usage, the word "law" thus appears only to apply metaphorically, or accidentally to natural things (TTP 4.5). For this reason, Spinoza sees it as preferable to work with a more particularly human definition of law as a self-given "rule of living," an expedient or means for the practical purposes of individual or social life (4.5).[40] One might think he is, in this case, simply equating "rule of living" with "command." Quite to the contrary, his discussion reveals the inadequacy of the latter as a definition of law. To identify law with command would be to elide a surplus of meaning that Spinoza's broader notion of *ratio vivendi* discloses. It is instructive to compare the two definitions:

(1) "commonly nothing is understood by law but a command which men can either carry out or neglect";
(2) "law . . . is a rule of living which man prescribes to himself and others for some end" (TTP 4.5).

Spinoza indicates that the common image or (mis)understanding of law, definition (1), refers obliquely to the fact that law confines human power within certain limits, regulating, modifying, or channeling those powers in view of attaining some social objective. Definition (2) only reinforces how, for Spinoza, it is not part of law's essential function to dispense any particular purpose or end for human life. Law rather facilitates the pursuit of particular ends that individuals have specified for themselves or others. Be that as it may, Spinoza holds that the true nature, operation, and broader social utility of law as a "rule of living" are not immediately apparent to legal subjects, with the consequence that law, the enforcement of which requires an apparatus of rule, appears to have ruling as its essential function. Law, then, comes to be experienced and implemented as "a rule of living prescribed to men by the command of others" (TTP 4.7). With that small but consequential shift in prepositions, from law as a rule *of* living to a rule *over* living, one switches from law as conceived within a problematic of empowerment to law as perceived within a problematic of securing obedience.

Given the qualified definition of law as a *ratio vivendi* that "men prescribe to themselves or to others for some end," Spinoza further distinguishes between human and divine rules of living. He calls human law a rule of living that "serves only to protect life and the republic." Divine law, by contrast, is a rule of living that "aims only at the supreme good, i.e., the true knowledge and love of God" (TTP 4.9). Here again, Spinoza's argument should be handled with some care. For while it may be tempting to shorthand the difference between human and divine rules of living as a distinction between political and ethical laws, one would then lose sight of the extramoral but decidedly political meaning that divine law carries in Spinoza's text (and conversely, the necessarily moral, or theological-political, aspect of state law, which I examine in the next chapter). To be sure, Spinoza expressly claims that a full elaboration of divine law pertains to a "universal ethics" that would account for the precise means and rule of living required by this "end of all human actions" (4.13; cf. Ep 23, 27). But he also says tantalizingly, before dropping the issue, that it belongs to a universal ethics to articulate *"how the foundations of the best republic and the rule of living among men"* follow from the natural divine law (4.13, my emphasis).

A similarly puzzling feature of Spinoza's presentation of the divine law concerns the very idea of prescribing rules, for it remains unclear who is doing the prescribing and how they are doing it. Immediately after citing the commonsense conception of law (a command prescribed by some to others), Spinoza posits a distinction between legal personalities that seems to offer some clues about the prescriptive character of divine law. Here he presents a "just" person "who gives to each his due because he knows the true reason for laws and their necessity" and who "acts from his own decision" (*ex proprio decreto*). Spinoza juxtaposes to this person a slavish figure who "gives each one his due because he fears the gallows," one who acts, or rather reacts "according to the command of another (*ex alterius imperio*) and . . . coerced by evil," and who, therefore, "cannot be called just." (4.7).[41] It helps to consider both of these enigmatic aspects of divine law—its political meaning and its prescriptive character—in connection with Spinoza's understanding of *sui juris* status. In the remainder of the section, I discuss the prescriptive, or better, jurisgenerative character of the natural divine law; the next section examines its political meaning.

In the *Political Treatise*, Spinoza initially proposes that one "is *sui juris* so long as he can fend off every force and avenge an injury done to him, as seems good to him, and absolutely, insofar as he can live according to his own complexion" (TP 2.9, trans. modified). Here Spinoza signals that one is *sui juris* in an unqualified sense ("absolutely") insofar as it is in one's power (*potestas*) to live according to one's own discretion (*ingenium*). By contrast, an individual—call him Bento—remains subject to the power (*potestas*) of another insofar as that other person has done any of the following: (a) physically constrained Bento; (b) deprived Bento of weapons or other means of self-defense and escape; (c) instilled fear in Bento; or (d) bound Bento through hope of some benefit such that Bento desires to live according to the other's desires and opinions (i.e., according to his complexion) rather than his own. Both Bento's mind and body are subjugated in cases (c) and (d), but only for as long as the fear or hope that sustains his subjection endures. If either of these passions is taken away, he remains *sui juris* (2.10).

However, Spinoza specifies a second meaning of *esse sui juris* in the paragraph immediately following this initial exposition:

> A mind is completely *sui juris* just to the extent that it can use reason rightly. Indeed, because we ought to reckon human power not so much by the strength of the body as by the strength of the mind, it follows that people are most *sui juris* when they can exert the most power with their reason, and are most guided by reason. So I call a man completely free just insofar as he is guided by reason, because to that extent he is determined to action by causes which can be understood adequately through his nature alone, even though they determine him to act necessarily. (TP 2.11)

If the first definition of *sui juris* depicts an individual who pursues his natural right according to his own complexion (*ingenium*), free from domination (from living at the pleasure, or *ingenium* of another), then the second definition depicts an individual who acts powerfully (or rationally, or virtuously), which, as I have noted, is always a matter of degree. The strength of mind or causal activity at issue here is a perspicuous grasp of one's constitutive relations with other bodies and minds. One who is *sui juris* in this second sense "understands himself as an active participant in the causality that makes him an effect."[42] Hence Spinoza will say both that "no citizen is *sui juris*," in reference to the constituted juridical power of the state, *and* that anyone can become *sui juris,* in reference to the natural causal power that is an inalienably common resource (3.5, 2.11). The difference (and complementarity) between the conception of *sui juris* as not dominated and the conception of *sui juris* as empowered features centrally in the *Theological-Political Treatise.* On one hand, Spinoza defends the natural right to judge according to one's own *complexion,* with "each one . . . the defender of his own freedom" (pref 29). On the other hand, as a condition for the preservation and augmentation of that freedom of human nature—for becoming *sui juris,* or empowered—Spinoza requires that everyone forswear the right to act arbitrarily, "solely according to the decision of his own mind," so that all may live instead by a common law (pref 29, 20.13). Law, properly understood, makes for freedom, as I discuss below.

Spinoza's understanding of *sui juris* status diverges significantly from other early modern appropriations of the category, such as those found in Grotius or Locke, for whom the idea of being *sui juris* reinforces an understanding of freedom as subjective property and thus as a status that is essentially exclusive of others' rights.[43] For Spinoza, by contrast, *sui juris* status is inclusive of all others' rights because the freedom upon which it depends is a good "capable of communicating itself," viz. the power of intelligence (TIE 1). In Spinoza's articulation of the concept, one could say that natural juridical independence coincides with a communal and tendentially cosmopolitan agreement (*convenientia*) between singular and plural human powers—the federation, or co-implication of all those "who, from the guidance of reason, seek their own advantage [and consequently] want nothing for themselves that they do not desire for other men" (E IV 18s). Here, as in the Roman conception, *sui juris* status presupposes a natural capacity to form one's own judgment on common affairs. Indeed, for Spinoza, this is precisely because the right or power to judge, properly understood, is a communal and not a subjective right, a right that is held and developed in common.

Given these distinctive features of *sui juris* status, Spinozistically construed, I am now in a position to say more about the "prescriptive" or jurisgenerative activity of the "just" and "free" individual who, in TTP 4, acts in accordance with the natural divine law. Here it helps to read Spinoza through Canguilhem, whose work on the normative creativity of living beings offers a conceptual idiom better equipped than that of moral prescription or natural description to illuminate the immanent and constituent features of Spinozist normativity. Canguilhem, for his part, conceives of the biological health and pathology of living beings as a dynamic polarity. Each living thing is a composite entity that operates according to its own internal norms; it is "normative" in that it is capable of creating norms and conditions for the realization of its powers and continued health.[44] At the same time, Canguilhem distinguishes between a living being's homeostatic, conservative tendency toward organic normality and its self-transgressive, creative tendency to generate new norms of living.[45] A tendency toward normality or mere preservation would, in the context of Spinoza's system, mean that the force of a being's *conatus* is predominantly invested in a struggle against an imagined cause of sadness, such that the individual's capacity to create and live according to new norms—her capacity to affect and be affected—is diminished (E III p37).[46] By contrast, in the case of truly vital normativity, the force of the *conatus* pushes beyond itself, as it were, and the individual endeavors not just to preserve her existence but to augment her overall capacity to affect and be affected.

Read through Canguilhem, the "ethical" polarity that recurs in Spinoza, between life as lived under a norm of affect ("from impulse") and life as lived by a norm of reason (E IV p37s1), acquires further nuance. Both manners of living qualify as modes of effectuating normative power.[47] The difference between them concerns the relative amplification or abridgment of the scope of one's effectuations, which is to say, the complexity and diversity of one's normative power. To live under the norm of an affect is to operate with a restricted and fixated normativity. But to live by the norm of reason is to diversify and complexify one's capacity to affect and be affected, to persevere in becoming and not just to preserve one's state (IV p38). Canguilhemian normativity, in this fashion, comports with what Spinoza describes as the endeavor to become other and greater: to transform oneself by enlarging the scope of one's effectuations. After all, on Spinoza's view, it is of the "nature of existence" (to use his phrase at E II p45s) that each and every individual endeavors, whether she realizes it or not, to do all she can, not just to preserve herself in the face of external threats, but to bring about the greatest of self-transformations—changing corporeally into another body of maximal aptitude and mentally into a mind of maximal consciousness. "In this life," he proposes, "we endeavor especially that the infant's body may change . . . into another, capable of a great many things and related to a mind very much conscious of itself, of God, and of things" (E V p39s).

For Spinoza, that which gives rules of living their value—the norm of norms—is the norm of the useful (*utile*). His position on this score involves three key ideas. First, Spinoza takes as an initial premise the idea that all humans "want to seek their own advantage (*utile*), and are conscious of this appetite" (E Iapp). Regardless of whether individuals are mistaken or correct in their judgments about the useful, what is true for everyone is that judgment follows desire—not so much this or that momentary desire but the shape or complexion of desire over time. And this effectual truth points to the second key idea about the norm of *utile*. Ethically speaking, what matters most in the pursuit of the useful is not the achievement of a particular type of affect—a species of joy, for instance, may ultimately become a harmful preoccupation that threatens one's overall vitality—but the "strategic" trajectory of perseverance: the individual's vigilance or "care" she exercises, and the internal resilience she cultivates, while confronting and surmounting obstacles in her life course. As I noted above, "taking care not to kill oneself" is the minimal threshold for the maximal development of one's virtue or power, including the capacity to create new norms of living, new relations with other bodies, ideas, and their attendant powers. In Spinoza's usage, and this is the third key idea, reason represents the successful strategy of becoming active, *sui juris*, or empowered. "Our actions," he writes, "those desires that are defined by man's power, or reason—are always good" (E IVapp3). And further: "Acting absolutely from virtue is nothing else in us but acting, living, and preserving our being (these three signify the same thing) by the guidance of reason, from the foundation of seeking one's *utile*" (E IVp24). Living according to reason means pursuing one's *utile* on the basis of ideas of properties that are common to all humans. Therefore, to the degree that it is rationally determined, the norm of the useful operates necessarily as the norm of common action.[48]

In this account of immanent normativity, one can discern the twofold structure of Spinoza's transposed conception of "providence." Esposito captures something of this transposition when he characterizes Spinozist natural right as "the immanent rule that life gives itself in order to reach the maximum point of expansion." When viewed from "a general perspective," Esposito elaborates, "every form of existence, be it deviant or defective from a more limited point of view, has equal legitimacy for living according to its own possibilities as a whole in the relations in which it is inserted." From which he concludes: "Spinoza makes the norm the principle of unlimited equivalence for every single form of life."[49] This is true as far as it goes: as a description of "the general perspective" of natural right, where the right and *potentia* of each thing is considered as a part of God/Nature's power—viz. the "rules according to which all things happen," or "universal providence" (TP 2.4, KV 1.5.2). But what Esposito overlooks is how "the norm" carries another meaning when viewed as "particular providence," where "the norm" of natural right is considered in terms of the specific virtue, freedom, or power proper to an individual. Here the individual acts according to the laws of its own nature. In short, everyone acts by the same right of nature—just not with equal strength.

The Best Rule of Living

Given this account of Spinozist normativity, I want to examine in this section the political meaning of natural divine law. How does it figure into political life? In what respect do "the foundations of the best republic" and the "rule of living among men" follow from the natural divine law, as Spinoza proposes they do? The short answer is that the vital normativity of natural divine law corresponds to the jurisprudential power that generates and is generated by a republican constitution. Here the condition for the legitimacy of any positive legal order becomes the capacity of individuals critically to reconfigure existing legal and political relations in view of their perfect constitution, the constitution of a free or empowered people. From within a theory of natural right, Spinoza thus offers a variation on the maxim, *salus populi suprema lex*, which he construes as a constitutional meta-norm of empowerment.

I work out support for this reading of Spinozist constitutionalism, in part, through a comparison with Hobbes, who uses his own doctrine of natural right to argue, on the contrary, that constituent power simply means the capacity of a people, *solely by virtue of their incorporation as a sovereign state*, to author law. Spinoza is often said to offer a more realistic or dynamic version of the Hobbesian contract, wherein the right and power of the civil sovereign to make law is no longer obtained in a single legitimating act that captures in advance the constituent power of a people. Commentators routinely underscore how, in Spinoza's conception, the legitimate law-making power of the sovereign is always a provisional achievement, emerging from the continual negotiation between the respective powers of state and subjects. This common juxtaposition of Hobbes and Spinoza identifies an important difference in their conceptions of sovereignty. However, it takes for granted the idea that law is essentially an expression of sovereign power, which is precisely the assumption that Spinoza throws into question.

The through line of Hobbes's contract theory is familiar enough: from an unlivable condition of war, a multitude of individuals are impelled to make decisions in favor of peace and the preservation of life. On the basis of an agreement they make with one another, individuals transfer their natural right to live by their own powers and decisions to a civil sovereign who represents their collective power and who thereby makes, interprets, and enforces law on their behalf. In *Leviathan*, Hobbes employs a peculiar account of representation-as-authorization to specify the type of obligation that follows. If a "Person is the *Actor*," then "he that owneth his words and actions, is the AUTHOR: in which case the Actor acteth by Authority." Therefore, when I authorize an action, I may be identified as its author; I am "present" in and must own up to, or take full responsibility for that which my representative does in my name. Hobbes's social contract generalizes this mechanism: "by this Institution of a Commonwealth, every particular man is Author of all the Soveraigne doth; and consequently he that complaineth of injury from his Soveraigne, complaineth of that whereof he himself is Author; and therefore ought not to accuse any man but himself." The sovereign can commit no injury because its acts belong to each and every subject, and to "do injury to ones self, is impossible."[50]

Hobbes opposes the right of nature and the law of nature in order then to reconcile them through the use of reason—initially, the "right reason" of the individual, and, finally, the "Publique Reason" of the sovereign. By natural right, Hobbes intends "the Liberty each man hath, to use his own power, as he will himself, for the preservation of his own Nature." And by "law of nature," Hobbes means "a Precept, or generall Rule, found out by Reason, by which a man is forbidden to do, that, which is destructive of his life, or taketh away the means of preserving the same; and to omit, that, by which he thinketh it may be preserved."[51] Thus, in Hobbes's famous summation, "*Lex* and *Jus* are as different as *Obligation* and *Liberty*."[52] It is the work of reason, understood as the discovery of a certain prohibition and commission, to mediate this opposition between natural right and natural law. As Hobbes writes in *De cive*, "Neither by the word *right* is anything else signified than that liberty which every man hath to make use of his natural faculties according to right reason. Therefore the first foundation of natural right is this, that *every man as much as in him lies endeavor to protect his life and members*."[53] Reason dictates laws of nature in the form of hypothetical imperatives that command humans to seek peace where possible, and to resort to war when no other option presents itself.[54]

Although Hobbes insists that laws of nature are not laws in the proper sense—"the word of him that by right command over others"—they nonetheless define and delimit the natural right specific to humans, which consists in the liberty of encountering "no stop" in doing what one "has the will, desire, or inclination to doe."[55] Since, for Hobbes, any and all determination of the will to act implies a deliberation on the utility of the action for one's preservation, one's will is always already determined by a "precept of reason"—above all, the injunction to preserve oneself. Despite Hobbes's refusal to define human beings by reason, reason is presupposed in his account of their transition from the natural to the civil condition: each individual's effort to preserve himself implies and represents reason even before giving it an effective constitution.[56] Reason appears in the contract moment as a form of fear, "The Passion to be reckoned upon."[57] More than just one passion among others, Hobbes makes fear a rational sentiment, the primordial calculation by which an individual defends his life.[58] In the final analysis, humans enjoy the liberty to do "what their own reasons shall suggest, for the most profitable to themselves," but carry the obligation to defend themselves.[59] This same internal finality—at once a criterion of humanity—impels Hobbesian individuals to transfer their natural right to a sovereign.

According to Hobbes, individuals can be considered as a political entity, as "all together," only by virtue of having each individually authorized a sovereign representative to "beare their Person."[60] This representative does not represent a people in their plurality so much as the person of the state or *civitas*, which Hobbes posits as the true and original subject of sovereignty. As a consequence, Hobbes attributes juridical and political power exclusively to the sovereign, in relation to whom there can be no external criteria of legitimacy. Justice becomes simply the conformity of an action with the civil law established by the sovereign—synonymous with "Keeping of Covenant," which, Hobbes stipulates, is a "Rule of Reason, by which we are forbidden to do any thing destructive to our Life; and consequently a Law of Nature."[61] And injustice "is no other than the not performance of the covenant."[62] Crucially, the sovereign himself, precisely because he was not party to the contract, cannot himself introduce "a breach of Covenant . . . and consequently none of his Subjects, by any pretense of forfeiture, can be freed from his Subjection."[63]

Hobbes presents the absoluteness of the sovereign as the condition of possibility for civil relations *between legal subjects*: subjecting everyone to this supreme authority is the only way one can be assured that others will abide by the established law. Nevertheless, between the sovereign, who by definition is released from law (*absolutus*), and the subjects, who are wholly bound to law, there remains a natural, warlike relation. Paradoxically, the sovereign remains in the natural condition that everyone sought to escape by establishing his authority. What partially alleviates this paradox, as Dimitris Vardoulakis has recently shown, is Hobbes's narrative of exceptionality: the use of figures, from the savage to the fool, and, above all, the rebel, who are at once excluded from law and abandoned to its force because they are "irrational" in Hobbes's terms—incapable of submitting to obligations and therefore threatening to the state. The Hobbesian edifice of sovereignty hinges on a "codetermination" between the sovereign, who stands above the law, and those whose exclusion from law helps to justify the state violence to which they and others are subject.[64]

In the context of Spinoza's metaphysics of potentiality, the key terms of the contract, natural right and natural law, acquire a markedly different sense. It helps to recall, as a starting point, Spinoza's first presentation of natural right, in chapter 16 of the TTP. "By the right and established practice of nature," he means "nothing but the rules of the nature of each individual, according to which we conceive each thing to be naturally determined to existing and to working in a certain way" (TTP 16.2, trans. modified). Hence the "right of each thing extends as far as its determinate power does" (TTP 16.3). Natural right follows from the laws of each thing's functioning, which entails that, for humans, both laws of passion and laws of reason endow all individuals—"fools and madmen . . . sensible and sane"—with a natural right (16.5). And in Spinoza's telling, "the supreme law of nature," from which the right of each individual (human or otherwise) derives, is that "each thing strives to persevere in its state, as far as it can" (16.4). Here natural law is not something that humans discover and impose upon themselves by way of reflecting on their natural rights. It is rather an eternal truth from which natural right is deduced: "because the supreme law of nature is that each thing strives to persevere in its state . . . it follows that each individual has the supreme right to do this" (16.3). In this way, Spinoza articulates natural right less through the language of prescription than through that of *inscription*: "It's a universal law of human nature," he ventures, "that no one neglects to pursue what he judges to be good, unless he hopes for a greater good, or fears a greater harm. . . . This law is so firmly inscribed in human nature, that it ought to be numbered among the eternal truths, which no one can fail to know" (16.15–16).[65] With these conceptual maneuvers, Spinoza "performs an overhaul on the relationship between natural right and natural law, while eliminating the rationality of the natural law understood as the precept of a reason that obligates."[66] And this radical overhaul turns, in the words of Alexandre Matheron, on a "brutally simple principle," namely, "the absolute identification of right with fact."[67] Although I ultimately want to qualify Matheron's characterization, it helps to consider what aspects of Spinoza's natural right doctrine it accurately describes and what implications follow for a Spinozist account of constitutionalism.

Above all, Spinoza's "identification of right with fact" entails that the constituted legal order is a continuation of war by other means.[68] Positive laws furnish one of the primary means by which violence is made legitimate (a "civil" condition), and, as such, they are tokens of the state's present hegemony.[69] Consider how this view emerges from Spinoza's recasting of obligation and entitlement, the "objective" and "subjective" aspects of natural right. Each individual is determined, or "bound," by the supreme law of nature to do all it can do to "live, and to preserve themselves, as far as they can by their own power" (TTP 16.7). Correspondingly, each is "permitted, by supreme natural right" to want, to take, in short, to do whatever they judge to be useful, regardless of whether one's action entails force, or deception, entreaties, etcetera (16.8). Here individual right designates one's power (*potentia*) as a part of nature, or whatever an individual in fact does. "For whatever each thing does according to the laws of its nature, it does with supreme right, because it acts as it has been determined to do according to nature, and cannot do otherwise" (16.5).

By the same logic, the contract that establishes the state represents a promise or obligation that is co-extensive with *de facto* power relations. "For by natural right each person can act deceptively, and is bound to stand by the contract only by the hope of a greater good or the fear of a greater evil" (16.22; cf. TP 2.12). An individual is obliged only so long as she, in fact, keeps her promise. Hence a contract has no force except "by reason of its utility," or insofar as individuals judge it to benefit them, "whether . . . by certain reason . . . or merely . . . by opinion" (16.19). In the case of the social contract, the civil authorities retain the right of command "only so long as they really have the supreme power. If they should lose [that power], they also lose, at the same time, the right of commanding all things. [The right] falls to him or those who have acquired it and can retain it" (16.28).[70] The *Political Treatise* further elaborates how the "authorization" that subjects offer to any holder of sovereignty is, in Matheron's words, "given, at every moment, to each of his particular actions, by the fact alone that most of his subjects agree to cooperate actively or passively with him."[71] Note here the divergence from Hobbes, whose theory of natural right seeks to establish, philosophically, a hiatus between natural and civil conditions that legitimates *once and for all* the current holder(s) of sovereignty, and that renders irrelevant citizen judgments about existing law or matters of common concern more broadly.

Indeed, for Spinoza, the state's hegemony can never be established to the exclusion of individuals' freedom publicly to judge the utility of state law. And this freedom always operates, in part, as the bearer of vital normativity, the constituent power or virtue proper to a free people. As I showed in chapter 1, the surplus power of a people's judgments does more than occupy the negative space of sovereign jurisdiction—either as "conscientious judgments" that dissent from yet uphold the state's law or as "seditious opinions" that imply a counter-sovereignty, an *imperium in imperio*. Freedom of judgment, as Spinoza conceives it, also necessarily presents a surplus power that proceeds by another logic (jurisprudential) and that generates an alternative basis—beyond that of command and obedience, or legitimate domination—for the self-constitution of a people: rule of law.

The crucial point here, lost in the usual discussions of Spinoza's identification of right with fact, is that one must distinguish the state's factual rule *by* law from the people's jurisprudential creation of a rule *of* law.[72] There is an overwhelming tendency in the Spinoza literature to collapse the latter into the former, and thereby to reduce rule of law to a species of hegemony, in the course of emphasizing that Spinoza offers a more flexible or dynamic conception of state legitimation than that of Hobbes.[73] On the standard reading, Spinoza simply advances different means to the same end of becoming sovereign, different strategies of turning the natural rights and constituent powers of a people into the positive commands and constituted power of the state.[74] However, when viewed from the perspective of natural divine law, conceived as a "virtue and power" and pursuit of "the best rule of living," it is clear that Spinoza understands the circulation of judgments in society to engender more than just new reasons for (dis)obedience or a perpetual negotiation of the state's command. Rather, these judgments carry a vital normativity, a constituent power of transgressing established norms and creating new norms more conducive to the common endeavor of becoming maximally free, rational, powerful (*sui juris*). A people's judgments, in short, bear a power to transform the state's rule by law, or legal domination, into a rule of law where no one is dominated.[75]

Spinoza asserts in the fifth chapter of the TTP that "obedience has no place in a social order where government is in the hands of all and where laws are enacted by common consent." At this juncture in the text, he takes obedience to mean "following orders solely on the authority of a commander" (TTP 5.25).[76] It follows, he argues, that a people "remain equally free whether laws are multiplied or diminished" because in each case, rather than act "from the authority of another," they act from their "own consent." Spinoza rehearses here the idea that rule of law enables individuals to be free from domination, an idea famously captured in Cicero's claim that one subjects oneself to law so as not to have masters (and therefore to confirm one's natural status as *sui juris*). But what Spinoza leaves unclear in this early discussion of the rule of law—the immediate context, one should recall, is a discussion of how a system of law might be constituted so as to moderate the violence of the state—is what it means for an entire people to consent to law.[77] Stated otherwise, how does rule of law make for freedom?

In TTP 16, Spinoza tackles these questions through recourse to the idea of a republican constitution:

> In a republic, and a state (*in republica et imperio*) where the supreme law is the well-being of the whole people, not that of the ruler, someone who obeys the supreme power in everything should not be called a slave, useless to himself, but a subject. So that republic is most free whose laws are founded on sound reason. For there each person, when he wishes, can be free, i.e., live

> wholeheartedly by the guidance of reason. Similarly, even though children are bound to obey all the commands of their parents, they are still not slaves. For their parents' commands are primarily concerned with the advantage (*utile*) of the children. We recognize a great difference, then, between a slave, a son, and a subject, which we define as follows: a *slave* is someone who is bound to obey the commands of a master, which are concerned only with the advantage of he who commands; a *son* is someone who, in accordance with the command of a parent, does what is to his advantage; and a *subject*, finally, is one who does what is advantageous for the collective body—and hence, also for himself—in accordance with the command of the supreme power. (TTP 16.34–35)

I interpret this passage to mean that the freest state secures, through a rule of law, the possibility of becoming *sui juris*. Spinoza observes here that neither child nor subject is a slave, bound to act by the dictate and for the benefit (*utile*) of another. But neither the child nor the legal subject enjoys the freedom, virtue, and power—the *sui juris* status—that comes with being a citizen of the "most free" republic.[78] (The term "citizen" is conspicuously absent from this passage but fundamental to Spinoza's defense of free judgment in the concluding chapter of the *Treatise*.) In the most free republic, each can be free "when he wishes," which is not to say immediately, upon simply deciding to live by reason, but rather to the degree that one's desire or *conatus* comes to be rationally, actively, determined as strength—as a virtue exhibited by the "best citizens" (TTP 20.15).[79]

Recall Spinoza's insistence that in the "most free" republic and state—the one that "comes closest to the natural condition"—"no one so transfers his natural right to another that in the future there is no consultation with him" (*nemo jus suum naturale ita in alterum transfert, ut nulla sibi imposterum consultatio sit*) (TTP 20.38, 16.36, trans. modified). This claim implies that a republican constitution preserves for each constituent the occasion to form his own judgment in common and on common affairs, and, on that basis, to consent to an equal law. Each can confirm his natural *sui juris* status (as free from personal domination) and so all remain equally free "as they were before, in the state of nature," namely, free from having to submit one's judgment to the arbitrary powers and pleasures (*ingenium*) of another (16.36). Indeed, what everyone "transfers" is precisely the right to act arbitrarily, agreeing instead to be bound equally, if provisionally, by the decisions of a common legislative body. "Because not all men can equally think the same things," Spinoza explains, "they agreed that the measure which had the most votes would have the force of a decree, but that meanwhile they'd retain the authority to repeal these decrees when they saw better ones" (TTP 20.38, TP 3.5).

Attention to Spinoza's classical sources provides further illumination. The question of *consultatio*, of what it means to have the occasion—the time, space, and capacity—to reflect and consider appears, among other places, in Terence, one of the Roman writers to whom Spinoza periodically alludes.[80] In the fifteenth chapter of the TTP, for instance, Spinoza provides a line reminiscent of Terence's *Hecyra*, V, 650, "Pamphilus, there is no room now for deliberation" (*Nulla tibi, Pamphile, hie jam consultatiost*) (TTP 15.17).[81] And Spinoza was surely familiar with Crito's remark, in Terence's *Phormio*, that "we must deliberate further" (*amplius deliberandum*), likely a satirical allusion to the Roman judicial practice of "ampliatio," which meant to extend or defer a decision.[82] In the context of Spinoza's thought, however, the imperative to "deliberate further" is less satire than the normative endeavor of political life: judgment must be maintained as a live option for everyone, and beyond that, it must be amplified as a common capacity—diversified, complexified, expanded in scope (TP 9.14).

When Spinoza associates the freest republic with the "best rule of living," with laws based on "sound reason," or, in another of his formulations, with "what sound reason teaches to be useful to all men," he is invoking the "virtue" or normatively creative power of reasoning—represented, above all, by the *sui juris*, or maximally free and powerful individual—*as the common good*, or *salus publica* (TTP 16.34, 20.7, TP 3.7). As I have shown in previous chapters, Spinoza's appeals to the "common good" as determined by reason are not appeals to some substantive community. They are appeals to a "virtual" commonality—to the power of intelligence in which everyone partakes but which no one exclusively possesses—and a cosmopolitan alliance or agreement (*convenientia*) to which individuals give their reflective or active consent insofar as they are considered *sui juris* constituents of a free, self-organizing people. It is imperative to distinguish between two types of consent in Spinoza: on one hand, the consent or agreement through which a people constitute themselves as empowered and equally capable of giving law (co-authors of a perfect constitution); on the other hand, the consent or agreement (as co-subjects of positive law) that establishes the hegemony of the state, a factual rule by law that associates its addresses according to hierarchical relations of command and obedience, and that secures a civil condition where no one can arbitrarily deprive another of his or her rights.[83] This distinction between a people's perfect political constitution and their factual or civil constitution corresponds to the distinction between right as specific virtue, or maximal empowerment, and right as *de facto* power.

By Spinoza's account, the supreme law of a people exceeds the conventional or provisional determinations of law that the state makes in the interest of its order and security. For the supreme law issues from nature and bears critically on constituted law from the viewpoint of a people's perfect, most free, and powerful self-constitution—a people considered not in their existential actuality, as ordered according to a hierarchical division between rulers and ruled, but in their essential actuality, or what I have called here virtuality (E IV p36). Spinozistically understood, the supreme law of a people corresponds to their constituent power of judging in common the "true reason for laws," that is, the true meaning of common or public right.[84] This supreme law is enacted, so to speak, when individuals participate actively in reflecting on what rights and powers belong to a free people. Spinoza here anticipates the postrevolutionary understanding of constituent power, which "shifted the idea of the people's role from one estate among others (a mixed constitution), internal to constituted power and constituted law, to the form of public opinion that was exogenous to (constituted) law."[85]

A Vital Public Sphere

Following Spinoza, then, the demand for another occupation of common powers, for a use that reorients subjects around the endeavor to become *sui juris* citizens of a constituent people, arrives from outside the bounds of the established legal system, with its divisions between citizens and noncitizens, governors and governed, haves and have-nots, etcetera. Jacques Rancière has persistently pressed a variant of this argument in recent years, with his contention that a society only becomes political from the outside in, thanks to the constituent power of the "part that has no part" in the constituted order of the state.[86] Rancière's claim formalizes what is abundantly clear from the history of revolutionary politics, where the freedom asserted by excluded "parts," be they plebeians, proletarians, women, or slaves, subverts the established distribution of identities and activities, engendering an emancipatory reconstitution of the people as a whole. One could say, with Spinoza, that these bearers of constituent power arrive as if from a condition of nature, where a people organize themselves not on the basis of substantial identities or territorial demarcations but solely in terms of their free and equal capacity for law, or *sui juris* status. The natural condition of humans, it turns out, need not be imagined as anarchic in a purely privative and apolitical sense: by Spinoza's lights, this condition is better conceived as the anarchic space of exteriority to the form and finality of government. In closing, I want to consider further the features of this anarchic space without territory and its corresponding law.

By way of negative orientation, it helps to note the exclusions from citizenship that Spinoza justifies and to which he was subject as an inhabitant of the United Provinces. In the *Political Treatise*'s final, unfinished chapter on the democratic state, Spinoza declares his intention to discuss only that kind of democracy "in which absolutely everyone who is bound only by the laws of his native land, and who is, furthermore, *sui juris* and lives honorably, has the right to vote in the supreme council and to stand for political offices" (TP 11.3, trans. modified). He then hastens to enumerate the members of society who are to be excluded from citizenship so conceived: foreigners, women, servants, children, minors, and criminals.[87] Spinoza's position on this issue is not that unusual for his time and place—the comparatively "free" Dutch Republic of the First Stadholderless Period. Spinoza himself did not qualify for full citizenship. No Jews at the time did, even though they were granted roughly similar protections as other inhabitants. Dutch citizenship was then still a legacy of feudal privileges and it was a largely local distinction that granted its holders a voice in municipal government. On the basis of their membership in guilds and civic militias, those with citizenship rights wielded some capacity to influence the regents (who came from aristocratic families). Spinoza was, in short, one of many "ordinary people" excluded from these official privileges and informal powers of citizenship.[88]

However, Spinoza also numbered among the extraordinarily high proportion (relative to the rest of Europe) of literate individuals in the Netherlands—roughly two-thirds of men and one-third of women—that made for a thriving pamphlet culture and an unofficial sphere of political (and very often anonymous or pseudonymous) opinion.[89] My point here is to suggest, as Spinoza asserted both in the text of the *Theological-Political Treatise* and in the act of its publication, that "in a free republic everyone is permitted to think what he wishes and to say what he thinks," and that whoever partakes of this freedom through the public use of their reason can qualify as a citizen who helps to transform the constituted body of the people into a vital, self-organizing whole (20 title, 20.15). The historical Dutch Republic in which Spinoza lived, and which he extols at the beginning and end of the TTP, was manifestly not the "free republic" that extends to each and all a complete freedom of judgment. But the crucial theoretical insight is that true citizenship, or membership in a free republic, is by Spinoza's logic never simply a matter of including outsiders into the established body of the people, which, no matter how inclusive, always stands prejudged by the state. On the contrary, citizenship in his normative (or normatively creative) sense entails what I have called common alteration—understood here as a pluralizing exchange of opinions and places (between citizens and "ordinary people," etc.) and as a transformation of the factual, rank ordering of society.

To lend an image to the natural law that grants everyone the right to judge what rights belong to an empowered people, I would suggest the "law of the sea." Particularly in a country such as the Netherlands, the sea expresses a natural condition that persists within and continues to act on the established boundaries, channels, and dykes, always remaining in some measure "beyond" the state's territorializing efforts. The law by which the sea operates, in fact, leads the water recurrently to transgress and resediment land areas, just as the critical and constituent power borne by free judgments deterritorializes those individuals whose *sui juris* status is rooted in property ownership and reterritorializes them in a common space of opinion where all are granted the presumption of being of independent (*sui juris*) mind. As Grotius declares in his book *Mare Liberum* ("The Freedom of the Seas"), "the sea is common to all, because it is so limitless that it cannot become a possession of any one, and because it is adapted for the use of all."[90] Likewise, in the natural condition or anarchic space of judgment, no one possesses a right to an exclusive judgment or opinion: by nature, judgments are always in relation—singular and plural. One could say that this law of the sea, Spinoza's law of nature, defines the general condition within which the "constitution of judgment," a people's perfect constitution, must be developed.

By comparison, Spinoza's "natural divine law," which describes the virtue or powers proper to the human species, furnishes the specific condition for the development of such a constitution. The natural divine law denotes the means or the mode of becoming *sui juris*. It is a law or rule that cannot be commanded. Nor can it be internalized.[91] And to the extent that the natural divine law "prescribes" rules, it does so in accordance with one of the less prevalent connotations of *praescribere*—namely, as a mapping, an activity that requires judgments for its "enactment" or "application" to singular cases. Demonstrating the possibility of becoming *sui juris* is both a contingent action, in that there is no necessity to any particular exercise of the natural divine law, and the actualization of life's normative potentiality, the power of life as it relates to humans.[92] One can say that the reward of the natural divine law is the law itself—to act, to live, and to preserve the vitality of one's powers.

Seen from the vantage of the Spinozist constitution of judgment, rule of law assumes its truly facilitating role in political society whenever law is made to regulate rather than rule over common—that is, singular and plural—endeavors to persevere in becoming active. For properly conceived, law does not superimpose purposes on human life. Rather, law expresses, adverbially, conditions for the free development of that life.[93]

4
State of Judgment

What does Spinoza's vital republicanism owe to an idea of the sovereign state? What does the Spinozist state owe to religion? This chapter examines the constructive meanings that Spinoza accords to state and religion as they combine in a conception of civil religion that he develops over the course of the *Theological-Political Treatise.*

The portrait of Spinoza as an unsparing critic of religion and staunch advocate of secular politics has in recent years been supplemented if not supplanted by a Spinoza who appreciates the indispensable role of religion in creating and preserving political community. Even so, commentators tend to operate with, and find in Spinoza, an instrumental understanding of religion as an imaginative resource that rulers employ to secure obedience and promote civic solidarity. In addition to restricting the "political" role of religion to a single governmental function, this sort of approach implies that central features of his constructive account of the theological-political liaison—the absolutist defense of sovereign power, for example—might just as well be considered a contingent feature of his political theory, explicable in the context of the intellectual controversies he faced and the rhetorical strategy he consequently adopted but not something that performs any more fundamental conceptual work in his discourse.

In the following pages, I argue instead that the seemingly atavistic traces of seventeenth-century polemics in Spinoza's TTP, including and especially his discussion of theocracy, figure constitutively into his understanding of a civil religion and the free state it makes possible. As a first approximation, civil religion could be defined as a religion that motivates individuals to be good citizens. However, more specificity is needed both to prevent the concept from collapsing into a "baggy metaphor" (to borrow Mark Silk's phrase) and to grasp its theoretical significance in Spinoza and beyond.[1] Indeed, understanding the idea of civil religion requires taking seriously the prospect that some of the building blocks of Spinoza's political thought, and of modern republicanism more broadly, are intelligible only in light of theology.

This chapter proceeds on the hypothesis that Spinoza advances a modern idea of civil religion that has its intellectual origin in Machiavelli and its most famous exposition in Rousseau. Its premodern antecedents lie in Arabic and Jewish prophetology—philosophical conceptions of revealed religion that understand religion to be integral to political science and foundational to public, worldly happiness.[2] To be sure, one also finds in Spinoza a more instrumental conception of civil religion that comes much closer to the Roman idea of a "civil theology," viz. an official teaching about civil deities that all citizens, particularly priests, are required to know and administer in the interest of social cohesion. Spinoza is overwhelmingly critical of this instrumental idea of religion, which he depicts as paradigmatically "pagan superstition" employed by the one or the few to subjugate the masses, and to which he sees the Calvinist Church of his day (among other religious authorities) as having reduced the Christian faith (TTP pref 13). Instead, like Rousseau after him, Spinoza advances an interpretation of Christianity that renders its moral core—charity, or love of one's neighbor—wholly compatible with and conducive to the virtues of republican political life.

My approach in what follows is not so much to establish lines of influence or intellectual context for these distinct ideas of religion that are operative in Spinoza, but, rather more selectively and in combination with a close reading of Spinoza's text, to show how an awareness of non-Christian theological-political sources, in particular, helps to recast and resolve some interpretive puzzles that have bedeviled Spinoza scholarship. Chief among these puzzles is the question of why, in the so-called political chapters of the TTP, Spinoza's naturalistic account of the democratic state (TTP 16) and final vindication of free judgment (TTP 20) is mediated by a lengthy and approving analysis of the ancient Hebrew "theocracy" (TTP 17–19).[3] The apparent incongruity of these political-philosophical and theological-political moments has led commentators to grant Spinoza's examination of the Hebrews a historical significance but little or no theoretical justification. The model of the Hebrew state had long played a legitimating role for various theological-political purposes in the United Provinces; interpreters note how it enabled Spinoza, in particular, to enter pitched debates over *jus circa sacra* on the side of Erastian toleration, even if ultimately in service of a "secularizing political science" that would entail "religion truly has been banished from political life."[4] But is that solely or even primarily what the Hebrew case does for Spinoza?[5] In my view it is not, and reading his text from the perspective of civil religion can help to reveal the reasons.

More affirmatively put, the optic of civil religion helps to disaggregate the politically salient meanings of religion in Spinoza and, in turn, to approach the issue of the state's debt to religion less as an "either/or" question of dependence or independence than as a "both/and" question of interdependence along different dimensions (institutional, justificatory, cultural, etc.). This sort of differentiation matters not only for the study of Spinoza's thought but also, I suggest, for contemporary "postsecular" debates over whether and how religion plays a public or foundational role in modern constitutional democracy.

Moses, Civil Religion, and Acquisition of State

Spinoza's insistence that true religion stands as an essential condition for the prosperity of a well-governed republican state echoes Machiavelli's exhortation to re-interpret Christianity according to virtue rather than idleness.[6] With Machiavelli, Spinoza aims to vindicate a "civil" interpretation of religion as "always adapted to the advantage of the republic" (TTP 19.30), meaning a religion that fosters the military and political strengths of a citizenry.[7] A "spiritual" interpretation of religion, by contrast, privileges the otherworldly salvation of souls, orthodoxy in speculative matters, and the pastoral power of priests, all of which serve to enfeeble or "disarm" civil authorities and citizens alike.[8] In order to "reform" religion away from its corrupt and politically debilitating spiritualist form as priestcraft and superstition, Spinoza, like his Florentine counterpart, has recourse to exemplary figures of "ancient religion"—above all, those of Moses and the Hebrews. The early chapters of the TTP showcase the politically educative function of Moses's prophecy. Moses taught the Hebrews as a legislator, constraining them to live well by command of God's law, which he fashioned into a civil code and attached to a series of material threats and benefits (2.46–47). Spinoza accentuates the conjunctural quality of Moses's prophecy as a species of prudence:

> Moses . . . by revelation . . . perceived the way the people of Israel could best be united in a certain region of the world, and could form a whole social order, or set up a state. He also perceived the way that people could best be compelled to obedience. But he did not perceive, and it was not revealed to him, that that way is best—or even that the goal they were aiming at would necessarily follow from the general obedience of the people in such a region of the world. So he perceived all these things, not as eternal truths, but as instructions and precepts, and he prescribed them as laws of God. (4.29–30, trans. modified)

Rather than a translation of the necessary and true into reality—the classical idea of prudence, roughly speaking—Moses's prudence appears in this passage and throughout the TTP as a function of the collective security he afforded his people through the acquisition of state. His prophetic leadership becomes, in Spinoza's treatment, an art of turning the *aléas* of fortune to the specific benefit of the Israelites, and a way of transforming the contingent situation of a dispersed multitude into the destiny of a chosen people.

Spinoza's reading of the Jews' election, so often viewed as simply deflationary when compared with the prevailing Christian and Jewish theologies of the period, in reality also advances an affirmatively political idea of special divine providence oriented around the problem of public, earthly happiness (TTP 3).[9] Moses and his people received God's favor inasmuch as they "handled their security auspiciously (*foeliciter*)," overcoming threats both external and internal to their polity (3.17). The Hebrew nation was "chosen by God before others" in respect of "its society and the fortune by which it acquired a state and kept it for so many years," and not in respect of superior intellectual or ethical virtue, which, Spinoza explains, are gifts that cannot be exclusive to any nation (3.16, trans. modified; cf. 3.19, 3.26, 3.30).[10] Moreover, these other goods or "gifts" presuppose the collective good of "living securely and healthily," which is to say, they presuppose the good of *society*, a term that for Spinoza mediates between sheer chance and the self-sufficiency of human nature.[11] The means of living securely and healthily, Spinoza explains, are called gifts of fortune because they depend primarily on God/Nature acting through external causes rather than on God/Nature acting through causes internal to human nature. Nevertheless, "human governance (*directio*) and vigilance can be a great help" in procuring the necessary means to live in safety. Both reason and experience teach that the surest of these means are "to form a society with definite laws, to occupy a definite area of the world, and to gather (*redigere*) the powers of all, as it were, into one body, the body of society" (3.14, trans. modified). At this point in the text, Spinoza dwells only on the idea of society as a way of living together for mutual protection, and on the reasons for associating that project with the belief in God's special providence. One should expect a society founded and directed by prudent and vigilant men to be more secure and stable, or less vulnerable to fortune; conversely, a society composed of unskilled men should be more unstable, more susceptible to fortune.[12] If the latter society has managed, nonetheless, to survive and even thrive, "it will owe this to the guidance of another," and will thank God for its miraculous endurance in the face of adversity (3.15).

In discussing "the calling of the Hebrews" (TTP 3 title), Spinoza mentions but does not yet thematize the idea of state, which, at this textual juncture, one might think he views as simply synonymous with the *status* or good condition that comes from life in society. Nor has Spinoza done more than gesture toward the specific "manner" (laws) and "means" (revelation) by which the Hebrews acquired and maintained their state (3.26). "It is enough for my purposes," he writes, "to have shown that the Jews' election concerned nothing other than the temporal happiness and freedom of the body, that is, the state" (*temporaneam corporis foelicitatem, et libertatem, sive imperium*) (3.26, trans. modified). What is more, Spinoza argues that the Jews' centuries-long survival in exile, "scattered and without a state . . . is nothing to wonder at" given the persistence of their ceremonial law ("external customs") and "the sign of circumcision," which have separated them from and incurred the hatred of other nations. Experience has shown, he observes, that this hatred alone "has done much to preserve [the Jews]" (3.53). Almost in passing, Spinoza adds, "if the foundations of their religion did not make their hearts unmanly, I would absolutely believe that someday, given the opportunity, they would set up their state again, and God would choose them anew. That's how changeable human affairs are" (3.55). This passage is significant both for its reference to a certain messianism (about which I will say more in the concluding section), and for the way it echoes Machiavelli's charge that a spiritualist interpretation of the Christian religion has rendered the world "effeminate" and heaven "disarmed."[13] But despite the fact that Spinoza here singles out the Hebrews' religion as a politically debilitating force—alluding perhaps to the millenarian and messianic hopes shared in complex ways by many Calvinists and Jews in the seventeenth-century Netherlands—elsewhere he argues that the same religion played a politically fortifying role, encouraging the Hebrews to "bear everything with special constancy and virtue, for the sake of their country" (17.82). The key to these different assessments concerns the nature of the "foundations," and corresponding interpretations of salvation (spiritual or civil?), that the Hebrew religion received in different moments.

Spinoza's Moses employed religion in the "foundation" of a political way of life, that is, in the constitution of collective power from a condition of relative powerlessness.[14] And it is in relation to this constitutional endeavor, detailed in chapter 5 of the *Treatise*, that Spinoza first thematizes the idea of state (*imperium*). Here Moses ostensibly fits the profile of the mythical prophet-legislator whose divine virtue allows him to organize a dispersed, uncultivated, and slavish multitude in a discrete territory.[15] And yet, as I noted above, one must not lose sight of the fact that Spinoza conceptualizes the political quality of Moses's prudence less in the manner of classical political philosophy than in the post-Machiavellian terms of an experiential and conjunctural knowledge deployed in secular time and in a situation of insecurity. Spinoza recounts that after "having known the complexion and obstinate spirit of his nation" (*ingenium et animum suae nationis contumacem*), Moses "saw clearly that they could not finish what they had begun without the greatest miracles and special external aid of God—indeed, that they would necessarily perish without such aid" (3.41). So on one hand, Moses possessed exceptional knowledge of the character of his people, who would not allow themselves to be subjugated for force alone. On the other hand, he divined the need and the means to prepare for them for war (5.28).

Spinoza presents these features of Moses's prophetic virtue in view of some general rules of state acquisition. The reader learns how Moses acquired state—status in the eyes of his people, a command over them, and a vital body politic—by introducing what Machiavelli calls "new orders and methods," or what Spinoza calls "ceremonies" that habituate a population into a new form of life. Arguing from "universal foundations" (5.17), Spinoza posits, first, the necessity of society for "living securely from enemies, but also for doing many things more easily," and he cites the common benefit that accrues from dividing labor and cultivating arts and science (5.17–5.18). Spinoza moves next to acknowledge that people rarely act according to "what true reason teaches them to desire," which, in general terms, is to pursue their own advantage in and through alliance with others. Rather, people tend to judge what is advantageous on the basis of "immoderate desire . . . carried away by affects of mind which take no account of the future and of other things" (5.21). It follows, Spinoza argues, that the conditions for the existence and subsistence of society include "a power of command (*imperium*) and force, and hence, laws which moderate and restrain men's immoderate desires and unchecked impulses" (5.22, trans. modified).

The problem, however, is how to establish an organization of rule given the fact that "human nature does not allow itself to be compelled in everything." Here Spinoza takes as axiomatic Seneca's saying that "no one has sustained a violent rule for long; moderate rule lasts." Why so? Spinoza briefly rehearses some points about the affective basis for thought and action: violent or direct command inspires fear in a population, and fear constrains individuals to act contrary to their desire—unwillingly and reactively—so that they endeavor chiefly to avoid, say, the immediate evil of punishment, without conscious regard for "the advantage, even the necessity, of doing what they're doing." So disposed, individuals can desire only the downfall of their leaders—especially, Spinoza indicates, given the more general human aversion to "being subservient to equals." Finally, he proposes, "nothing is more difficult than to take freedom away from men again, once it has been granted" (5.22).

From these foundations, Spinoza draws several implications. First, there are two ways of establishing a state: either the whole society as a body shares command such that no one is subject to an equal; or *imperium* is monopolized by one or a few persons widely perceived as quasi-divine (5.23). Second, to encourage subjects to fulfill their civic obligations eagerly (*cupide*), laws should be made less to instill fear than to inspire hope of some urgently desired good (5.24; cf. TP 10.8). And third, obedience (*obsequium*) in the strict sense of action taken under the personal authority of another has no place in a republic, a "society where sovereignty (*imperium*) is in the hands of everyone and laws are enacted by common consent." From this last point, Spinoza draws the conclusion that a people remain "equally free" whether or not laws are increased or diminished, because they act consensually. The opposite occurs in the case of absolute sovereignty, or rule by one, where "everyone carries out the commands of the state solely because of the authority of one person, with the result that, unless they have been educated from the beginning to hang on the words of the ruler, it will be difficult for him to institute new laws when it is necessary, and to take away a freedom once it has been granted to the people" (5.25).

Spinoza applies these three general rules of statecraft to the specific case of the Hebrews. He notes that, upon leaving Egypt, the Hebrews were free in principle to give themselves laws and to acquire a state and territory of their own, though in practice they proved incapable of holding power collectively, habituated as they were to a slavish way of life. Consequently, rule remained "in the hands of one person," Moses, who could command and compel the others, in addition to prescribing and interpreting the entirety of their laws (5.27). Spinoza contends, furthermore, that Moses employed religion as a moderating, motivating, and educating force, so "that the people would do their duty not so much from fear as voluntarily (*sponte*)" (5.28). In a nearly identical passage a few lines below, Spinoza uses the term *devotione* rather than *sponte*, noting that Moses "introduced religion into the republic so that the people would do their duty not so much from fear as from *devotion*" (5.29). Devotion, then, functioned as an essential component in the governmental art of inciting the Hebrew subjects to conduct themselves in ways that resemble the comportment of a "free man," namely, one who "willingly (*sponte*)" and directly pursues "what is really useful" to himself and others (5.20).[16] Crucially, Moses insured that the devotional bond of the Hebrews—who were acutely and reflexively resistant to oppression—was not just another form of bondage. So while he implemented a system of drill and discipline for a people not yet capable of exercising their own right (*sui juris esse non poterat*), arranging for them a long schooling in military and civic discipline, the point was not to bind them to his own rule as an absolute monarch but to the rule of an absolute God who commands love of one's neighbor, above all else.[17] To the extent that Moses induced the Hebrews to "hang on the words of the ruler," one could say that he achieved this nobly and for common welfare, rather than through deception and for the sake of elite domination (cf. TTP 20.5). In sum, the Mosaic religion moderated the necessary violence of state command by entraining the Hebrews to charity, justice, and the "spontaneous" rhythms of mutual assistance in civic life, all while encouraging them to become citizen-soldiers in defense of their country (5.28).[18]

In this first presentation, Spinoza approaches the Hebrew state as a particular instance of a general category. His main ambition at this point is to foreground the essentially civil, as opposed to "spiritual," function of religion in founding a system of authority where a relationship of command and obedience obtains. In Spinoza's second and more sustained presentation of the Hebrew state (TTP 17–18), its singularity becomes much more pronounced, both in relation to other ancient examples of "civil religion" and in relation to early modern political theologies of sovereignty. Consider, in this respect, Spinoza's reprise in TTP 17 of his earlier claim about the two ways of establishing the security of rule (either sharing *imperium* equally or granting it to one or a few on the basis of some "religious" entitlement). Following a brief survey, drawn from Roman history, of attempts by kings of "archaic times" (*olim*) to sacralize their rule, Spinoza writes:

> Others have had better success . . . in persuading men that majesty is sacred and carries the place of God on earth (*vicem Dei in terra gerrere*), that it has been established, not by men's vote and consent (*ab hominem suffragio et consensu*), but by God, and that it is preserved and defended by God's particular providence and aid. And in this way monarchs have devised other means to secure their rule, which I'll omit. To get to the conclusion I want to reach, I shall, as I've said, note and weigh only those things divine revelation taught Moses for this purpose. (17.24–25)

The assertion here that "others have had better success" in sacralizing kingship may well refer to the difference between early modern monarchs, who claimed the eternity of a monotheistic God as their source of power, and the royal republics of antiquity, with their many occasional gods and civil theologies. In practice, the Roman kings were nowhere near as absolute as rulers such as Louis XIV or the Spanish Habsburgs, who, far from meeting any requirements for popular consent (as in Rome), virtually absorbed or stood in for their bodies politic.[19] Similar to these monarchs, Moses made political use of divine revelation rather than the largely ineffectual hodgepodge of superstitions employed by rulers such as Alexander. ("Only men who are complete barbarians allow themselves to be deceived so openly and to turn from subjects to slaves," Spinoza writes in reference to one of Alexander's schemes [17.24].) Despite playing a majestic role in this respect, Moses was a founder of a constitution and not a king. And the rule to which he bound his people absolutely was not his own but that of God. These features of Moses's undertaking come to the fore in Spinoza's second discussion of the Hebrew state, which, it helps to recall, he frames as part of an inquiry into the place of free judgment in a free republic. The orientation of Spinoza's analysis of the Hebrews changes accordingly, from "general considerations" of state acquisition to a consideration of the type of civil religion most suited for republican political life (5.26). Whereas Moses appears in TTP 5 as a charismatic founder, TTP 17 offers a reflection on the routinization of his power. In short, Spinoza moves from the theme of state acquisition to the theme of state preservation via constitutionalism.

The Mosaic Constitution between Theocracy and Democracy

In his second and more extended discussion of the Hebrews, Spinoza employs the idea of theocracy to elaborate the specific "excellence" (*praestantia*) of their state. The first-century historian Josephus had coined the term "theocracy" (θεοκρατία) in order to argue that Moses accorded the ancient Israelites a political constitution that was uniquely superior to the classical Greek paradigms of monarchy, aristocracy, and democracy. Theocracy, as defined by Josephus, placed all "authority and power" (*archè kai kratos*) in the hands of God.[20] Though one finds some basis in Josephus's writings for the narrowly political, post-Enlightenment conception of theocracy as rule by priests ("hierocracy"), its primary meaning for Josephus concerned, more broadly, the form of Jewish life as ordered by monotheistic beliefs, God-given laws, and diverse practices of piety.[21] Josephus foregrounded the comprehensive sweep of God's jurisdiction, which covered everything from dietary laws to criminal procedure. Somewhat less straightforwardly, but crucially for the recuperation of Josephus in early modern thought, his texts supported the position that God vested the administration of *all* laws, whether pertaining to "civil" or "religious" affairs—a distinction the Mosaic constitution did not recognize—to the supreme civil magistrate (initially Moses, and subsequently Joshua, the judges, kings, and Sanhedrin).[22] Hence one finds a host of sixteenth- and seventeenth-century political writers drawing on Josephus to launch an Erastian argument that theocracy, God's authoritative constitutional model, entails the subordination of clerical to civil authority. Spinoza can certainly be included in such company (see esp. TTP 19). However, what distinguishes his creative appropriation of the Hebrew state is the radical equivalence he posits between theocracy and democracy.[23]

When Spinoza introduces the term "theocracy" into his own discussion, it is to highlight the performative force of the Hebrews' conviction that they had submitted themselves exclusively to the rule of God. "By the very fact that they believed they could be preserved by the power of God alone, they transferred to God all their natural power to preserve themselves" (17.29). This belief and its myriad corollaries took hold in all facets of the Hebrews' collective life: they regarded their state as "the Kingdom of God"; they treated enemies of state as "enemies of God" and judged any would-be usurpers of his authority to be guilty of "treason against God's majesty"; and most fundamentally, the Hebrews viewed the laws of their state as "laws and commands of God" (17.30). Spinoza underscores, further, how religious principles found expression entirely in and as civic practice: "The doctrines (*dogmata*) of religion were not teachings (*documenta*), but laws and commands. Piety was regarded as justice, and impiety a crime and an injustice. Anyone who abandoned religion ceased to be a citizen and, for this alone, was he considered an enemy. Anyone who died for religion was thought to have died for his country."[24] In short, the Hebrews made "absolutely no distinction . . . between civil law and religion," and "for that reason," Spinoza concludes, "this state could be called a theocracy, since its citizens weren't bound by any law except the one revealed by God" (17.31, trans. modified). He adds an immediate and important qualification: all of these features of the Hebrew theocracy consisted "more in opinion than in fact," for in truth, the Hebrews "retained the right of the state absolutely" (17.32). As Spinoza goes on to elaborate, the democratic constitution or structure of their theocratic covenant with God consisted and persisted in its effects. The Hebrew theocracy achieved its worldly realization in the form of democracy; that is, a republic in which no single individual or group in society exercised command over the people as a whole.

Spinoza's treatment of ancient Israel becomes in TTP 17 a case study of how, to use a contemporary idiom, a people acquired and preserved a state of nondomination. His history of this "divine Republic" (TTP 17 title), prior to the period of the kings, resolves it analytically into three distinct forms—call them direct theocracy, Mosaic theocracy, and theodemocracy—that the Hebrews' political constitution assumed in the course of its history. Only the third appears as a state capable of enduring, precisely because it operates a synthesis of the first, which represents a society free from human rule, with elements of the second, which represents a society coordinated entirely by the quasi-regal command of a charismatic figure.

To appreciate the reasons for the "excellence" of the Hebrew theodemocracy, then, it helps to follow Spinoza's analytic-synthetic order of presentation. In a first moment, Spinoza introduces the idea, absent in his earlier rendition of the Hebrew state, that the Sinai covenant consisted of a free and equal transfer of rights from the Hebrews directly to God. Following on from his natural-right account of the social contract in TTP 16, Spinoza now has a conceptual language for articulating the covenantal structure of the Hebrews' direct theocracy.

> For after they'd been freed from the intolerable oppression of the Egyptians, and were not attached to any mortal by any contract, they regained their natural right to do anything they could. Each of them could decide again whether he wanted to keep it, or to surrender it and transfer it to someone else. When they'd been placed in this natural condition, they decided to transfer their right only to God, not to any mortal. That was Moses' advice and they had the utmost trust in him. Without further delay they all promised equally, in one voice, to obey all God's commands absolutely, and not to recognize any other law except what he would establish as law by Prophetic revelation. And this promise, or transfer of right, to God, was made in the same way as we've conceived it to be done in ordinary society, when men decide to surrender their natural right. For by an explicit covenant and an oath they freely surrendered their natural right and transferred it to God, without being compelled by force or terrified by threats. (17.26–28)

The Hebrews sought to secure their "freedom from human rule" (17.82) in the same way that members of an "ordinary society" do. In other words, the Hebrews' theological conviction is formally equivalent to the democratic promise—at once an aspiration and an agreement to live by reason's dictate—underlying the idea of society as such.[25] (Recall that in the TTP democracy functions as the generic state.) "As in a democracy," the Hebrews surrendered their natural right on equal terms, subjecting themselves to an authoritative law so as not to obey any of their equals. They "cried out in one voice 'whatever God says' (without any explicit mediator) 'we will do'" (TTP 17.33; cf. 16.25–27). It follows, for Spinoza, that "everyone remained completely equal by this covenant": each one of the Hebrews, renouncing the unrestricted right to act at his own discretion and thereby assuming the responsibility to abide by the revealed communal norms, remained equally free from any obligation to subordinate his judgment to another (cf. 5.25, 16.36, 20.14). All maintained an equal "right to consult God, and to receive and interpret his laws." And in this respect, "everyone held the whole administration of the state equally, without qualification" (17.33). Even Moses enters the picture here not as a ruler but as a trusted adviser who facilitated the Hebrews' decision, made "freely" and without compulsion or threat, to credit God with sovereignty.

It bears emphasizing how Spinoza's "democratic" account of the Sinai covenant coincides with the biblical narrative of a people who form themselves (immanently) in and through the divine revelation (transcendence).[26] According to this narrative, the covenant between God and people required that both parties consent, a consent predicated in turn upon the Hebrews' freedom of judgment. After all, they did not initially follow Moses's advice, disheartened as they were by the labors of their servitude (Exod. 6:9). Only after a process of collective deliberation did the Hebrews, first, consent to do "whatever God says" and, second, expressly affirm Moses in his intermediary function.[27]

If, in Spinoza's telling, the Hebrews' direct theocracy exemplifies the aspiration to form a society free from domination, their promise to obey only God's commands also illustrates, on one hand, the problem of ratifying the pact and establishing the conditions for its stability (see TTP 16.15—*Qua autem ratione pactum hoc iniri debeat, ut ratum fixumque sit . . .*), which requires an agency of enforcement and hence command; and, on the other hand, the problem of applying law to particular cases, which requires an authoritative agency of interpretation or judgment. Glossing Exodus 19–20, Spinoza relates that when the Hebrews "equally went to God the first time to hear what he commanded" they were so thunderstruck by his voice that they selected Moses to become their explicit mediator (17.34–35). In so doing, "they clearly abolished the first covenant and transferred to Moses, unconditionally, their right to consult God and to interpret his edicts," promising to obey whatever God said to Moses (17.36). Although the Hebrews had initially hoped to obey God's commands while retaining equal rights of interpretation, a crisis arose when they sought to determine what his commands were. Why so? What might Spinoza take the Hebrews' fear of the theophany to mean? Quite possibly, as Morfino suggests, they were astonished by the "deafening roar of a crowd that imagines God in a thousand different ways," faced as they were with the challenge of arriving at a univocal decision on what God's law requires of all subjects.[28] Thus Moses, as armed prophet, vested with exclusive rights of interpretation and command, resolved the twofold problem of stability and application for the Hebrews.

Spinoza's allusions to the violence Moses employed are certainly much more muted than those found in Machiavelli, who baldly states "that if Moses was to put his laws and regulations into effect, he was forced to kill countless men who, moved by nothing else than envy, were opposed to his plans."[29] Likewise for the biblical text: where Spinoza's language in the early pages of

TTP 17 characterizes the passage from the direct to Mosaic theocracy in the volitional terms of a popular election or choice (17.38), albeit one made on the basis of acute fear, Exodus reveals this "transfer of right" to be the effect of an outright massacre visited upon the people, the violent imposition of Moses's interpretation or prophecy over another, namely, the worship of the golden calf.[30] Spinoza does, nonetheless, retain this biblical figure of an originary violence as a symbol of the exceptional, "tyrannical" basis of the Hebrews' constitutional regime, as I will discuss shortly. More generally speaking, throughout the TTP Spinoza very openly affirms the indissociable link between the validity of any law or principle of right—be it the Mosaic constitution, the "universal faith" of justice and charity, or the dictates of reason—and its facticity or force, which can be established only through an agency of public command (see esp. TTP 19).

Spinoza considers Moses's prophetic "introduction" of religion into the Hebrew republic as part and parcel of the latter's acquisition of state, or command over the population (5.29, 17.112). Moses's divine vision of a chosen people with unique laws and a singular purpose, Spinoza argues, included a perception about the artful use of violence, or how this people could "best be compelled to obedience" (4.29). So even as the TTP focuses mainly on the nonrepressive, institutional ("civil"), and devotional forms into which Moses transmuted the sheer violence of his command, Spinoza shows the persistence of this extraordinary, prelegal violence in times of emergency. Here, for instance, is Spinoza's account of the Korah rebellion:

> As soon as the people began to flourish in tranquility in the desert, many men, not from the ordinary people, began to be bitter about this choice, and from this they took the opportunity to believe that Moses had instituted nothing by divine command, but had done everything according to his own pleasure, because he'd chosen his own tribe before all others, and had given the right of priesthood to his own brother forever. With a great commotion, they approached him claiming that everyone was equally holy and that he was unjustly raised above everyone else. He could not quiet them in any way, but when he used a miracle as a sign of his good faith, all the rebels were annihilated [Numbers 16:31–35]. This gave rise to a new and general rebellion of the whole people [Numbers 16:41–50], who believed that the first rebels had been annihilated, not by God's judgment, but by Moses' cunning. He finally quieted them after they had been worn out by a great calamity or plague, but in such a way that they all preferred death to life. So at that time it was more that the rebellion had ended than that harmony had begun. (17.103–4)

One could say that the schooling in disciplined obedience Moses offered his people, their education into military and civic virtue, made for a continual demonstration of his theological-political authority, weaving it into the rhythms of everyday life.[31] But in exceptional circumstances, when, as Machiavelli puts it, "the multitude began not believe," Moses ascended to absolute status.

The key question Spinoza raises with his depiction of the Hebrews' second pact is the precise meaning of Moses's command. How, for instance, to understand Spinoza's occasional references to Moses as the personal embodiment of God's majesty (*vicem Dei, hoc est, supremam majestum habuit*) (17.37)? One possibility is to read Spinoza through a Hobbesian lens. So when Spinoza writes that, after the Hebrews transferred their right of command to Moses, "he remained king absolutely and only through Him did God reign over the Hebrews" (19.11), one could see in these lines Hobbes's assertion that "there is no covenant with God but by mediation of some body that represents God's person."[32] And yet, if the goal was simply to advance a theory of lieutenancy—and by extension, an Erastian arrangement that denied clergy independent authority—wherein Moses, as a human sovereign, "becomes God . . . and acts instead of him," Spinoza could have presented the Sinai covenant as a direct transfer of rights to Moses and left it at that.[33] Instead, Spinoza takes pains to present the Hebrews' covenant as one made directly with God and, after pausing briefly to note the absoluteness of Moses's command, he turns quickly to the question of Moses's succession. Spinoza devotes most of his energy to an analysis of the federal, constitutional features of the post-Mosaic theodemocracy, where, strictly speaking, no one ruled.

What, then, to make of the second contract with Moses? It is better, I suggest, to see Moses here as a vanishing mediator. Moses carried the place of God as a charismatic authority, mediating the Hebrews' transition from a liberated but relatively powerless multitude to an armed people capable of remaining free from external oppression, or, in short, from the challenge of acquiring a state to that of preserving one. In this capacity, Moses "alone had the authority to make and repeal laws in God's name, to choose the ministers of sacred affairs, to judge, to teach, to punish, and to command absolutely all things to all people" (18.4). Nevertheless, Moses deliberately avoided choosing a successor for fear that such an arrangement would have made the Hebrew state "nothing more than a monarchy" (17.39). Instead, Spinoza insists, Moses opted to give the Hebrew theocracy the form of a republican constitution, implementing measures that enlisted the support of all constituents of society, rulers and ruled, so as to make the state last.

In Spinoza's account, these distinct elements of the Hebrews' political history combine in the form of a relatively stable republican state where the Mosaic constitution divides the people's unitary constituent power into different governmental powers that check each other and are checked in turn by the armed citizenry (17.50–60). Hence the first feature that accounts for the temporal prosperity of the Hebrews, according to Spinoza, was their good "laws and mores," understood broadly as the quality of the constitution of the state.[34] Moses's constitutional arrangement of state power guarded against monarchy by instituting in the state an absence of God, "the supreme majesty of that state" (17.42, 19.36).[35] Moses "left the state to be administered by his successors in such a way that it couldn't be called either popular, or aristocratic, or monarchic, but Theocratic" (17.41).[36] God's constituent power—housed, as it were, in the tabernacle or "dwelling-place" built entirely from communal resources and subject to communal oversight—remained the extraordinary source of all constituted offices and laws (17.42).

In Spinoza's initial description of this "theocratic" arrangement of governmental offices, the high priest, Aaron, and the Levites possessed the sole right to interpret God's decrees, whereas Joshua, the supreme commander of the army, alone wielded the executive power of administering matters of war and peace (17.41, 17.43–49).[37] But following Joshua's death, and on the basis of a distribution of territory conquered in war, the regime became a federation of autonomous tribes. Joshua's powers of command devolved, accordingly, to tribal leaders, who each assumed "responsibility for his own share, i.e., the responsibility for consulting God through the high priest about the affairs of his own tribe, for commanding his own army, for founding and fortifying cities, for establishing judges in each city, for attacking the enemy of his own particular state, and of administering all matters of war and peace without exception" (TTP 17.55). The tribes, Spinoza says, remained united as fellow citizens "in relation to God and Religion," but allies in relation to one another, much like the "Sovereign Federated States of the Netherlands" (17.54).[38] Summing up, Spinoza adds further texture to his definition of theocracy:

> After Moses' death no one had all the functions of the supreme commander. These things didn't all depend on the decision of one man, or of one council, or of the people. Some were administered by one tribe, and others by the other tribes, with equal right for each one. From this it follows most clearly that after Moses' death the state was neither monarchical, nor aristocratic, nor popular, but, as we have said, Theocratic: I) because the temple was the royal house of the state and, as we've shown, it was the only reason why all the tribes were fellow citizens; II) because all the citizens had to swear allegiance to God as their supreme judge; he was the only one they had promised to obey absolutely in everything; and finally, III) because, when it was necessary to appoint a supreme commander over everyone, only God chose that commander. (17.60–61)

Spinoza thus accommodates the Hebrews' shift to a federation of tribal republics within his understanding of theocracy and even adduces the absence of a permanent commander-in-chief as another reason to characterize the regime as theocratic.

Spinoza uses his account of the Mosaic constitution to show, in the spirit of Machiavelli, that for the Hebrews good laws followed from "good arms," which in turn followed from the goodness of a civil religion capable of undergirding constitutional arrangements.[39] As I noted above, Spinoza's Moses counted the need to prepare for war with external enemies as one of the basic reasons for introducing a new religion that could unify and motivate his people. Spinoza's emphasis in TTP 17 on the Hebrew state's internal stability leads him to foreground, in addition, the "moderating" force of its theocratic arrangements, which divided and balanced power in order to restrain rulers and ruled alike (17.62, 17.112). The Levites' authority to interpret the law, for example, prevented the tribal leaders from disguising any crimes they committed with the trappings of legality. Moreover, since the people as a whole were commanded to assemble every seventh year to learn the law from the priest, each on his own being required continuously and attentively to study the book of law, the tribal leaders "had to be very careful (if only in their interest) to administer everything according to the prescribed laws." To the extent that the leaders performed in this charge, the people venerated them as ministers of God's Kingdom; if the leaders deviated, however, "they could not escape their subjects' greatest hatred" (17.65). By the same token, arming the people as guardians of God's Law helped to deepen their own investment in the perseverance of the state.

Another, more "material" reason for the resilience of the Hebrew theodemocracy, in Spinoza's telling, was that "the principle of *utile*, the mainstay and life of all human actions," found "exceptionally strong" economic, political, and social articulation in this state (TTP 17.84–85). Spinoza emphasizes how Hebrew citizens possessed a strong right to property ownership and an equal share of lands and fields. And redistributive measures such as the jubilee served as bulwarks against inequality: "If poverty compelled anyone to sell his estate or field, it had to be restored to him once again when the jubilee year came. They instituted other similar practices, so that no one could be alienated from his real property." (17.85). Nowhere, Spinoza argues, was poverty more bearable than in this state, where "the people had to cultivate, with the utmost piety, charity toward their neighbor (i.e., toward their fellow citizen), so that God, their King, would favor them." Yet the "Hebrew citizens could prosper only in their own country," he adds, for "outside it they faced great harm and dishonor" (17.86, trans. modified). The Hebrews faced these things, Spinoza contends, because their conceptions of solidarity and equality, so scrupulously cultivated through a host of practices and institutions, proved inseparable from a chauvinism and a mimetically sustained hatred of others—the sort of intolerance that Rousseau would later criticize as an inherent feature of particularistic "religions of the citizen."[40]

Crafting a Modern Civil Religion

Despite its many noteworthy features, Spinoza registers the limitations of the Hebrew theodemocracy as a constitutional model for "modern" states like the Dutch Republic, which differ from ancient Israel in their experience of political and religious liberty. For one thing, the prosperity of the Hebrew state was premised on a type of political, cultural, and economic autarky that Spinoza claims is no longer useful under modern conditions of interdependence. He also offers a more theological-political reason for the inimitability of the Hebrew state: God can no longer be imagined as the God of one nation alone. A people cannot covenant with God as the ancient Israelites did because "God . . . has revealed through his Apostles that his covenant is no longer written with ink, or on stone tablets, but written on the heart, by the very spirit of God" (TTP 18.2). Spinoza writes, "before the coming of Christ the Prophets were accustomed to preach religion as the law of their Country and by the power of the covenant entered into in the time of Moses; but after the coming of Christ the Apostles preached the same [religion] to everyone as a universal law, solely by the power of the passion of Christ" (12.24). With the Christian spiritualization of the law, it becomes possible and necessary, Spinoza contends, for a republican state to give determinate political form and force to the kind of universal religion sketched in TTP 14, a faith gleaned from monotheistic religions but identified with no religion in particular. What emerges from Spinoza's line of argument here is a new conception of civil religion.

By describing the universal faith that Spinoza sets out in chapter 14 of the TTP as the basis of a modern *civil religion*, I mean to highlight a continuity with and not only a departure from his treatment of the ancient Hebrew state. The continuity consists in the fact that Spinoza still understands religion to play a constructive, foundational role for the creation and maintenance of a people's collective "salvation" or worldly happiness. Recall that Spinoza contrasts Moses's (and the Hebrews') interpretation of religion, first, with a more "spiritual" conception as otherworldly salvation, and, second, with a more instrumental notion of "civil religion" as political imposture, or the use of falsehoods by one or a few to dominate the many—illustrated largely by Roman examples.[41] The modern civil religion that Spinoza develops in the TTP, similarly, takes its distance from both an apolitical, spiritual conception of faith and a particularistic religion of the city and citizen. How, then, to understand its universalistic dimension?

Spinoza's contemporaries typically employed the term "universal religion" (*religio catholica*) to denote a "natural religion" (*religio naturalis*) that stood as the distillation of and essential structure for revealed religion.[42] For his part, Spinoza speaks of a universal religion revealed by both "the natural light and the prophets" (*lumine naturali & Prophetico revelata*) (Ep 43). As he develops this view in the TTP, it becomes clear that Spinoza wishes to displace the received way of thinking about the relationship between reason and faith, namely, in terms of a primacy of one over the other. Spinoza thus initiates a double move: he denies that religion consists of mysteries whose interpretation would require either a "supernatural" light (special intuition about God's will) or a philosophical education in metaphysics, and he affirms that an indefinite diversity of opinions is compatible with, or necessitated by, faith properly understood as the practice of charity.

The form of Spinoza's argument, captured in the title of chapter 15, is that "Theology should not be the handmaiden of Reason, nor Reason the handmaid of Theology" (TTP 15 title). Rather than a relation of dependence or subordination of one to the other, Spinoza argues for a mutual independence and complementarity between faith and reason "which brings no slight advantage to the republic" (15.35). This principled separation, which turns on a distinction between the ends and the foundations of each—philosophy, based on common notions, aims at truth, whereas faith, based on the histories and language of scripture, aims only at obedience and piety—corresponds with a practical agreement between the faculties. Spinoza's position here also entails a differentiated understanding of reason understood not only in its theoretical, and one could say authoritative, guise as apodictic demonstration, but also, crucially, in its practical and radically democratic or common aspect as the capacity of all individuals, "no matter how slow," to perceive, discern, and make sense (13.4). After all, Spinoza holds that there is nothing in what scripture "expressly teaches" that conflicts or that would "contradict the intellect" (pref 24). The biblical teachings consist not of "lofty speculations, or philosophical matters," but only of "simple things that everyone could easily perceive," thanks to the poetic ingenuity of the prophets, who confirmed the biblical teachings "with those reasons by which they could most readily move the mind of the multitude toward devotion to God" (13.4, pref 24). As such, the knowledge of God, the theo-logos, that each is bound to have concerns the true way of living: "God is supremely just and supremely merciful," or, in short, "he is the unique model of the true life" (13.23).

Spinoza's distinction between faith and reason entails that true religion is necessarily social: religion furnishes the basis for the morality required by human society and it requires human society for its realization. Recall Spinoza's view that moral laws are not eternal truths of nature but "rules of living" that follow from human decision. Even though, as I showed last chapter, the true function of law is not to establish a relation of command and obedience, it is still the case that everyone is in principle capable of seeing the utility of law in these moral terms, either because she can grasp the true reason for society or because she perceives some particular benefit to come from obeying (or harm from disobeying) (4.6). Likewise, even though everyone can in some fashion grasp the utility of living with others in society and can in principle agree with others to form society, everyone is also by nature within her rights to act in antisocial ways and to break her promise to others if she perceives it to be in her interest (*utile*). Hence the requirement (following from natural right) that humans establish an agency of public command to determine and enforce a common standard of good/bad, right/wrong, pious/impious (E IV p37s2, TTP 19). In Spinoza's view, this public morality has its foundation in biblical faith, the sole aim of which is to "teach obedience" to a law commanding "love of one's neighbor" (14.6). Further, Spinoza understands faith to "grant" or necessitate an interpretive freedom that allows everyone to understand this command by their own lights, and thus to assume full responsibility for adhering to it or not. True religion, in short, offers a training in the obedience that makes society (neighborly love) possible. Reciprocally, religion conceived in this truly universal sense requires the authoritative interpretation (sovereign jurisdiction) of a state in order to have a public, concrete, and determinate application (TTP 19).

Commentators often interpret the functional equivalence that Spinoza sets up between prophets and sovereign powers (TTP 1.4n4), along with his insistence that the latter must be "interpreters and defenders," through analogy with Hobbes's treatment of religion.[43] However, the prophetic dimension of public or civil religion in Spinoza has more in common with the prophetology of Maimonides and Alfarabi, for whom the figure of the prophet is at once a legislator and a philosopher: a legislator in that he enables the worldly happiness of a people by providing them with a constitution, and a philosopher in that he ensures that the fundamental laws guiding the people are rational, or oriented toward their common benefit. Focusing here on Alfarabi, three features of such prophetology are worth noting. First,

Alfarabi emphasizes that revelation rather than philosophy offers the form of instruction—"persuasion and imaginative representation"—most rhetorically suited to educating the many into political life.[44] Second, he stresses that the highest wisdom or theoretical science should be employed "for the benefit of others" in attaining supreme happiness and worldly perfection, if it is not to be "defective philosophy."[45] Finally, Alfarabi observes that revealed law finds its proper articulation in and through politics. If philosophy gives an account of the ultimate principles, "religion sets their images by means of similitudes . . . and imitates them by their likenesses among political offices. It imitates the divine acts by means of the functions of political offices."[46] Thus political life furnishes the means through which humans come to know and imitate God. Here "political theology" does not depend on the authority of priests or philosophers with special knowledge of divine mysteries. The many can know God just as much and as well as the few, since this knowledge, as Maimonides in particular underscores, concerns God's ethical traits or attributes of action.

Likewise, for Spinoza, universal faith furnishes the basis for a public reason, a reason aimed at "constitutional essentials" (to borrow from Rawls), and articulated in a language that is accessible from all viewpoints (i.e., avoiding scientific/philosophical technicalities and faith-based or prophetic intuitions). The first of the seven tenets of this faith, for example, stipulates that "God exists, i.e., there is a supreme being, supremely just and merciful, or a model of true life" (TTP 14.25).[47] What God *is*, however, and what it means that he is a model of true life is a matter for everyone to interpret for themselves (14.30). Is God to be understood in anthropomorphic fashion as a being with a "just and merciful heart," an example to be imitated? Or is God to be understood in some other way, such as the vital principle of the natural universe? On the latter view, it is not because God is just and merciful that one ought to be just and merciful. Rather, it is because God is God that individuals are these things, "because all things exist and act through him and consequently we, too, understand through him, and through him (and hence that we too understand through him, and see through him, what is truly right, and good)" (TTP 14.30). These divergent interpretations imply the existence of an indefinite multiplicity of others, more and less "theological" or "philosophical."[48] The decision as to which interpretation is true—traditionally, the concern of theology—is irrelevant to faith and thus to civil obligation. One need not justify in a definitive way what moves one to undertake works of charity and justice. Intellectually, then, this sort of civil religion authorizes a plurality of interpretations.[49] As Susan James notes, what distinguishes Spinoza's understanding of the universal faith "is the fact that each tenet is in effect a variable, to be filled in by each believer as they see fit; and this is what makes them universal."[50]

One of the most significant features of civil religion, conceived along these Spinozist lines, is that it addresses the challenge of how to motivate civil solidarity. To put this in terms Rousseau will later come to use, civil religion allows republican institutions to embody a universal solidarity and charity, such that a certain tolerance—or intolerance of persecution—becomes the religion of the citizen. For Spinoza, it is evident that a wholly rational account of the reciprocal utility of human beings is ill-equipped to inspire everyone to respect universal equality, that is, to love one's neighbor as oneself. Everyone in his own way nonetheless desires salvation or freedom or happiness. Hence the promise of scripture: "We can't perceive by the natural light that simple obedience is a path to salvation. Only revelation teaches that this happens. . . . Everyone without exception can obey. But only a very few (compared to the whole human race) acquire a habit of virtue from the guidance of reason alone. So, if we didn't have this testimony of Scripture, we would doubt nearly everyone's salvation" (15.45). Following Spinoza, civil religion makes a public use of a salvation narrative insofar as the state gives determinate (if provisional) form and force to the idea of loving one's neighbor. In other words, the state gives an account of public happiness aimed at motivating all individuals to act justly and charitably.

From a contemporary liberal viewpoint, such a public use of religion might appear untenable or inappropriate. Should the state not just remain neutral on the issue of how to pursue happiness?[51] A Spinozist response might run as follows. The state must be concerned about whether and how its citizens can achieve a temporal and public happiness by subscribing to its laws, even though it must allow individuals to imagine and pursue their personal happiness in their own ways. This is why, for example, the maintenance of economic equality through redistributive measures such as the jubilee acquires importance in Spinoza and other republican thought: it offers a condition for public happiness. If the state is not attentive to the conditions for public happiness, it runs the risk that individuals' capacities to act as free and equal citizens become captured by and diverted—or as Spinoza might say, *sacrificed*—to other pursuits (TTP pref 11). Individuals may choose to adhere to decidedly uncivil or antisocial conceptions of religion that provide a sense of belonging and a promise of happiness in the beyond. Alternatively, individuals' public virtue may become corrupted or overtaken by a preoccupation with some private pursuit of happiness such as the acquisition of money.[52] Attention to Spinoza's republican idea of civil religion thus suggests that a state cannot allow political life to be steered in any significant way by belief systems and ideologies that would require, say, religious martyrdom or laissez-faire economics.

Popular Sovereignty and Political Messianism

Let me return to the opening question of the modern state's "debt" to religion. Spinoza's development of a republican civil religion, by way of a critique of spiritual and instrumental interpretations of religion, on the one hand, and a selective appropriation and affirmation of key features of the Hebrew state, on the other, demonstrates the inadequacy of framing the issue of conceptual indebtedness as an either/or question of the modern state's dependence on or independence from religion.[53] Therefore, the idea that Spinoza uses the Hebrew case "to undermine the authority of Scripture, in the service of a secularizing political science" (Nelson) holds only if one adds that Spinoza undermines the authority of Scripture *to prop up hierocracy*, that is, a conception of religion that would require priests or a church to play an intermediary role between God and a people organized according to a republican or democratic constitution. It would be a distortion to conclude, though, that Spinoza's deflationary political agenda renders God "merely an anthropomorphizing illusion," or that Spinoza's reading of the Hebrew state entails that "religion truly has been banished from political life" (Nelson), for these sorts of assertions deny the foundational role Spinoza assigns to civil religion, in line with the prophetology of Alfarabi and in the tradition of modern republicanism as articulated by Machiavelli, Rousseau, and others.[54] Neither would it be accurate to say, conversely, that Spinoza's engagement with political theology confirms Schmitt's thesis that all significant concepts of the modern state are secularized theological (read: Christian) concepts. Spinoza shows, instead, that a "both-and" account of the complex interdependence between state and religion is more conceptually adequate and normatively desirable.

By complicating the received—implicitly or explicitly Hobbesian—picture of the modern state and disclosing the outlines of an alternative, republican state of nondomination, Spinoza's thought helps to reframe the topic of "sovereign debt" in still another sense, one related to a question that the recent financial crisis has posed anew: what happens to public debt when the only person capable of incurring and redeeming it, the juridical person of the state, appears increasingly to be stripped of its sovereignty, ineffectual if not yet extinct?[55] Agamben and Esposito contend that what is at stake in this question is not so much the waning of sovereignty and the eclipse of political theology as the migration of sovereignty into the domain of economic theology, conceived as the immanent, providential ordering or government (*oikonomia*) of social life.[56] Writes Esposito, "the fact that all states, divided by a clear inequality of resources, are now indebted to an entity as elusive as global finance means that for the first time, perhaps, the world will experience a condition of shared suffering."[57] Esposito proposes that, to find a way out of such a condition, "we would need to change the way we interpret it," namely, by reversing the meaning of universal indebtedness so that it signifies rather a "circuit of solidarity" or common debt akin to the original sense of *communitas*.[58] What Spinoza stands to contribute to this interpretive project, as articulated by Esposito, is greater political specificity and purchase: the concept of a republican state whose "debt" to theology—a universalistic civil religion—consists in the endeavor to transform sovereignty in and through works of the common. In closing, I will speculate on one other respect in which Spinoza incorporates an irreducibly "providential" element into his conception of the republican state: through the messianic idea.

To be sure, Spinoza maintains that there are no more prophets such as Moses in the modern age (TTP 1.7, 19.62). Neither are there peoples who find themselves in the position of the ancient Hebrews. As Spinoza notes, the ancient Hebrews' *ingenium* or "memory" following their exodus was profoundly contoured by their experience as slaves. After escaping Egyptian oppression, they persisted "in a state of nature," no longer under the dominion of another and yet still possessed of a slave mentality. They needed—and Moses delivered to them—an education into the freedom of political life, a freedom that they maintained until transferring their right to a human king (19.13). Spinoza's contemporary Dutch readers, of course, had a memory of subjection to the Spanish Habsburg rule, but they had a more profound image of themselves as constituents of a republic that had been free since time immemorial—a self-image to which Spinoza appeals at the beginning and end of the TTP. The States of Holland, he stresses, have never transferred their sovereignty to a king, but only to counts who have held the people's power in trust. Consequently, the states have always retained the ultimate right and power to defend their citizens' freedom and, if necessary, to depose tyrannical leaders (18.36). As Spinoza adds in the *Political Treatise*, "If someone retorts that this state of the Hollanders has not lasted long without a Count, or a Representative who could act in his place, I would reply: the Hollanders thought that to maintain their freedom it was enough to renounce their Count and cut the head off the body of the state. They didn't think about reforming it, but left all its members as they'd been set up before, so that Holland remained a county without a Count, or a body without a head" (TP 9.14). According to Spinoza, then, the Dutch did not fit the profile of a dispersed multitude in need of a prophet-founder—they already possessed a "headless" body politic along with the strength and desire to maintain it as such. Why then speak of messianism at all?

Here it helps to note how, over the course of the TTP, the change in Spinoza's constitutional focus from Hebrew theodemocracy to modern republican state parallels a shift in the different way he talks about God's Kingdom: no longer in the Mosaic vein, which is to say in terms of an armed legislator-prophet, but rather in terms that resemble a redemption—viz. a return to and worldly realization of the divine principles of justice and charity. In Jewish political theology, such a redemption finds expression in the messianic idea, which stands for a repudiation of human sovereignty and a return to the beginning of God's divine republic.[59] Spinoza's exhortation in the TTP to "reform" both state and religion within a horizon of democracy and justice, when read through the lens of Jewish messianism, allows one to see how his appropriation of political theology—and his preoccupation with theocracy, in particular—is consistent with his philosophical or naturalistic account (in TTP 16 and 20) of the democratic state. As Spinoza underscores, prior to the period of Kings, God's command over his people took the form of a republic that was free from human rule. In their *direct* covenant with God, the Hebrews organized themselves as a democracy of equals. "The Hebrews didn't transfer their right to anyone else, but everyone surrendered his right equally, as in a democracy, and they cried out in one voice 'whatever God says' (without any explicit mediator) 'we will do'." It follows, Spinoza concludes, that "everyone remained completely equal by this covenant, that the right to consult God, and to receive and interpret his laws, was equal for everyone. Everyone held the whole administration of the state equally, without qualification" (17.33). By comparison, in his natural-right accounts of the state, Spinoza justifies his exclusive attention to democracy on the grounds that it comes closest to nature and that it facilitates a collective transfer of right wherein everyone "remains equal," as in the natural condition (16.36, 20.38; cf. 5.25). The Hebrew theocracy in its most perfect form, that most (specifically) favored by God, thus resembles the state that most nearly approaches "the freedom which nature concedes to everyone" (16.36). Or, as Spinoza also indicates, the Hebrew theodemocracy resembles the pact that all of humankind makes with God "as equals" (16.55–56).[60]

The key implication is that Spinoza preserves a sense in which the "supreme majesty" of the republican state that he constructs in TTP 16 can be made to represent, however provisionally or imperfectly, not God, but God's *covenant* with His people, His Kingdom on earth, which exists wherever and whenever "justice and charity have the force of law and command" (TTP 19.4, trans. modified).[61] Spinoza's civil religion, one could say, represents divine justice and charity as an obligation to uphold the principle of human rights (equality of all with all). In naturalistic terms, however, loving one's neighbor as oneself is not a moral duty but a necessity to take one's power to the limit through an alteration or exchange with the powers of others (*sui juris* individuals considered adequately, as singular constituents of common power). It belongs to a citizen-driven use of reason to fully immanentize God in a democracy of equals and to enact complete justice, as we shall see in the next chapter.

5

Democracy of Judgment

How much the more must we grant freedom of judgment, which not only can't be suppressed, but is undoubtedly a virtue.

SPINOZA

The essential work of politics is the configuration of its own space.

JACQUES RANCIÈRE

What would it mean to treat judgment as a political virtue in its own right? Spinoza's writings provoke this question even if they do not expressly pursue it. His most extended analysis of judgment, the vindication of *libertas philosophandi* in the *Theological-Political Treatise*, proceeds in primarily negative terms as a series of arguments aimed at demonstrating why freedom of judgment should not and cannot be suppressed. When Spinoza positively articulates what such judgment is and what it does, he stresses above all its virtue as a means to preserve piety and the stability of the state. On the face of it, he offers a theological-political and instrumental defense of judgment: one must remain free to interpret how best to assume responsibility as a subject of law. But from the perspective of Spinoza's naturalism—wherein right or power (*potentia*) operates as a means without end, exception, or limit—the "virtue" at stake in individuals' right to judge concerns, more fundamentally, a common capacity to (re)configure a political constitution that fosters the vitality of shared and singular powers. Hence Spinoza's provocation: animating every individual's natural right of judging is, so to speak, a query about how best to participate in common potentiality, a query that assumes a paradigmatically "jurisprudential" form when individuals employ their reason to philosophize or judge publicly the utility of the state's laws.

In this chapter, I delineate further what I take to be the core features of Spinoza's jurisprudential line of thinking, reflecting in particular on its connection to and implications for democracy. Gathering and amplifying some interpretive threads from the preceding chapters, I employ the notion of "citizen jurisprudence" as a Spinozist tool for conceptualizing the radical relationship between democracy and judgment. Although Spinoza's affirmative and affirmatively political case for judgment stands as a largely neglected dimension of his thought that merits scholarly attention, my chief aim here is not simply to repair oversights in the current reception of Spinoza. Rather, the chapter's more synthetic focus on citizen jurisprudence allows me to return more directly to the larger problem that launched the sequence of Spinozist reflections offered in this book: what makes judgment democratic?

In contemporary political theory, discussions about the judging power of the people are largely a function of how two distinct "deliberation" and "judgment" literatures have emerged and evolved, with the former now something of an orthodoxy that the latter seeks to challenge. Indeed, many of today's theorists of political judgment see in the prevailing deliberative paradigm a turn away from the very phenomenon of judgment, if not from democratic politics as such.[1] These critics argue that the political specificity of judgment falls out of view when deliberative democrats subsume first-order practices of judgment into second-order discourses of moral justification. The "specificity" at issue pertains to the social-historical particularity of the political subjects and scenes of judgment; it also encompasses the specifically political *form* that judging takes when diverse perspectives on a particular matter (*this* law, *this* policy) engender a commonality. In thus emphasizing the contexts, encounters, and processes by which judging becomes political rather than the procedural or discursive norms said to guide the judging process, a new cohort of political theorists is insisting on a more "reflective" than "determinative" approach to judgment. Without that additional reflexivity, the argument goes, deliberativists threaten to perpetuate rather than mitigate oppressive forms of rationalism in politics.[2]

Still, if deliberative theory tends to lose sight of judgment's political specificity, the question of how to understand that specificity as *democratic* remains elusive even for those theorists who take (reflective) judgment to be their central concern. It may well be that a certain intellectualist image of judgment as "an explicit and propositional intellectual activity" makes it difficult to conceptualize the practice of judgment as it manifests itself in broader political struggles and everyday life.[3] But more fundamentally, the elusiveness of democratic judgment is bound up with the challenge of theorizing politics in its own terms. For if one argues (rightly, I believe) that the deliberative approach too easily assimilates judgment to a norm of justification and politics to a form of government, there remains the risk that such a critique, in its attempt to demarcate a uniquely democratic practice of judging, might itself presume an authentic or "pure" sphere of the political.[4] This kind of presumption reintroduces a circularity in which the proper subjects, objects, and forms of political judgment are already given and thus the action of politics to configure its own field is obscured. How, then, to grasp the democratic specificity of judgment without, as it were, prejudging politics?

This chapter develops the Spinozist concept of "citizen jurisprudence" as a way of addressing this problem of democratic judgment. By citizen jurisprudence, I understand a right (*jus*) and a power (*potentia*) of judging that is internally related to the "power of the people." Citizen jurisprudence operates both as figure and effect of democracy conceived expansively: not solely as a state form but as an activity of equally free (*sui juris*) individuals determining the sense and the scope of common affairs. In what follows, I set out the core features of this concept in three steps. I demonstrate, first, that citizen jurisprudence, both as a right of equal freedom and as a collaborative activity of reasoning, presupposes a certain *publicity*. I then consider how a particular capacity for being acted upon, or a *passibility*, corresponds essentially to this judging activity. And in a final step, I argue that citizen jurisprudence comes into its own as a democratic practice of illuminating the constitutive premises of public right.

Citizen jurisprudence is a felicitous term for my purposes, not only because it conveys key aspects of prudential and bottom-up reasoning about matters of public right but also in that it connotes a combination of general principles (a philosophy of law) and concrete cases (judgments relative to specific situations).[5] In this way, the term marks the explicit connection that Spinoza himself establishes in the TTP between philosophizing and judging. More broadly, the concept registers the complex interweaving, in Spinoza's system, between the geometric or formal-generic order of reason and the specific events of language, passion, and history.[6] As I detailed in chapter 2, Spinoza's treatment of *ingenium* is a prime example of such complementarity. So too is his construal of the republican concept of *sui juris* status, both in an ostensibly traditional juridical sense, as independence, and in a more technical sense, as the maximal causal power to affect and be affected. In its connection with democratic power, citizen jurisprudence similarly combines geometrical or juridical formalism (as the *figure* of a democracy of equals) with the question of activity and affective capacity (as the *effect* of such a democracy). If, according to the ancient republican ideal of citizenship, the distinctly political relationship was that of partaking in a form of ruling and being ruled, Spinoza's vital republicanism embraces a decidedly modern notion of citizenship as partaking in the activity of co-authoring the basic law to which one is subject. In Spinoza, citizenship operates less as the condition for the free activity of jurisprudence than as its immanent effect: judging is the activity in which subjects become citizens of a free people and matters of fact become matters of common concern. Citizen jurisprudence, in short, is the democratic activity of subjects and objects becoming political.

Another Public "Use" of Reason

Recall that in the TTP Spinoza defines and defends freedom of judgment as a basic right of citizenship. Without exaggeration, one could say that, for him, the possibility of a free political life turns on this right. Political domination, which, Spinoza asserts, "the Turks" have most successfully achieved, is foremost a matter of colonizing subjects' judgments with superstitious prejudice. But no endeavor could be more ruinous "in a free republic," where it is "completely repugnant to common freedom to occupy with prejudice or in any way constrain the free judgment of each and every one" (pref 10, trans. modified). If, in proposing this thesis, Spinoza (via Tacitus) plays on the pre-eminence of free judgment in the contemporary Dutch self-image—"We happen to have that rare good fortune that we live in a republic in which everyone is granted complete freedom of judgment . . . and nothing is thought to be dearer or sweeter than freedom"—he also takes at its word the prevailing contractarian discourse on the state (pref 12). In so doing, Spinoza presents freedom of judgment as the figure of a generalized juridical independence. Indeed, the foundation of the state is precisely the "natural right of each," a right that "extends as far as each individual's desire and power extend" (pref 29). Each individual "transfers" his natural right in the pact that forms a political society, but only conditionally. This right remains at the disposal of the state insofar as the state wields the effective power to make and enforce law. However, no one can wholly surrender "his faculty of reasoning freely and of judging concerning anything whatever" (20.2). Strictly speaking, it is not within a subject's control to dispose of his basic capacity to judge, which is itself disposed in a multiplicity of ways according to ambient networks of affect. Individuals cannot help but continuously render more and less reflective judgments on the conditions for their own perseverance, and thus on the utility of their civic status (16.15–22, TP 3.3, TP 3.8).

Even though this natural right of judging is in some manner prior to the state, it is not natural in the sense that it is grounded in any primordial fact or substantial features of human nature; nor, in the context of Spinoza's anti-teleological naturalism, does it correspond to any sort of natural duty or obligation. These peculiarities might account for why Spinoza initially describes freedom of judgment as being rooted in a *quasi*-natural right to one's rights. It is "as if by natural right" that "subjects retain . . . certain things which cannot be taken from them without great danger to the state" (TTP pref 31, trans.

modified). The as-if (*quasi*) structure of this statement conveys how such a right is, on the one hand, an uncodifiable and *de facto* inalienable power (*potentia*). On the other hand, the subjunctive as-if underscores that this individual right-power of judging remains scarcely conceivable outside of a political society in which singular individuals "join forces" and "have common rights" (TP 2.13–16; E IV p18s, IV p35s). Thus, in contrast to the usual image of subjective rights—liberties that are conceived against externally imposed limits (legal or moral) and that, as such, are always already negative—Spinoza characterizes each individual's right of judging as a potentiality that is internally related to the *absence* of given legal mandates or predetermined finality and to the *presence* of co-equal freedoms of judgment.

The relation between individual rights and collective power here is one of mutual composition and expansion rather than mutual limitation, as Spinoza indicates in his treatment of the state's right to "limit" citizens' freedom of judgment (TTP 20). Rather than determine such a limit in view of a prior norm of good government, Spinoza decenters the traditional question of rule (that of the best regime) by making free judgment an end in itself. As a result, he gives the issue of limits an entirely different valence: the radical extension of freedom of judgment, encapsulated in the figure of the "free republic," becomes itself the touchstone for political order and vitality. Conversely, corruption takes on a new meaning. No longer simply the idea of one's neglect of the "common good" in favor of private interest, corruption becomes the usurpation of the equal freedom of judging even or especially under the cover of duly constituted laws and institutions (20.21). It follows, as I have argued in previous chapters, that Spinoza's conception of freedom of judgment cannot be reduced to the idea of an individual immunity against community. If it were—for example, if it were treated as simply an extension of private liberty of conscience—then by Spinoza's logic the state would be, in some measure, prejudging the form and finality of its constituents' judgments and depriving the people of their equal freedom of judging "anything whatever." By the same token, this freedom effectively decouples the judgment of public utility from sovereign prerogative and relocates such judgment within the activity of citizen-driven reasoning.[7] The exemplary (*optimus*) citizen exercises his right to judge in scrutinizing public right; he "shows that a law is contrary to sound reason" and, submitting his judgment to the sovereign, advocates the law's repeal (20.15). What remains underelaborated in Spinoza's illustration of the exemplary citizen, and in the TTP generally, is the nature of an appeal to "sound reason."

Broadly speaking, Spinoza defines reasoning as the effort to select encounters that are good (*utile*), namely, those that preserve and enhance one's concurrent powers of mental and bodily activity. These powers concern the aptitude of a body to affect and be affected by other bodies, together with the aptitude of a mind to comprehend the causes of ideas. Individuals experience transitions to greater and lesser power, respectively, as joy and sadness, and as the myriad affective states that derive in complex combinations from these primary affects. The effort to organize life in a way that brings about joy thus involves a rudimentary use of reason, a way of knowing what "agrees with reason."[8] This could include the simple fact of opting to live in society rather than in isolation or the calculation that it is better to abide by than to disregard the law (TTP 16.12, TP 3.3).

In addition to this initial aspect, Spinoza describes reason as a higher-order reflexivity whereby one grasps the causes of enabling or enfeebling encounters—their internal logic—rather than simply confront them according to the "external" order of chance (E IIp29s). By internally determining ideas, a mind experiences its power and contribution as an "adequate cause" amidst a larger causal network of ideas (III def 1). It thus produces joyful affects that are "born of reason."[9] With this second aspect, as the power to grasp the causes of ideas, reason emerges from what Spinoza calls "common notions" (II p37–40).[10] A common notion is an idea of a compositional cause shared between some or all bodies. At the most general level, all bodies have something in common, which is extension, motion, and rest. But common notions pertain equally to more local levels of similarity and difference, such as those found in a political community, where "men hold their rights in common." The myriad encounters between human and nonhuman constituents in a given society create complex circuits of desire, joy, and sadness—climates of hope or fear, for example—that dispose multiple bodies to be affected in similar ways. Spinoza thinks that this collusion and collision of affections (bodies, ideas, and their concomitant affects) make it likelier for reason to emerge than would be the case if one were to withdraw altogether from collective life, as the mind's power of thought, its aptitude to think in and through commonalities with other bodies, varies with the complexity and scope of a body's affectivity (II p13s, II p39c). The experience of joyful or agreeable encounters spurs reflection on the causes of these fruitful combinations and, in turn, on a range of other constitutive commonalities and their absence—on, say, the enabling conditions for civic friendship or civil war.

On the basis of this sketch, I want to press two further points about reason's "public use" in Spinoza. The first concerns the manner in which common notions furnish an alternative to top-down or subsumptive forms of judgment. More specifically, common notions afford a genetic perspective from which to critique putatively "Universal notions" (*notiones Universales*)

(II p40s). Spinoza argues that these "Universals" convey the sorts of abstract similarities that are highly equivocal because they are, in fact, projections of a particular history of experience, signs of a specific affective complexion. Take "dog," one of the examples Spinoza adduces as a "Universal." His logic is something like the following. For a given Muslim Yemeni, "dog" might conjure an image of an accursed creature, and this image might be linked to memories of fearful encounters with rabid stray dogs as a boy. Yet the same word may evoke fond memories of a champion sledding team for an Inuit in northern Canada. At the immediate and unreflective level, supposedly universal ideas such as these are akin to "conclusions without premises" (II p28). How these image-ideas arose in their unique configuration and how they support particular sensual and ideological investments remain unthought. Absent an understanding of the conditions for a given idea, one imagines simply that ferocity belongs to the nature of "dog" or that "dog" universally signifies the thrill of competition. In a political context, agents may be convinced that it is of the nature of law to be a command, or that free speech is an unassailable right, without reflecting on what moves them (and these ideas) to such conclusions. Spinoza calls such ideas "inadequate" because of their partial, impressionistic, and inexpressive character. They indicate the momentary affective disposition of one's body more than they explicate the nature of external bodies and ideas themselves (II p16c2). By contrast, Spinoza designates as "adequate" those ideas that express their causes. Adequate ideas "express" their causes in a twofold way: they emerge from and develop individuals' power of thinking (as part of Nature's infinite power of thought), and they include an apprehension of the other ideas that brought them into being. In other words, adequate ideas grasp at least some of the constitutive commonalities or relations between bodies. I propose below how this genetic perspective might obtain when political judgments about the character of public right express or "internally determine" its cause in common powers of minds and bodies.

As an illustration of how common notions are formed, let me take for now the less political and more "biological" example of surfing—as related by William Finnegan in his memoir *Barbarian Days: A Surfing Life*.[11] As a young teen, Finnegan recalls, "Waves were the playing field. They were the goal. They were the object of your deepest desire and adoration. At the same time, they were your adversary, your nemesis, even your mortal enemy."[12] In his youth, it seems, Finnegan's experience of surfing is something of a morality play. He maintains a largely extrinsic and haphazard relationship with the waves, knowing and feeling them from their effects and thereby imagining them in almost personal terms: in one moment, a joyful exhilaration when they propel him along "the playing field," leaving traces of "desire and adoration" like a secret lover he wants to embrace; in the next moment, a fear at the waves' seemingly murderous intention to knock him unconscious and drown him in their swell. Of course, even at this early stage, Finnegan possesses enough *savoir-faire*—enough adequate ideas of his own causal power, of what he can do safely to navigate the waves—that he is not simply passive, helplessly bowled over by the surf (as I would be).

And it is on the basis of that initial knowledge, a prudence regarding what makes for a joyful encounter with a wave, that he proceeds to build over time an understanding of the nature of waves and of the possibilities and limits of fruitfully combining with their power. Consider, in this regard, a second image that Finnegan presents:

> The close, painstaking study of a tiny patch of coast, every eddy and angle, even down to individual rocks, and in every combination of tide and wind and swell—a longitudinal study, through season after season—is the basic occupation of surfers at their local break. Getting a spot wired—truly understanding it—can take years. At very complex breaks, it's a lifetime's work, never completed . . . Wave judgment is fundamental, but how to unpack it? You're sitting in a trough between waves, and you can't see past the approaching swell, which will not become a wave you can catch. You start paddling seaward. Why? If the moment were frozen, you could explain that, by your reckoning, there's a fifty-fifty chance that the next wave will have a good take-off spot about ten yards over and a little farther out from where you are now. This calculation is based on: your last two or three glimpses of the swells outside, each glimpse caught from the crest of a previous swell; the hundred-plus waves you have seen break in the past hour and a half; your cumulative experience of three or four hundred sessions at this spot, including fifteen or twenty days that were much like this one in terms of swell size, swell direction, wind speed, wind direction, tide, season, and sandbar configuration; the way the water seems to be moving across the bottom; the surface texture and the water color; and, beneath these elements, innumerable subcortical perceptions too subtle and fleeting to express.[13]

If, in this passage, Finnegan explicates in largely scientific terms the embodied understanding of an experienced surfer, elsewhere he compares surfers' oceanographic knowledge to a musical fluency: "To a surfer sitting in the lineup trying to decipher the structure of a swell, the problem can indeed present itself musically. Are these waves approaching in 13/8 time, perhaps, with seven sets an hour, and the third wave of every set swinging wide in a sort of dissonant crescendo? Or is this swell one of God's jazz solos, whose structure is beyond our understanding?"[14] Here Finnegan depicts wave judgment, in a way that is arguably truer to the practical formation of common notions, as an art of composition. Whereas the previous passage on wave judgment suggested a knowledge that can be articulated in a priori fashion (if "the moment were frozen"), as a mathematical grasp of the relationship between the wave's dynamically complex structure and that of his body, Finnegan now observes that, in the order of experience, the knowledge that wave judgment presumes and produces entails something more like a rhythm sense. The surfer intuits how his body, characterized by a certain ratio of parts (E II p13), might directly combine with the characteristic relations of the wave so as to commune with it—he judges when to paddle, how to "pull into" the wave's barrel, etc.—thereby producing a new, more powerful composition (swimmer/surfer/wave) and a causal knowledge thereof.[15] This kind of judgment constitutes a more intrinsic, "adequate" grasp of the relations between surfer and wave than the perceived confrontation between self and wave, or knowledge-by-effects, that Finnegan recalls from his teen years.[16]

My second point about Spinozist reason concerns some "utilitarian" features of common notions that do not come through in the wave example. After all, in Spinoza reason operates as a prudential judgment about what is truly useful (*utile*) for oneself, and this judgment implies a certain mutual utility, or better, synergy between reasoning individuals. So Spinoza takes utility, in the sense of alliance and mutual composition, to be a common notion—a generality drawn out from experience and posited by reason—and it is in this vein that he delineates several practical implications or "dictates" of reason in the *Ethics* (E IV p18s). Common notions have, in this respect, an immediately ethical-political dimension despite the fact that they are not prescriptive norms as ordinarily understood. Acting from an understanding of these commonalities or "laws" of (human) nature, Spinoza proposes, is acting from "virtue" or strength and for its own sake, that is, not for the sake of anything perceived to be more useful (E IV def 8, E IV p18s, E IV p24; TP 2.7).

Both of these "utilitarian" features—the prudential judgment about one's vital interest and its essential connection to the "use" of others' powers—inform Spinoza's famous assertion that "nothing is more useful to man than man" (E IV p18s). This passage and its surrounding context could be glossed as follows: others are useful to me and I am useful to others to the degree that we desire what is equally good for all, that is, to the degree that we all become *sui juris*, "independent" judges of what is good and right. Note that no other purpose governs this alliance: no prior interests, identities, truths, objectifiable goods—no-*thing* but the common development of singular powers. The cause or reason for this society, to put it in seemingly paradoxical terms, is a non-instrumental utility. As one might suspect, given his critique of "Universal" notions and his antifinalism, Spinoza nowhere suggests that this universalizing dynamic of reason is a matter of establishing the maxim of one's action as a moral law, or of recognizing the "humanity" of others by abstracting from the nontrivial, material differences between individuals.

Indeed, on Spinoza's account, "sound reason" demonstrates—and experience attests—that it is in everyone's nature to be different, irreducible to one another and to oneself over time (E III p51). The essence of "man" is desire, the common life force that perpetually individuates and individualizes (III def aff 1). And "since everyone according to his affect judges what is good, what is bad, what is better and worse, it follows," Spinoza argues "that men vary as much in judgment as in affect" (III p51s). Nevertheless, in demonstrating that singularity is *implied* in but not *explicated* by the general laws of nature, and even as the affective charge of common notions inspires in individuals the desire to know more and better, Spinoza's geometric or causal order of reason shows its own limitations for distinguishing things and events in their specificity. This "formal" aspect of reason finds its completion only in the realm of experience, with the concrete grasp of historical, linguistic, and institutional matrices of power, desire, and knowledge. As I noted above, the plurality and impropriety of affect is a central premise of the TTP. In that text, Spinoza is at pains to explicate, by way of singular cases (e.g., ancient Israel) what follows for religious faith and civil obedience. Relatedly, the TTP is also where the figure of citizen jurisprudence as right and reason finds its effect—and affect—as democracy.

Passibility, or the Power and the Glory

Before exploring more directly the relationship between citizen jurisprudence and public right, I want to underscore how, along with publicity, a certain disposition to be acted upon, or "passibility," is essential to this activity of judging. I borrow the term from Timothy Reiss's *Mirages of the Selfe*, which recovers a premodern sense of personhood wherein "material world, society, family, animal being, rational mind, divine, named some of the 'circles' which were a person. These circles," Reiss explains, "did not 'surround' a person who somehow fit into them. They *were* what a person was: integral to my very substance. At the same time they were public and collective, common to everyone *qua* human." Reiss goes on to note that via Plato, the Hippocratics and Aristotle, Cicero, Seneca, and Plutarch, this antique conception of relationality was captured under the Latin name of passibility: "This is not passivity. Passibility names experiences of being whose common denominator was a sense of being *embedded in and acted on by* these circles—including the material world and immediate biological, familial, and social ambiences, as well as the soul's (or 'animate') and cosmic, spiritual or divine life."[17] To be sure, Spinoza rejects many of the metaphysical premises espoused by these premodern thinkers, even while sharing with them a certain exteriority to the predominantly personalist and subjectivist lexicon of modern philosophy.[18] The crucial point I want to underline, at any rate, is that the antonym of the passivity or passionate servitude Spinoza so carefully and comprehensively studies (explicitly thematized in E IV, "On Human Bondage") is not so much "activity" as a form of *passibility*—one that he calls *acquiescentia in se ipso.*[19]

Few readers of Spinoza would deny that he understands one's basic power to exist and to act as a capacity to affect *and to be affected.* Even so, a prevalent interpretation assigns these constitutive tendencies of finite modal agency—acting, being acted upon—to determinate subjects (the rational few vs. the appetitive many) and discrete spheres (ethical solitude vs. political society). Such a reading treats passibility as separable from truly free or powerful action, as if the latter is "emancipation not only from the passions and affects but from the needs and society of others."[20] Here the effective power to judge for oneself is assumed to be a properly private endeavor of judging *by* oneself, a species of "personal autonomy" for which political freedom is at best an instrumental good. According to Steven B. Smith, for instance, Spinoza "urges us to seek out the company of others and to live with them peaceably and sociably, but largely as a means to increase one's own sense of power."[21]

Granted, Smith touches on a key point for interpretation: the transition to greater power coincides, at its maximal point of expansion, with "the greatest thing we can hope for," that which Spinoza describes as the affection of *acquiescentia in se ipso* (E IV p52s). Spinoza employs this term in different contexts to denote an affection of "self" or "mind" (IV p52s, IV app 4, V p10, V p27, V p36s, V p42s). In each instance, the term signifies an optimal conjunction of activity and passivity, wherein one's power to act is effectuated through a radical receptivity to "the goings-on of the universe," to speak with Wordsworth.[22] *Acquiescentia* is thus aptly characterized as a "sense" of power. It is a joy arising from the self-reflexive grasp of one's finite power to act in and as part of the infinite power of nature. Far from epitomizing a solitary and suprasensual ethic of individual perfection, however, Spinoza's *acquiescentia* bespeaks a maximally inclusive and intensive collaboration with ambient powers, together with a maximally discerning ability to grasp them in their singularity.

Indeed, at all levels, Spinoza's relational ontology undercuts the presumption that one could be the exclusive cause of one's thoughts, feelings, and actions, like an "empire within an empire (*imperium in imperio*) (E III pref). The human individual is a thoroughly embodied and embedded "part of Nature," part of the infinitely encompassing substance that articulates itself in infinitely many attributes, of which humans know two. These two attributive powers, thought and extension, find expression in infinitely many things or "modes"—ideas in thought and bodies in extension. Finite things such as human bodies modify the existing aspects of substance as they affect and are affected by the power mediated through other bodies. Modes are thus "parts" of nature in that they participate in nature's power (*potentia*). They are determined intrinsically as modifications of the attributes and extrinsically through the co-affection of other modes.

Within such an ontological frame, Spinoza envisages even the passage to the superior form of "intuitive knowledge" and the "greatest human perfection" not so much as the achievement of an Archimedean perspective on being and a freedom of sovereign subjectivity than as the activation of an exemplary power in passibility, a *mentis acquiescentia* (E V p27). As a model of knowing, "intuition" is the ability to judge the singularity of things as emerging through common powers. Notably, Spinoza describes the "superiority" of this knowledge in terms of affective capacity, of "how much the knowledge of singular things . . . can accomplish, how much more powerful it is" than the formal knowledge of common properties. Formal reasoning does not, he remarks, "affect our mind as much" as when one grasps the immanent relation between the infinite power of God/Nature and a finite modification of that power in its singular composition and intensity (E V p36s). It is the optimal participation between activity and passivity that enables intuition and its corresponding "sense of power," or *acquiescentia*, to complement or complete the power of reasoning. At once cognitive and conative, Spinoza characterizes such knowledge as an "intellectual love of God, which . . . is eternal" (V p33).

Remember that Spinoza situates this experience of eternity within a theory of divine providence, according to which God favors, so to speak, those individuals who successfully—that is, rationally—cultivate their essential freedom, virtue, or power. In Ethics V, he puts the matter as follows: "Salvation, or blessedness, or freedom, consists . . . in a constant and eternal love of God, or in God's love for men. And this love, or blessedness, is called glory in the Holy Scriptures—not without reason. For whether this love is related to God or to mind, it can rightly be called *acquiescentia*, which is really not distinguished from glory (by Defs Aff. XXV and XXX)."[23] Spinoza devotes most of proposition 36, along with its demonstrations, corollary, and scholium to elucidating the features of this divine auto-affection. The key point for my argument here is that God does not know and love himself through his absoluteness but only through the minds of human beings who know him thanks to an intuitive knowledge of singular essences. In other words, God needs to demonstrate a particular providence toward humans in order to achieve full knowledge of himself. "From this it follows that insofar as God loves himself, he loves men, and consequently that God's love of men and the mind's intellectual love of God are one and the same" (V 36c). Why might Spinoza characterize God's particular providence as available only in and through the highest power of thinking?

As I noted in chapter 3, those who act in accordance with the natural divine law exercise an exemplary virtue or power that is at once philosophical and political—both an intellectual knowledge and love of God/Nature and a normative capacity to "prescribe" rules. Otherwise put, the normativity of the natural divine law is a constituent power, a way of creating rules of living that is not a form of ruling by law. Spinoza's reference to glory in the passage above thus raises the question again of the political meaning of this specific prudence and maximal "freedom of human nature," given that the biblical idea of glory refers on one hand to the glory of God as King and on the other side to the glorification offered by God's people (TP 4.5). What might Spinoza mean by equating *acquiescentia* and glory?

On this question, Agamben's recent work on political and economic theology offers some clues. According to Agamben, the theological idea of glory derives from the political practice whereby an individual was raised, by virtue of the glorification or acclamation of an assembly, onto the throne of sovereignty.[24] Cast in theological terms, God receives his glory—he is elevated and sustained in his sovereign throne or resting place—thanks to the prayers, hymns, and sacrifices of the faithful. Agamben finds in the theology of the Brahmana some further insight into the "essence of liturgy," in particular, the circular relationship between glory and glorification. Following some of Mauss's research, Agamben notes that the Brahmana understand the gods to "nourish themselves with hymns, and men, who ritually sing the *viraj* [or "nourishment-hymn"], provide for the gods' nourishment in this way (and indirectly for their own as well)."[25] Set in the context of Spinoza's discussion of *acquiescentia*, this would imply a vision of God's power and glory as that which nourishes and is nourished by the human species in its most "absolute" pursuit of natural right—that is, in the "freedom of human nature" to philosophize and thereby to care most vigilantly for the life that each and all have thanks to God. The question then becomes one of discerning how such freedom finds expression in political life.[26]

Public Right and the People's Power

In the final pages of the *Theological-Political Treatise*, Spinoza declares, almost in passing, that "freedom of judgment . . . not only can't be suppressed, but is undoubtedly a virtue" (TTP 20.25). My interpretive focus in this chapter has been to explicate the premises for and political implications of that positive assertion. In so doing, I have sought to think with Spinoza the conditions in which judgment becomes a political virtue in its own right, a form of citizen jurisprudence. "The free republic" of the TTP, the common notions and *acquiescentia* of the *Ethics*: these motifs figure citizen jurisprudence as a right-power that is effectuated through a form of collective action and the passibility corresponding to such action.[27] To shift back now from an ontological to a political register, what I am calling citizen jurisprudence is internally related to the "power of the people," as Spinoza presents it. More precisely put, this form of judgment is essential for the people to be an active presence in political life, which requires in turn that the people's power not be conflated with the sovereign or governmental powers of the state. For the people to be powerful, citizens' public use of reason (jurisprudence) must remain a critical alternative to the compelling "reason" (jurisdiction) of the sovereign state. Citizen jurisprudence must, in short, continue to pose the problem of public right, reflecting on and reconfiguring the sense and scope of what is equally good for all.

At first blush, Spinoza seems to position public right at a distant remove from popular scrutiny. In general terms, every state is just by its very existence, that is, by virtue of the "transfer" of natural right that authorizes it to prescribe and enforce a normative order of common rules as "civil right" (TP 5.1; TTP 16.39). By the same logic, every state, no matter how its offices of government are organized, is in some sense democratic or republican because the "power of the people" functions as the originary and effective ground for all constituted forms of common right (TTP 16.37; TP 2.16–17). The obvious risk, here, is that the generic name of "the people" might simply function as the ideological fig leaf for the particular purposes of a state. So what accounts for the quality of "civil right," of the state's justice, if the mechanisms of authorization are too blunt of an instrument?

The answer, for Spinoza, is an index of the degree to which democracy approaches the "quasi-natural" status of the "free republic" wherein everyone, by right, is possessed of his full powers of judgment (TTP 16.36). In a democracy, all citizens submit their arbitrary wills to a common will that regulates their conduct, the better to enhance their powers of intelligence. Majority decision is an expedient that enables common decisions to be passed and that, more importantly, preserves the occasion for each and all to judge the utility of positive laws (20.38). By distinguishing sovereign decision from citizen judgment in this way, democracy figures a condition in which "everyone remains equal, as they were before, in the state of nature": equal in the sense of equally free from any obligation to align one's sentiments and sensibilities with those of another, and thus equally free to "judge what is true or false, good or bad, right or wrong" according to one's own *ingenium* (16.36, 20.1, trans. modified). In this regard, democracy secures the possibility of being an independent source of right and a judge in one's own right (*sui juris*). Further, democracy allows for the development and expansion of natural right, or potentiality. It allows anyone and everyone to enhance their ability to reason—to actively discern what is useful (*utile*)—and thus to become maximally possessed of their natural right (*maxime sui juris*), that is, empowered (TP 2.11). Consequently, for Spinoza, the ultimate standard for justice is less the instituted representation of the people's power in sovereign commands than the active and plural "use" of this power. By this I mean the degree to which reason circulates in a multiplicity of judgments and, through these judgments, articulates adequate ideas of public right as expressive of citizens' shared and singular powers. To clarify what this entails, it helps first to consider Spinoza's critique of the specious forms of right to which a people's power so often become captive.

As with the "Universals" of the *Ethics*, images (*species*) of right are nominally similar to the phenomena they purport to represent but are inadequate at the level of both thought and practice. Spinoza alludes to the "fateful example" of "the English people, who sought causes with the appearance of right (*specie juris*) for removing a monarch from their midst. . . . After much bloodshed they resorted to hailing a new monarch by a different name" (TTP 18.33, trans. modified). On his reading, this was a case of mistaking effect for cause, symptom for source, and thereby removing a tyrant but not the conditions for tyranny. An "appearance of right" (*specie juris*) served the English as a "conclusion without premises," a way of imagining injustice and the course for its remedy by subsuming these phenomena under an abstract category or "Universal." Arguably, the "Universal" by which the English Parliamentarians' conception of right remained most governed was that of sovereignty. Captive to that image and its associations with the arbitrary rule of the king, their desire and power (hence, their right) was not their own. Instead, it was overwhelmingly determined by—invested in—the ordinary customs, extraordinary fantasies, and painful legacies of royal absolutism. This meant, at the level of thought, that the ascendant notions of justice and freedom remained shackled to conceits about control, supremacy, constraint, and caprice. At the level of practice, "the English people" (or those who acted in its name) found more power and pleasure in regicide than in establishing the broader political conditions for their collective flourishing. They acted out, or reacted—"conscious of their actions and ignorant of the causes by which they [were] determined"—more than they acted from virtue or strength (E II p35s, III p2s).

The important theoretical point here is not that Spinoza blames the English for violating the legitimate right of their king. Nor is it that he condemns their ignorance. In fact, Spinoza regards simple denunciations of mass ignorance and prejudice as themselves enacting a prejudice inasmuch as they prejudge the very phenomena requiring explanation. Taking up the moralistic abstraction that "there is no truth or judgment in the common people," Spinoza responds that "this is not surprising, since the important affairs of state are conducted without their knowledge, and from the little that cannot be concealed they can only make conjecture. For to seek to suspend judgment is not a common virtue. So to seek to conduct all business without the knowledge of citizens and then to expect them not to misjudge things and to put a bad interpretation on everything, is the height of folly" (TP 7.27). This passage appears in a chapter on monarchy and in a text that takes given regimes (monarchy, aristocracy) "as they are" in order then to illuminate the possibilities within these polities for empowering the people—in order, that is, to theorize the conditions for a "free republic."

Spinoza's own critique of monarchy centers, accordingly, on how this regime privatizes public affairs by maintaining an arbitrary control over governmental institutions, and, more basically, by deploying specious forms (images and institutions) of religion and sovereignty to usurp subjects' powers of judgment (TTP pref 10; TP 7.29). It helps to recall that, for Spinoza, judgment is everywhere and always being exercised. Subjects' rights and powers are always actual (as signaled in Spinoza's claim that "to suspend judgment is not a common virtue"). The crucial consideration relates to the circumstances of judgments and the degree to which they dispose individuals' powers either to compound and expand or to disperse and contract. It is with this consideration in mind that Spinoza theorizes a measure of right beyond that which is commanded by the state or demanded in a violent mirroring of sovereign force and will.

Within a constituted legal order, injustice is the act of "taking away from someone, under the pretext of right (*specie juris*), what belongs to him according to the true interpretation of the laws" (TTP 16.42). Again, Spinoza's definition points to inadequacy of both thought and practice. On the one hand, the formation of an image (*species*) of right goes together with the act of depriving someone of the enjoyment of his rights, that is, it coincides with the act of separating him from the full exercise of his powers. On the other hand, relating to others justly and thereby "apportioning to each person what belongs to him according to civil law" is never simply a question of aligning one's conduct with the state's edicts (16.42).[28] Strictly speaking, justice in Spinoza is not an attunement of right and fact; it does not reflect conformity with an object such as the decision of the sovereign body or a particular distribution of entitlements. Justice "proper" is rather an activity in the sense of a practice, and in the peculiarly Spinozist sense of causal activity, viz. being the preponderant cause of one's effects and affects. A "just man," Spinoza writes, "gives to each his due because he knows the true reason (*ratio*) for the laws and their necessity." As such, he "acts from a constant heart and by his own decision, not that of another" (*ex proprio, non vero alieno decreto*) (4.7). Indeed, being just is co-extensive with being *sui juris* and acting freely (E IV p66s).

Being just, being *sui juris*, as Spinoza's language here conveys, is a matter of being one's "self" considered adequately.[29] This is to "use" reason, to think and act from common notions such as mutual utility and the joyful affects that they afford. Otherwise put, attributing to each his own through a judgment that considers existing law in light of its "true rationale" is a process of thinking and acting by way of an adequate idea of civil or public right. Such an idea would, so to speak, acknowledge its debts by expressing its formal and material causes or "premises." In other words, it would be explained by the common powers of judgment that generate it in a particular case and it would express its enabling conditions in other ideas. At the level of practice, this mode of political judgment would have both constructive and critical elements. For it is a practice where individuals link law as a principle (*ratio*) or premise of equal empowerment—the common notion of mutual utility—to a set of political circumstances, thus building a case for the reciprocal connections between a specific right and what it entails for the community. The critical element comes from the manner in which this practice illuminates what is unreasonable ("against sound reason") about a given configuration, or *species*, of individual and public right. Justice thus emerges as a norm that is internal to the radically public or common "use" of citizen jurisprudence, which one might also characterize Spinozistically as a practice of illuminating and adequating the constitutive premises of public right.

For a contemporary illustration of citizen jurisprudence, consider the case of the Movement for Black Lives (M4BL) as it has evolved from a string of relatively local and loosely coordinated protests against police violence into a self-organizing communal movement consisting of "federated" groups in solidarity with one another.[30] Three key features of M4BL deserve emphasis for the purposes of this chapter. First, in the most immediate sense, the movement began as a political antibody or co-immunity defending against an excess of defense on the part of those agents of legitimate state violence, the police, who are authorized, as the expression goes, to "serve and protect" their communities. Building on and with the momentum and horizontality that the 2011 Occupy movements had brought back into the streets, ground-level outrage and protests against the extrajudicial killing of young black women and men such as Trayvon Martin began to acquire a certain viral or contagious quality, spreading nationally, along with the hashtag #blacklivesmatter, created by Alicia Garza following the acquittal of Martin's killer, George Zimmerman. The declaration that "black lives matter" circulated widely, becoming a common rallying cry in the face of police violence against black people. Amid the uprising in the weeks and months after Michael Brown's killing, Garza joined with other activists to transform the hashtag into an organization of the same name. It is crucial to note that, from the outset, the movement that was building around Black Lives Matter challenged the jurisdictional logic of the state, which continually worked to localize both the issue of police violence and the mounting protests by treating the former as an issue of "accountability" and the latter as complaints about the deprivation of civil liberty or as demands for the redistribution of resources.[31] What is more, this incipient movement mounted its challenge to state violence intersectionally, through alliance with other actors and "parts with no part" in the status quo, such as fast-food workers agitating for a livable minimum wage.

The second feature worth highlighting about M4BL is its systemic vision. The members and organizations in the movement have taken care in their public statements to situate the specific wrongs of policing in a wider context of state-sanctioned violence and racialized capitalism. One could say that judging in this manner moves political analysis and action beyond a fixation on the level of effects so as to "see" these effects in relation to causal matrices; that is, to see them, as much as possible, in their systematicity. This move, this difference, can be expressed in Spinozist terms as the transition from judging what is right according "the fortuitous run of circumstance" (from being determined externally) to a jurisprudence that reflects on "several things at the same time, [understanding] their agreements, their differences, their opposition" (to being determined internally) (E II p29s). Take, for instance, the Movement for Black Lives platform. This platform covers issues from economic justice to environmental racism and articulates persuasively, if provisionally, an alternative vision of public right that is radically connected to a people's constituent power.[32] In this way, M4BL has endeavored to frame the issue of police brutality as an issue of common concern and thereby to transform the common sense of who and what counts politically.[33]

Finally, the case of M4BL demonstrates how the transformative praxis of citizen jurisprudence should be understood as extending well before and beyond any isolable speech act or political event. Strictly speaking, the Movement for Black Lives did not begin with a hashtag but with ordinary people in their localities learning or relearning the art of democratic politics, building commonalities—above all, the common notion of equal empowerment—with diverse others through the dissensual work of judging publicly the utility of prevailing images, institutions, and justifications of public right. And this whole learning process itself reaches back into previous generations of political struggles—whether those of black activism, feminism, or radical labor—that endeavored in their own way to reconstitute a people and a public sphere. The emergence of Black Lives Matter and M4BL reveals a new point of inflection in a larger process of becoming political, a process that, in many ways, is a long patience.

Coda

A Right to Problems

> As if we would not remain slaves so long as we do not control the problems themselves, so long as we do not possess a right to problems, to a participation in and management of the problems.
>
> GILLES DELEUZE

In addition to its soixante-huitard overtones, the epigraph above bears distinct echoes of Spinoza.[1] I repeat it here, at this book's point of arrival, as a prompt for reflecting back on the preceding chapters and for considering how their theoretical significance might be carried forward. In a sense, I have been talking about a "right to problems" all along. For when viewed through the paradigm of Spinoza's vital republicanism, the democratic power of judgment entails just such a right, which I understand as a natural, or, so to speak, biopolitical right to take part in constituting a people and a public sphere. And in keeping with the aspectival character of Spinoza's thought, the theoretical import of a "right to problems" can be conceptualized from at least two perspectives: control and constitution, republicanism and biopolitics. Let me elaborate.

Most obviously, a right to "management of the problems" would seem, first, to evoke the principle of workers' control, the idea that "anyone actively engaged in a certain project of action should be able to have an equal say in how the project is carried out."[2] Relative to the contemporary debate on the common and commons, this right bespeaks something like the deconstructed "entrepreneurship of the common and innovation of cooperative social networks" advocated by Hardt and Negri.[3] Somewhat more concretely, this right could take the form of the democratized public-service management that Ostrom calls "coproduction."[4] Further still, and in a more traditionally political sense, a right to manage or control common problems denotes popular control over government.[5] At stake here is an assurance, backed by the force of positive law, that individuals may jointly undertake the project of their empowerment more deliberately and less haphazardly, without being subject to the arbitrary control of other members of society. If a right to problems construed in this fashion postulates a public agency of command, or state, this state need not take the form of sovereignty in the Hobbesian mold, as I argued in chapter 4. Spinoza has inspired important critiques of the state form, and rightly so, but his work can also serve as a useful reminder today that the power of state institutions might be enlisted for more than authoritarian projects—perhaps even for the purposes of nondomination.

Second, and more profoundly, a right to what Deleuze rather cryptically calls "participation in the problems" might usefully be understood along the lines of the Q.O.T. principle that "whatever touches all must be approved by all" (*quod omnes tangit, ab omnibus approbetur*). Chapter 3 demonstrated how this principle was operative in Spinoza's idea of the agreement (*convenientia*) uniting the *sui juris* constituents of a free, self-organizing people. In this case, individuals give their reflective judgment or approval to law insofar as they can be considered the co-authors of a "perfect constitution." Here a right to problems names a "right" to constituent power, or an effective capacity (*potentia*) to demonstrate how public right is premised on the jurisprudential activity of citizens determining the sense and scope of common affairs. It is a right of designating things as politically problematic in the first place. Spinoza's texts conceive of it, moreover, as a right that citizen-subjects assert and augment in concert, which is to say, as an empowerment of their ability to see, feel, think, and speak about disparate matters of "fact" as matters of common concern. From this viewpoint, a right to problems expresses the radically constitutive rather than derivative character of judging. Neither the subjects ("the people") nor the objects (issues of "public right")—the basic terms or form of the problem—are given in advance of such activity, which, to be sure, is provoked by given perceptions of contentious identities, interests, obligations, entitlements, and their coincident affects.

In the preceding chapters, I have shown how, in Spinoza's political thought, the dimensions of control and constitution stand in an agonistic rather than exclusionary relationship with logics of rule or domination. The first chapter presented the paradigmatic form of this agonism in the relationship between jurisdiction and jurisprudence. Much as jurisprudence endeavors to contest and convert rather than simply negate the negation of jurisdiction, I showed in chapter 2 that Spinoza's conception of the reason at play in the psychosocial dynamics of the common proceeds not by absolving itself from or frontally attacking the exclusionary forms of mimetic desire but rather by transmuting them into forms of alliance and alteration. Chapter 3 argued that, for Spinoza, the vital impulse of a people's judgment finds its most powerful realization in the process of transforming rule by law into rule of law. In chapter 4, the story I told was one of a republican state and civil religion involving people in a political way of life and a form of equal liberty that they might ultimately undertake of their own accord, through the democratic exercise of what I called, in chapter 5, citizen jurisprudence.

As for its theoretical implications going forward, the right to problems at the heart of Spinoza's vital republicanism testifies to an elective affinity of sorts between modern revolutionary republican political thought and the new "commune-ism," theorized by the Italian school of biopolitics, among others, as an emancipatory discourse on life-in-common.[6] To speak of an elective affinity here means to see in the relationship between these lines of thinking the properties of an emergent third form of political theory focused on the dynamic interplay and overlap between public things, the common(s), and their citizen-custodians.[7] There are, of course, important and highly "useable archives" that document earlier experiments in conjoining republicanism with communal movements and thinking.[8] Kristin Ross, for instance, has given new life to the thought and culture of the Paris Commune, with its internationalist vision of a "universal republic" (self-consciously distinguished from the national republicanism of the bourgeois state) and its innovations in pedagogy, labor practices, aesthetics, ecology, and more.[9] In a contemporary context, Yves Citton's argument, in *The Ecology of Attention*, for converting the prevailing "attention economy" metaphor of the digital age into an ecological paradigm theorizes and, to some degree, performs the critical and creative jurisprudence involved in claiming a right to reconceptualize the very forms of the multifaceted political problems that "touch everyone" (per the Q.O.T. principle).[10] And Frédéric Lordon's formulation of a "re-commune" capable of challenging the affective servitude of post-Fordist capitalism effectively conjoins the socialist principle of worker control and the republican principle of *quod omnes tangit*, much as it conjoins a novel reading of Marx and Spinoza.[11] In the spirit and often with the material of Spinoza, these contributions signal the way toward a political-theoretical formation that could be of great use today: a constitutionalism and jurisprudence of the radically public, that is, common.

Notes

Introduction

1. A representative example is Sullivan, "Democracies End When They Are Too Democratic."

2. See Rancière, *Hatred of Democracy.*

3. Purdy, "What Trump's Rise Means for Democracy."

4. See Zerilli, "Judgment."

5. See Arendt, *Between Past and Future*; Rancière, *Disagreement*; Zerilli, *A Democratic Theory of Judgment*; Urbinati, *Democracy Disfigured.*

6. I borrow the term "people-judge" from Rosanvallon, *Counter-Democracy.*

7. Moreau, "Le jugement," 177.

8. Campos, "Introduction."

9. See Vatter, *The Republic of the Living*, 5, and the Afterword to Vatter, *Between Form and Event*, 307–17. See also Wootton, *Republicanism, Liberty, and Commercial Society.* Cf. Israel, *Enlightenment Contested*, chap. 10, for an intellectual-historical argument distinguishing the "democratic republicanism" of seventeenth-century Dutch political thought, including that of Spinoza, from the better-known and more heralded English republicanism of the same period.

10. See Connelly, *Spinoza, Right and Absolute Freedom*, chap. 5.

11. On the "strategy" of *conatus* in Spinoza, see Bove, *La stratégie du conatus.*

12. See, for example, Agamben, *The Omnibus Homo Sacer*; Negri, *Empire and Beyond*; Esposito, *Bíos*; Skinner, *Liberty before Liberalism*; Pettit, *Republicanism*; Laborde, *Critical Republicanism.*

Chapter One

1. Arendt, *Lectures on Kant's Political Philosophy*, 39.

2. Smith, *Spinoza, Liberalism, and the Question of Jewish Identity*, 22–26, 133–44; and Den Uyl, *Power, State and Freedom*, 96–128. Other influential discussions of Spinoza's political thought, while less insistent on classifying it as strictly liberal, align his *libertas philosophandi* broadly with the tolerationism of modern secular liberalism. See, for example, Israel, *Enlightenment Contested*, 155–63; Nadler, *A Book Forged in Hell*, chap. 9. Though critical of Spinoza's putative liberalism in general and his *libertas philosophandi* in particular, Leo Strauss helped to

establish the prevailing Anglophone interpretation of Spinoza as "the philosopher who founded liberal democracy." See Strauss, *Spinoza's Critique of Religion*, 16.

3. See Negri, *The Savage Anomaly*, 108; Negri, *The Subversive Spinoza*, 44; Montag, *Bodies, Masses, Power*, 22–25, 58–60; and Balibar, "Spinoza, the Anti-Orwell," 31–35. Balibar offers a particularly insightful analysis of why, on Spinozist grounds, freedom of judgment cannot be reduced to an abstract entitlement, or merely formal right. His largely appreciative critique assumes, nonetheless, that Spinoza's juridical formulation of free philosophizing/judging is plagued by an "an intrinsic weakness" that Spinoza rectifies when he turns later to theorize politics in terms of the effective power (*potentia*) of the multitude, which Balibar describes as the "real conditions of freedom" and the "true matter of politics." See Balibar, *Spinoza and Politics*, 117, 120.

4. Esposito, *Bíos*, 70–71.

5. Esposito, *Terms of the Political*, 50.

6. See Santner, *The Royal Remains*, 6.

7. Horkheimer and Adorno, *Dialectic of Enlightenment.*

8. Derrida, *Rogues*, 34.

9. See Agamben, *The Omnibus Homo Sacer.*

10. See Esposito, *Bíos*, 45–77.

11. *Ibid.*, 46.

12. *Ibid.*, 55.

13. Santner, *The Royal Remains*, 16.

14. Esposito, *Terms of the Political*, 71, 130.

15. *Ibid.*, 59.

16. *Ibid.*, 62, 132.

17. Esposito, *Bíos*, 147; Esposito, *Terms of the Political*, 76.

18. Cohen, *A Body Worth Defending*, 42–43. If a theorist like Agamben understands immunity in terms of an impersonal logic of sovereignty, Judith Butler tends to emphasize the "subjective" dimensions of immunity as a violent fantasy of sovereign mastery. In a discussion of the "split subject of US nationalism," Butler writes: "This is a schism in which the subject asserts its own righteous destructiveness at the same time as it seeks to immunize itself against the thought of its own precariousness." See Butler, *Frames of War*, 48.

19. Cohen, *A Body Worth Defending*, 43.

20. Esposito, *Terms of the Political*, 65.

21. *Ibid.*, 55.

22. Esposito and Campbell, "Interview," 53–54. See Lemm, "Nietzsche, *Einverleibung* and the Politics of Immunity," which develops the concept of common immunity through a discussion of "embodiment" in Nietzsche.

23. See, for example, Esposito, *Terms of the Political*, 134; Esposito, *Immunitas*, 169–71. For a critique of Esposito's exclusively metaphorical discussions of pregnancy and birth, in the context of a broader appraisal of contemporary biopolitical theory's inattention to issues of reproduction, see Catherine Mills, "Biopolitics and Human Reproduction."

24. Esposito, *Terms of the Political*, 65.

25. *Ibid.*, 68, 114. For his most developed critique of the "person," see Esposito, *The Third Person.*

26. Amendola, "The Law of the Living."

27. Esposito, *Bíos*, 185–94. See Vatter, "Biopolitics."

28. Esposito, *Bíos*, 72.

29. Leibniz, "The Controversy of Controversies," 8.

30. Hunter, *Rival Enlightenments*, xi.

31. See Lærke, "Jus Circa Sacra," 42–43.

32. James, *Spinoza on Philosophy, Religion, and Politics*, 8.

33. Van Bunge, "Philosophy," 323.

34. Stewart, "*Libertas Philosophandi*," 41.

35. Israel, *Radical Enlightenment*, 28.

36. Stewart, "*Libertas Philosophandi*," 41; Israel, *Radical Enlightenment*, 28.

37. See Van Bunge, "Philosophy," 320–44.

38. Constans, *Du Droit des Ecclésiastiques.*

39. Hobbes, *Leviathan*, 414; 306.

40. Constans, *Du Droit des Ecclésiastiques*, IV, 56–57.

41. See Moreau, "Spinoza et le *jus circa sacra*," 67.

42. See Lagrée, *La raison* ardente, 237.

43. Moreau, *Spinoza et le spinozisme*, 59.

44. I borrow this phrase from Curley, "Kissinger, Spinoza, and Genghis Khan," 315.

45. The expression "conscientious judgment" appears in Beiner, "Three Versions of the Politics of Conscience." The current reading of Spinoza's *libertas philosophandi* as an inversion and dialectical development of Hobbes's "private reason" is anticipated by Carl Schmitt's critical treatment of Spinoza in *The Leviathan in the State Theory of Thomas* Hobbes, 57–58. In other words, much of the recent discussion of Spinoza's "liberal" political legacy shares Schmitt's (not to mention Strauss's) interpretation while reversing his negative evaluation.

46. Steinberg, "Spinoza's Political Philosophy."

47. Spinoza identifies faith and theology in TTP 14.37.

48. Lagrée, *Spinoza et le débat réligieux*, 195.

49. Moreau, "Introduction," 11.

50. See Vardoulakis, *Sovereignty and Its Other*, 125–26.

51. Moreau, "Introduction," 11.

52. See Garver, "Spinoza on Constitutional Interpretation," 290–95.

53. See Vardoulakis, *Sovereignty and Its Other*, 127–40.

54. *Ibid.*, 127.

55. Montag, *Bodies, Masses*, Power, 58–60.

56. Balibar, *Spinoza and Politics*, 119.

57. Cohen, *A Body Worth Defending*, 5; original emphasis.

58. Laursen observes that Spinoza's examples of seditious opinions "were standard whipping boys: republican rebels against monarchies claimed the first, Machiavellians claimed the second, and libertines were commonly accused of 'living as they pleased.'" See Laursen, "Spinoza on Toleration," 190.

59. Differently stated, freedom is an "end" only in the specifically Spinozist sense of appetite, or the determination of what one can do. "By the end for the sake of which we do something, I understand appetite" (EIVdef7). Cf. E IV app4.

60. Sharp, *Spinoza and the Politics of Renaturalization*, 26.

61. For an argument that Spinoza's God/Nature is more profitably read as an ontology of relation than a metaphysics of substance, see Morfino, *Plural Temporality*, chap. 2. Cf. Williams, "'Subjectivity without the Subject.'"

62. See Moreau, *Spinoza: l'expérience et l'éternité*, 369–76.

63. Cf. Montag, *Bodies, Masses, Power*, 59.

64. Negri, *Spinoza for Our Time*, 50.

65. Ibid., 40. Cf. Negri, *The Savage Anomaly*; Negri, *Insurgencies*. See also Jason Read's *Unemployed Negativity* blog post, "Still Anomalous after All These Years."

66. See Hardt and Negri, *Empire*; Hardt and Negri, *Multitude*; Hardt and Negri, *Commonwealth*. On the "excess" of biopolitical labor-power in particular, see *Commonwealth*, 135–36, 151–52, 176, 242–43, 270–71, 312–21, 373.

67. Negri, *Savage Anomaly*, 229.

68. Negri, *Spinoza for Our Time*, 9–10.

69. Vatter, "Legality and Resistance," 66–76; Lemke, *Biopolitics*, 75.

70. Vatter, "Legality and Resistance," 66; Rancière, *Dissensus*, 86–88, 215–16. Morfino, *Plural Temporality*, 8–9.

Chapter Two

1. Ostrom, *Governing the Commons*; Hardin, "The Tragedy of the Commons."

2. Ostrom, *Governing the Commons*, 8–18.

3. *Ibid.*, 7–8, 21–23.

4. See, for example, Harvey, *Rebel Cities*; Klein, *This Changes Everything*; and Caffentzis, "Commons" for an overview of recent scholarship and activism related to the common and commons.

5. Fleming, *The Mythology of Work*, 6. On "competitive individualism" and alternative, non-individualist modes of imagining collective life, see the wide-ranging discussion in Gilbert, *Common Ground*.

6. See Hardt, "The Common in Communism." For ongoing discussions of the "idea of communism," see Douzinas and Žižek, *The Idea of Communism*; Žižek, *The Idea of Communism 2*; and Taek-Gwang Lee and Žižek, *The Idea of Communism 3*.

7. Hardt and Negri include the so-called natural commons in their definition but focus more on the common as social production. See Hardt, "The Common in Communism," 136; and Hardt and Negri, *Commonwealth*, viii.

8. Casarino, in "Surplus Common," offers the clarifying example of language via a reading of Dante (12–15). See also Agamben, *The Coming Community* and *Means without End*.

9. Hardt, "The Common in Communism," 136. In *Multitude*, Hardt and Negri write, "A theory of the relation between labor and value today must be based on the common. The common appears at both ends of immaterial production, as presupposition and as result. . . . The common, in fact, appears not only as the beginning and the end of production but also in the middle, since the production processes themselves are common, collaborative, and communicative. Labor and value have become biopolitical in the sense that living and producing tend to be indistinguishable" (148).

10. Hardt and Negri, *Multitude*, 204; original emphasis. In their understanding, singularity "refers externally to a multiplicity of others; is internally divided or multiple; and constitutes a multiplicity over time—that is, a process of becoming" (Harvey, Hardt, and Negri, "Commonwealth: An Exchange"). Cf. Hardt and Negri, *Commonwealth*, 338–39.

11. Hardt, "The Common in Communism," 131.

12. *Ibid.*, 135. See Hardt and Negri, *Multitude*, 205–6, and *Commonwealth*, 283. Hardt and Negri's point of departure in *Commonwealth* is a demonstration of "how capital and law inter-

twined together," creating what they call "the republic of property" to "determine and dictate the conditions of possibility of social life in all its facets and phases." Their ambition is to emancipate "the living labor that is closed within capital and the multitude that is corralled within its republic" (9). While they acknowledge no "necessary or intrinsic link between the concept of republic and the rule of property," and concede that "one could try to restore an alternative or create new notions of republic that are not based on property," they stress, nonetheless, that "the republic of property emerged historically as the dominant concept" (10). In their text *Declaration*, written in response to the uprisings of 2011, Hardt and Negri assert in more unequivocal terms that there is nothing redeemable in the modern republican constitutions that emerged in the Atlantic revolutions (88).

13. Dean, *Communist Horizon*, 120; 148, 152–55. Cf. Martel, "Division Is Common," 707.

14. Dean, *Communist Horizon*, 156. Jacques Rancière is arguably the premier thinker of an essentially divided, or, in his terms, dissensual common, though he insists that his notion of a *partage du sensible*, a sharing and division of the sensible, is an aesthetic and political rather than ontological concept. See, for example, his assertion, "There is politics because the common is divided" (Rancière, "The Thinking of Dissensus"); and more generally, Rancière, *Disagreement*.

15. Simondon coined the concept of transindividuality in his *L'individuation psychique et collective*. For its use in understanding Spinoza's thought, see Balibar, *Spinoza: From Individuality to Transindividuality*; Read, *The Politics of Transindividuality*; Sharp, *Spinoza and the Politics of Renaturalization*; Morfino, *Plural Temporality*.

16. Cf. Guattari, *The Three Ecologies*.

17. Lordon, *Willing Slaves of Capital*, 23. In the fourth section of this chapter, I use the language of strategy, bearing in mind Lordon's cautionary note about understanding the term in an "overtly conscious or calculating sense—although this sense should not be excluded, of course. . . . By strategic one should rather understand, more fundamentally, *the very logic of desire* and the full range of ways in which it cuts itself a path, whether these ways follow from calm calculation or from conduct governed by affects" (*Willing Slaves of Capital*, 22–23, original emphasis). See also Bove, *La stratégie du conatus*.

18. See Moreau, *Spinoza: l'expérience et l'éternité*, chap. 3.

19. Historically, the term "complexion" encompasses a similar range of meanings that refer, on the one hand, to the physiological features and physical constitution of an individual considered in relation to her biography and environment, and, on the other hand, to the combined mental and physical dispositions of an individual, her inclinations or tendencies. See Jaquet, *Les transclasses*, 99–102.

20. *Ibid.*, 99.

21. Read, *The Politics of Transindividuality*, 25.

22. Smith, "Preface: The Multitude and the Moving Train," xiv.

23. See Sharp, *Spinoza and the Politics of Renaturalization*, chap. 1; Morfino, *Plural Temporality*, 62–67.

24. Douglas, "The Affects."

25. Moreau, "Imitation of the Affects," 168.

26. "Between appetite and desire there is no difference," Spinoza writes, "except that desire is generally related to men insofar as they are conscious of their appetite" (E III p9s).

27. Moreau, "Imitation of the Affects," 168.

28. Moreau, *Spinoza: l'expérience et l'éternité*, 383.

29. Morfino, taking Spinoza's theory of affects as the privileged example, shows how the

latter's notion of God/Nature is more profitably read as an ontology of relation than as one of "substance." On this reading, the so-called primary affects as well as Spinoza's metaphor of ocean waves acquire another sense: "If these affects are 'primary' with respect to the individual," argues Morfino, "they are not primary from the point of view of immanent causality, this causality that gives rise to the individual as a *connexio singularis*, a singular interweaving, a stitch or a knot. . . . These affects cannot exist in a pure form, as originary elements whose combinations give birth to all the others. These affects 'exist' only in and through the infinity of metamorphoses that external relations impose upon them." The three primary affects appear, then, "less as substrates than as determined abstractions (common notions, in Spinoza's terms) necessary to conceptualise the composed affects." Hence "the singular thing can metaphorically assume the figure of the ripple or wave [*flutto*], the brief, momentary form that gives individuality to the otherwise undifferentiated sea." See Morfino, *Plural Temporality*, 64–66.

30. Moreau, *Spinoza: l'expérience et l'éternité*, 395.

31. *Ibid.*, 396.

32. *Ibid.*

33. Spinoza defines emulation as affective imitation when related to desire, and therefore as "the desire for a thing which is generated in us from the fact that we imagine others like us to have the same desire" (E III p27s). Recall that Spinoza sees no real difference between appetite and desire. In what follows, I will use "appetite for emulation" generally to name the striving to have others live according to one's complexion, an endeavor that Spinoza poses as a problem across his major texts. See, for example, E III p31, Vp4s; TTP 17.14; TP 1.5.

34. Spinoza appends a note to this proposition that reads, "Here and in what follows you should understand men toward whom we do not have any affect."

35. Spinoza clearly believes that other "things like us," with whom humans identify and whose affects they imitate, include nonhumans such as God-persons and animals. See, for example, E IV p68, and TTP 13 ("Showing that Scripture teaches only the simplest matters, that it aims only at obedience, and that it teaches nothing about the divine Nature, except what men can imitate by a certain manner of living").

36. Cited in Lagioia, "'Writing Is an Act of Pride'" (my emphasis).

37. Ovid, *Amores*, II, 19.

38. Cf. Girard, "Triangular Desire."

39. At E IV p37 s1, Spinoza defines "piety" as "the desire to do good generated in us by our living according to the guidance of reason." In the alternative demonstration to E IV p37, he writes, "The good which man wants for himself and loves, he will love more constantly if he sees that others love it (by IIIP31). So (by IIIP31C), he will strive to have the others love the same thing. And because this good is common to all (by P36), and all can enjoy it, he will therefore (by the same reason) strive that all may enjoy it. And this striving will be the greater, the more he enjoys this good (by IIIP37) q.e.d."

40. Moreau, "La place de la politique dans l'*Éthique*," 51.

41. Curley translates *gloria*, in this context, as "love of esteem."

42. Morvan, "Admiration dans le Spinozisme et fascination dans la psychanalyse," 39, 42; Read, *Politics of Transindividuality*, 33.

43. See Bove, *La stratégie du conatus*, 84.

44. *Ibid.*

45. Nevertheless, as Sharp notes, "Spinoza considers someone driven exclusively by ambition to suffer from a 'species of madness', for such an individual's *conatus* is transfixed by a particular source of power, remaining blind both to the complexity of its causal environment and

to the 'great many other ways' in which it might enlarge its power of thinking and acting. When the mind is 'possessed', captured, or occupied by a single source of joy or pleasure, neglecting everything in the world that does not point to one's preoccupation, one is properly called 'mad' (E IV p44s)" (*Spinoza and the Politics of Renaturalization*, 142).

46. Girard, "Mimesis and Violence," 13.

47. Spinoza writes, "In this life, then, we strive especially that the infant's body may change (as much as its nature allows and assists) into another, capable of a great many things and related to a mind very much conscious of itself, of God, and of things" (E V p39s).

48. In Laurent Bove's elaboration, Spinoza presents reason in *Ethics* IV "in an extrinsic manner as the form of an *imperium* and its dictates (*dictamina*). However, these forms only order that which nature affirms in and through its own self-arrangement; reason itself cannot realize this directly because of our own weakness and/or the passive affections of our body which is subjected to external forces" ("*Hilaritas* and *Acquiescentia in se ipso*," 218).

49. On the identity of the *exemplar* and the "free man" in Ethics IV, see now Nadler, "On Spinoza's 'Free Man.'"

50. Moreau, *Spinoza: l'expérience et l'éternité*, 415.

51. "In Spinoza, then, the opposition between *ego* and *alter ego* turns out to be purely fictitious, or better, imaginary, because the *alter* is not what is external to the space of interiority of the *ego*, something originally excluded from it. Rather, it is what always-already traverses or crosses through it, what constitutes it as a complex weave of bodies, practices, passions, ideas, words" (Morfino, *Plural Temporality*, 10–11).

52. Balibar, *Spinoza: From Individuality to Transindividuality*, 30.

53. Balibar, *Spinoza and Politics*, 76–98, 109–13.

54. See Israel, *Radical Enlightenment* and Israel, *Enlightenment Contested*; cf. Hardt and Negri, *Commonwealth*.

55. Israel, "Introduction," xxx.

56. Moreau, *Spinoza: l'expérience et l'éternité*, 403.

Chapter Three

1. See Rancière, "Occupation."

2. See Wark, "How to Occupy an Abstraction," 4.

3. See Mitchell, "Image, Space, Revolution," 105.

4. One should not overstate this "absence" of demands given that OWS protesters called for tax and campaign finance and the elimination of corporate personhood, among other things.

5. See the English translation on Wikipedia, https://en.wikipedia.org/wiki/Anti-austerity_movement_in_Greece#/media/File:Vote_of_the_People%27s_Assembly_of_the_White_Tower_Square.svg, taken from the original at http://www.realdemocracy.gr.

6. See Markell, "The Moment Has Passed," 131–32; Mitchell, "Image, Space, Revolution," 105–6.

7. Arendt, *On Revolution*, remains the key discussion of this issue. For a recent treatment, see Ochoa Espejo, *The Time of Popular Sovereignty*.

8. Graeber, *The Democracy Project*, 237.

9. See Loughlin, "What Is Constitutionalisation?"

10. For another recent interpretation of constituent power in Spinoza, see Del Lucchese, "Spinoza and Constituent Power."

11. As Spinoza emphasizes, the actual behavior of human individuals, what they in fact do,

results from a combination of their own power of acting and the power of other individuals (human and nonhuman) acting upon them.

12. Hauke Brunkhorst, in his magisterial *Critical Theory of Legal Revolutions*, advances a materialist evolutionary systems theory wherein he defines juridical-political constitutions as "evolutionary universals," viz. both functional advances and practical mindsets (10). Brunkhorst begins his text on a rather Spinozist note by situating revolutionary change within an all-encompassing and ongoing (nonteleological) evolutionary process: "Everything is evolution. Revolutions and collective normative learning processes are also evolutionary processes. Evolution never stops. But while evolution is, in rough distinction, a process beyond plan and control, revolutions and (revolutionary and non-revolutionary) normative learning processes are specific kinds of evolutionary developments which not only proceed automatically as blind natural occurrences (*naturwüchsig*), but also express and perform our plans, intentions and ideas" (9).

For a treatment of Spinoza's metaphysics in relation to the ideas of complexity and self-organization, see Atlan, "Immanent Causality." Bove, *La stratégie du conatus*, offers the most systematic interpretation of Spinoza's thought, metaphysical *and* political, as a logic of self-organization.

13. Consider also Foucault's treatment of this distinction: "Law, by definition, is always referred to a juridical system, and order is referred to an administrative system, to a state's specific order" ("The Political Technology of Individuals," 417).

14. See Rawls, *Political Liberalism*, and Habermas, *The Inclusion of the Other.*

15. Koselleck, *Critique and Crisis*; Israel, *A Revolution of the Mind.*

16. Whoever persecutes in this manner, Spinoza argues, merits the label "antichrist" (14.19).

17. See Benjamin, "Critique of Violence," 281.

18. Del Lucchese, "Sedition and Modernity," 3.

19. Derrida writes, "The state is afraid of *founding* violence—that is, violence able to justify, to legitimate, or transform the relations of law, and so to present itself as having a right to right and to law" ("Force of Law," 268). Cf. Benjamin, "Critique of Violence," on the threat of declaring a new law (283).

20. For an analysis of the relationship between "conventional" prejudice and the prejudice that Spinoza qualifies as superstition, see Dobbs-Weinstein, "The Power of Prejudice and the Force of Law."

21. Esposito, *Terms of the Political*, 129.

22. Spinoza's reference to blood circulation evokes another contrast with Hobbes, "for whom political institutions are an additional means for the individual conatus to defend themselves, but who defines the conatus as the reflex movements of the living body aimed at preserving the vital function of blood circulation, therefore with an end of mere self-conservation" (Lordon, *Willing Slaves of Capital*, 62n14).

23. As I noted last chapter in my discussion of affective imitation, Spinoza does not operate with an anthropology that clearly or definitively distinguishes humans from nonhuman beings.

24. Bove, "Bêtes ou automates," 161. See also Clemens, "Spinoza's Ass."

25. Consider, for instance, Spinoza's contrasting discussions of *titilattio* (EIV34) and *hilaritas* (EIV42). See Bove, "*Hilaritas* and *Acquiescentia in se ipso.*"

26. In chapter 4, I discuss how Spinoza takes up the issue of providence in a more theological-political key. Chapter 5 brings his naturalistic or political-philosophic account of providence together with his theological-political account of providence.

27. Rutherford, "Spinoza's Conception of Law," 164.

28. Den Uyl, in *Power, State and Freedom*, writes, "The total equation of right with power has a number of interesting and provocative implications. The most fundamental of these implications is that *Spinoza's doctrine of natural right is without normative content*. In contrast to prior teleological conceptions, Spinoza's notion of natural right only looks at the given act itself, and then only to the degree of power manifested by that act" (7, my emphasis).

29. Rutherford, "Spinoza's Conception of Law," 165; original emphasis.

30. *Ibid.*, 151.

31. On normation and normalization, see Foucault, *Security, Territory, Population*, 57–63.

32. On Spinoza's use of this metaphor in his elaboration of truth as "norm both of itself and falsity" (TIE 38), see Macherey, *Introduction à l'Éthique de Spinoza: La deuxième partie*, 334–35.

33. Steinberg, "Following a *Recta Ratio Vivendi*."

34. Esposito, *Bíos*, 186–87. On the revolutionary character of Spinoza's theory of law, see now Connelly, *Spinoza, Right and Absolute Freedom*; and Campos, *Spinoza's Revolutions in Natural Law*.

35. As Wirszubski notes, in Roman law "the term '*persona sui iuris*' . . . implies that to be free means to be capable of possessing rights of one's own, and this is possible only if one is not subjected to someone else's *dominium* (or *patria potestas*)" (*Libertas as a Political Idea at Rome during the Late Republic and Early Principate*, 1). A number of early modern thinkers take the idea of *sui juris* status from Roman private law and apply it to matters of public right. For its function in Spinoza, see Cristofolini "*Esse sui juris* and Political Science"; Campos, *Spinoza's Revolutions in Natural Law*, chap. 6; and Steinberg, "Spinoza on Being *Sui Juris* and the Republican Conception of Liberty."

36. See Bove, *La stratégie du conatus*.

37. Bove, "*Hilaritas* and *Acquiescentia in se ipso*," 221.

38. Nadler, "Spinoza's Theory of Divine Providence," 20.

39. On prudence and vigilance in Spinoza, see Jaquet, *Spinoza ou la prudence*; and Israël, *Spinoza: Le temps de la vigilance*.

40. Throughout, I modify Curley's translation of *ratio vivendi*, rendering it as "rule of living" rather than "principle of living," as he does.

41. Rutherford puts the interpretive puzzle as follows: "In Spinoza's view, the person who *lives lawfully* . . . prescribes a rule of living to himself for the safe of a safer or more comfortable life. In this case, Spinoza believes, the lawgiver must comprehend the connection between the end and the means, and desire the means because of the perceived necessity of the law . . . To say just this, however, is to leave unclear still the precise sense in which the just (or, more generally, lawful) person *prescribes* law to himself—a law that he subsequently takes to command his actions" ("Spinoza's Conception of Law," 153–54; original emphasis).

42. Campos, *Spinoza's Revolutions in Natural Law*, 165.

43. See Locke, *Second Treatise*, V, 27, and V, 44 ("every Man has a Property in his own Person. This no Body has any Right to but himself. The Labour of his Body and the Work of his Hands, we may say, are properly his"; and "though the things of Nature are given in common, yet Man (by being Master of himself, and Proprietor of his Person, and the Actions or Labour of it), had still in himself the great foundation of Property"). See Grotius, *De Iure Praedae*, 18. Grotius writes, "God made man *autechousios, liberum suique juris*," which, Van Gelderen notes, is "perhaps best translated as 'fully autonomous, free and in one's own right'. . . . In Grotius's lines, the notions of being 'fully autonomous', 'free' and 'in one's own right' go smoothly hand in hand, though analytically they were quite distinct. . . . To be free, he argues, means that in

our actions and in our use of the things that belong to us we are not subject to any other human will. Thus, from the start, Grotius explicitly associates the concept of freedom, of *libertas*, with notions of ownership and property, or, in the Latin, with the rich and complicated concept of *dominium*." See Van Gelderen, "Arminian Trouble," 25–26.

44. Canguilhem, *A Vital Rationalist*, 351.

45. *Ibid*; Canguilhem, *The Normal and the Pathological*, 228; Muhle, "A Genealogy of Biopolitics," 85.

46. LeBlanc and Sévérac, "Spinoza et la normativité du conatus" 125.

47. See LeBlanc and Sévérac, "Spinoza et la normativité du conatus," 129–30, on how "actualization" in Spinoza must not be understood as the actualization of a power in recess, i.e., as the realization of mere possibility.

48. *Ibid.*, 133.

49. Esposito, *Bíos*, 186.

50. Hobbes, *Leviathan*, 124. Matheron, "The Theoretical Function of Democracy in Spinoza and Hobbes," 212.

51. Hobbes, *Leviathan*, 91.

52. *Ibid.* 150.

53. Hobbes, *Man and Citizen*, 115.

54. *Ibid.*, 123; cf. *Leviathan*, 92. In this paragraph, I draw on the discussion in Lærke, *Leibniz lecteur de Spinoza*, 195–97.

55. Hobbes, *Leviathan*, 111, 146.

56. Moreau, *Spinoza: l'expérience et l'éternité*, 413.

57. Hobbes, *Leviathan*, 99.

58. *Ibid.* Moreau characterizes Hobbes's "refusal" of reason as only a methodological precaution. Spinoza, by contrast, takes passions to define natural right in the strong sense: they engender consequences that determine the conduct of individuals when these individuals are not limited by the power of the state. (Passions don't determine individual conduct completely, or adequately, Moreau writes, but positively.) Spinoza insists that natural right prohibits "nothing except what no one desires and no one can do." Therefore, disputes, hatreds, anger, deception, madness, in short, "anything appetite urges" are not obstacles to natural right but rather its effective content (TTP 16.9). See Moreau, *Spinoza: l'expérience et l'éternité*, 413.

59. Hobbes, *Leviathan*, 147.

60. Ibid., 120.

61. Ibid., 103.

62. Ibid., 100.

63. Ibid., 122.

64. Vardoulakis, *Sovereignty and Its Other*, 98.

65. On the "inscriptive" quality of Spinozist natural right, see Campos, *Spinoza's Revolutions in Natural Law*, 67–88.

66. Lazzeri, *Droit, pouvoir et liberté*, 103.

67. Matheron, *Individu et communauté chez Spinoza*, 292.

68. The "contract is defended . . . by right of war" (TP 4.6, trans. modified). Cf. Machiavelli, *The Prince*, chap. 18; Foucault, *Society Must Be Defended*, 16–17.

69. As I noted in the second section, Spinoza acknowledges multiple other "indirect" means by which a regime attains hegemony, all of which entail capturing in some measure the affective sphere of its subjects' opinions and beliefs.

70. See Matheron on the conditionality of this transfer, that is, the idea that "*transfer of right* means *transfer of power*," and, consequently, that subjects are only "obligated to obey, here and now, what is commanded to them *in fact* here and now" ("The Theoretical Function of Democracy in Spinoza and Hobbes," 214).

71. Ibid., 216. For Matheron, this is why Spinoza, in the TP, "no longer speaks of the social contract," namely, because political society "is not created by a contract; it is engendered and reengendered at each moment by a consensus that must be permanently renewed" (216).

72. See Meador's discussion of the "distinction between government under law and government by law" in *Habeas Corpus and Magna Carta*, 14–15.

73. For example, Goldenbaum writes, "In contrast to Hobbes's inflexible model, Spinoza understood the relation between the sovereign and the subjects/citizens as a balance of power. . . . The power of the sovereign depends on the transferred power of the united subjects or citizens, but the amount of that power is not constant over time. . . . *Spinoza makes the process of the constitution of the state in some way permanent.* As the agreement of the subjects or citizens cannot be won by suppression of their opinions, but only by engaging in a free discourse between the subjects/citizens and the sovereign, freedom of speech is clearly a precondition for the higher stability of the state and the greater obedience of the subjects/citizens to the sovereign. This is clear from the subtitle of the *Theologico-Political Treatise*" (Goldenbaum, "Sovereignty and Obedience," 8, my emphasis).

74. See especially Susan James, "Law and Sovereignty in Spinoza's Politics"; and James, *Spinoza on Philosophy, Religion, and Politics*, chap. 12.

75. Vatter, *Machiavelli's The Prince*, 129.

76. Cf. TTP 16.25, where Spinoza notes that a democratic constitution requires that "each person will be bound to obey" the sovereign power (*imperium*) of society "either freely, or from fear of the supreme punishment."

77. On the Roman idea of popular consent as the basis for law, see McIlwain, *Constitutionalism*, 47.

78. See also the *Political Treatise*, which defines a citizen not in terms of one's participation in ruling but in terms of one's participation in all the advantages of political society (TP 3.1).

79. As Spinoza underscores in the *Political Treatise*, "if it were as much in our power to live according to the precept of reason as it is to be led by blind desire, everyone would be led by reason and organize his life wisely. But this is far from true" (TP 2.6).

80. See Akkerman, Lagrée, and Moreau's edition of Spinoza's TTP, 767n20.

81. Cf. 16.22, alluding to Vergil: "Everyone is drawn by his own pleasure. Most of the time the mind is so occupied by greed, ambition, envy, anger, etc., that there's no room for reason" (trans. modified). See Moreau, *Spinoza: l'expérience et l'éternité*, 415.

82. Terence, *Phormio* I, iii, 457. See http://www.gutenberg.org/files/22188/22188-h/files/terence5_6.html#phor_note56.

83. Loughlin notes, "Constituent power expresses a virtual equality of citizens. This is generated *inter homines* (establishing the principle of unity) but it founds an actual association divided into rulers and ruled in a relation of domination (establishing the principle of hierarchy)" ("The Concept of Constituent Power," 229).

84. "Constituent *power* might just as appropriately be termed constituent *right* since this struggle entails the attempt to explicate the meaning of political right" (Loughlin, "The Concept of Constituent Power," 232, original emphasis).

85. Loughlin, *The Idea of Public Law*, 107.

86. Rancière, *Disagreement*, 11.

87. See the discussion in Montag, *Bodies, Masses, Power*, 83–86; and on Spinoza's treatment of sexual inequality in particular, see Sharp, "Eve's Perfection."

88. On the category of "ordinary people," see Te Brake, *Shaping History*.

89. Frijhoff and Spies, *Dutch Culture in a European Perspective*, 237; Koekkoek, "Spinoza Conception of Political Liberty and the Dutch Republic," 38–42.

90. Grotius, *The Freedom of the Seas*, 28.

91. Belaeif writes, "It is, so to speak, as if each gives himself the law insofar as by its very nature, the law, requiring the development of man's reason, can and must arise from each individual—a man cannot be forced and compelled to understand or seek his own true perfection" (*Spinoza's Philosophy of Law*, 62).

92. *Ibid.*

93. See here Oakeshott's discussion of law as "non-instrumental adverbial conditions" (*On History and Other Essays*, 142).

Chapter Four

1. Silk, "Numa Pompilius and the Idea of Civil Religion in the West," 864.

2. On prophetology, see Strauss, *Philosophy and Law*.

3. Beiner, *Civil Religion*, 124.

4. Nelson, *The Hebrew Republic*, 130; James, *Spinoza on Philosophy, Religion, and Politics*, chaps. 5, 11, and 12; Rosenthal, "Why Spinoza Chose the Hebrews."

5. For another exploration of this question, see Cooper, "Reevaluating Spinoza's Legacy for Jewish Political Thought."

6. See Machiavelli, *Discourses* II, 2.

7. Spinoza borrows Machiavelli's language to speak of the "introduction of religion into the republic" or "state" three times in the TTP. Two of the references refer to Moses and the Hebrews, and the salutary combination of religion and politics as civil religion. The third refers, on the contrary, to a harmful combination of religion and politics, namely, when Christian ecclesiastics, long accustomed to teaching their religion "in private Churches" as "private men" and "without any concern for the sovereign" began to introduce this religion into the state. These clerics "had to teach the Emperors this religion, as they had defined it" and "were easily able to succeed in being recognized as its teachers and interpreters"; moreover, "they looked out very well for their own interests, so that afterward Christian Kings would not be able to take this authority for themselves, by prohibiting marriage to the supreme ministers of the Church and the supreme interpreter of religion." Finally, they "increased the doctrines of religion to such a great number, and confused them so much with philosophy, that the supreme interpreter of religion had to be a supreme philosopher and theologian, and had to have time for a great many useless speculations, which can fall to the lot only of private men who have abundant leisure" (19.52–54).

8. On this civil/spiritual distinction and on Machiavelli's conception of civil religion more broadly, see Vatter, "Machiavelli, 'Ancient Theology', and the Problem of Civil Religion."

9. For emphasis on the deflationary aspects of Spinoza's reading, see, for example, James, *Spinoza on Philosophy, Religion, and Politics*, 68; Nelson, *The Hebrew Republic*, 130, 134.

10. Note that Spinoza does not claim that the Hebrews were any less intelligent or virtuous than others. He says rather that "they were equal to other nations and only a very few were

chosen" (3.18). Later in the TTP, Spinoza entertains and ultimately rejects the notion that the Hebrews' famous obstinacy was simply given by nature (17.93–94).

11. See Moreau, "The Necessary Incompleteness of the Republic," 150.

12. *Ibid.*, 150–51.

13. See Machiavelli, *Discourses* II, 2. For discussions of the messianism and millenarianism of Spinoza's day, see James, *Spinoza on Philosophy, Religion, and Politics*, 76–80; Popkin, *Spinoza*, chap. 4; and Nadler *Spinoza*, 249–54.

14. Stephen Holmes observes, "The primary function of the ancient constitutions was not to limit preexisting power but to create power out of powerlessness" ("Constitutions and Constitutionalism" 195).

15. On this theme, see Syros, "Founders and Kings versus Orators."

16. Later in the TTP, amid a discussion of the Hebrews' "extreme training in obedience," Spinoza will claim that "nothing captures the mind (*capiuntur animi*) more than the joy which arises from devotion, i.e., from love and wonder (*admiratio*) together" (17.90, trans. modified). Cf. E III p52s, E III def aff 10.

17. On how "drill and discipline" relates essentially to the ancient idea of "constitution," see Holmes, "Constitutions and Constitutionalism," 194–97.

18. Spinoza alludes to the expressly "violent" or fear-based elements of Moses's command elsewhere—for example, in the second chapter of the *Treatise*: "For he commanded them to love God and to keep his law, that they might acknowledge the goods they had received from God, such as their freedom from bondage in Egypt. Next he terrified them with threats, if they transgressed those commands, and he promised them many goods if they respected them. So he taught them in the same way parents usually do children who are lacking in all reason. Hence, it is certain that they did not know the excellence of virtue and true blessedness" (TTP 2.47). It is worth underlining that, in this passage, Spinoza is speaking generically about what all legislators do in some measure, which is that they back law with the threat of violent sanction. Given the singular circumstances and complexion (*ingenium*) of the ancient Israelites—above all, their characteristic desire not to be oppressed—Moses realized that the cultivation of forms of love or devotion (to God alone) would work better both theologically-politically and affectively to secure their obedience.

19. On this point, see Vatter, "Republics Are a Species of State," 226, 230–33.

20. Flatto notes that Josephus employed the term "theocracy" to capture the primacy that the Mosaic constitution assigns to "the rule of law over the personal and unpredictable governance of men" ("Theocracy and the Rule of Law, 8).

21. Barclay, *Pauline Churches and Diaspora Jews*, 85.

22. Nelson, *Hebrew Republic*, 91.

23. For recent analyses of this connection, see Cooper, "Reevaluating Spinoza's Legacy for Jewish Political Thought"; Hammill, *The Mosaic Constitution*, 95–96; Balibar, *Spinoza and Politics*, 47–48, and Balibar, "*Jus, Pactum, Lex*," 182–205; Levene, *Spinoza's Revelation*, 202–7; and James, *Spinoza on Philosophy, Religion, and Politics*, 270.

24. See Dobbs-Weinstein, *Spinoza's Critique of Religion and Its Heirs*, 96, for a discussion of the importance of this passage for Marx.

25. "For prophetically revealed religion to have the force of law among the Hebrews, it was necessary for each of them to surrender first his natural right, and for everyone to resolve, according to a common agreement, that they would obey only those commands which were revealed to them prophetically by God, in exactly the same way as we have shown happens in a

democratic state where everyone resolves, by common agreement, to live only according to the dictate of reason" (TTP 19.10).

26. See Trigano, "The Politics of the Ban of Representation."

27. In his description of the Hebrews' first, direct covenant with God, Spinoza appears to cite Exodus 19.8, whereas in his narration of their second covenant (with Moses), Spinoza seems to base his exposition on Deuteronomy 5, vss. 24–27.

28. Morfino, *Plural Temporality*, 169.

29. Machiavelli, *Discourses*, III, 30.

30. Morfino, *Plural Temporality*, 171. Spinoza refers to the "Sin of the Calf" at numerous other junctures (TTP 2.44–5, 6.32, 8.53, 17.96). One that is particularly significant: in chapter 12, he notes that the Hebrews had made their covenant with God "null and void by worshipping the calf" (12.15).

31. See Melamed, *The Philosopher-King in Medieval and Renaissance Jewish Thought*, 181.

32. Hobbes, *Leviathan*, 122. See James, *Spinoza on Philosophy, Religion, and Politics*, 273.

33. See also Cooper, "Reevaluating Spinoza's Legacy for Jewish Political Thought," 475. The quote is from Constans, *Du Droit des Ecclésiastiques* (*De Jure Ecclesiasticorum*), 23.

34. "Only . . . laws and mores can lead a nation to have its singular complexion, its singular condition, and its singular prejudices" (TTP 17.94, trans. modified). Cf. TP 5.2–3.

35. As Martin Buber shows, early Jewish political theology identified the armed prophet with the "commander" but not the "king" of an armed people. Buber also emphasizes how the term "theocracy" served precisely to distinguish the Mosaic constitution from the rule of a monarch. See Buber, *Kingship of God*, especially chaps. 5 and 8.

36. Spinoza elaborates: "From Moses' commands to his successors we easily infer that he chose administrators, not rulers, of the state. For he gave no one the right to consult God alone and when he wanted to; so he gave no one the authority he himself had of making and repealing laws, deciding concerning war and peace, and choosing administrators both of the temple and the city. All these are functions of someone holding sovereignty" (17.49); "Moses chose no one to succeed to his rule, but distributed all its functions so that those who followed him were regarded as deputies, administering the state as if a king were absent, not dead" (19.36).

37. Spinoza qualifies the initial post-Mosaic regime as theocratic insofar as "one person had the right of interpreting the laws and of communicating God's replies, and another had the right and power to administer the state according to the laws already explained and the replies already communicated" (17.41).

38. See James, *Spinoza on Philosophy, Religion, and Politics*, 277ff. for a discussion of the intellectual history of this comparison in the Netherlands.

39. See Vatter, "Machiavelli, 'Ancient Theology', and the Problem of Civil Religion."

40. See Rousseau, *The Social Contract*, IV, 8.

41. For more on why the libertine conception of religion as imposture is incompatible with Spinoza's views, see Moreau, "La duperie de soi"; and Van Bunge, *Spinoza Past and Present*, chap. 5.

42. Lagrée, "Irrationality with or without Reason," 35. Cf. James, *Spinoza on Philosophy, Religion, and Politics*, ch. 8; and Bordoli, "*Fundamenta fidei*."

43. See, for example, Hammill, *The Mosaic Constitution*, 76; James, *Spinoza on Philosophy, Religion, and Politics*, 273.

44. Alfarabi, *Philosophy of Plato and Aristotle*, I, 38, 5–10.

45. *Ibid.*, I, 39, 10–15.

46. *Ibid.*, I, 41, 1–5.

47. The other tenets, omitting Spinoza's brief explication of each one, are: (2) "He is unique"; (3) "He is present everywhere"; (4) "He has the supreme right and dominion over all things, and does nothing because he is compelled by a law, but acts only according to his absolute good pleasure and special grace"; (5) "The worship of God and obedience to him consists only in justice and charity, or in love toward one's neighbor"; (6) "Everyone who obeys God by living in this way is saved; the rest, who live under the control of pleasures, are lost"; (7) "God pardons the sins of those who repent" (TTP 14.25–28, trans. modified).

48. Consider how Spinoza qualifies the other tenets: "It also doesn't matter, as far as faith is concerned, if someone believes: [iii] that God is everywhere according to his essence or according to his power, or; [iv] that he directs things from freedom or by a necessity of nature, or; [v] that he prescribes laws as a prince or teaches them as eternal truths, or; [vi] that man obeys God from freedom of the will or from the necessity of the divine decree, or finally; [vii] that the reward of the good and punishment of the evil are natural or supernatural" (TTP 14.31).

49. Lagrée, *Spinoza et le débat réligieux*, 200.

50. James, *Spinoza on Philosophy, Religion, and Politics*, 214.

51. For an elaboration and critical discussion of liberal neutrality (albeit one that does not consider civil religion), see Laborde, "Liberal Neutrality, Religion, and the Good."

52. Spinoza observes, in this connection, that since money has provided societies with "a token for all things," its "image usually occupies the mind of the multitude more than anything else. For they imagine hardly any species of joy without the accompanying idea of money as its cause" (E IV app 28; cf. TTP 20.28).

53. For another critique of the dependence vs. independence framing, see Brunkhorst, "All Nightmares Back."

54. Nelson, *The Hebrew Republic*, 130, 134.

55. The classic form of this problem is the focus of Kantorowicz's landmark study, *The King's Two Bodies*. For the contemporary reframing, see Esposito, *Two*, 204; and Vatter, "Law and Life beyond Incorporation," 256. Skinner, in "A Genealogy of the Modern State," concludes that the only way to make sense of the idea of public debt is through Hobbes's construction of the state as fictional person (364).

56. Agamben defends a reading of Trinitarian theology as a theory of divine government, according to which the divine "economy" or immanent ordering of nature complements or completes the divine kingship of the transcendent God. He writes, "One of the theses that we shall try to demonstrate is that two broadly speaking political paradigms, antinomical but functionally related to one another, derive from Christian theology: political theology, which founds the transcendence of sovereign power on the single God, and economic theology, which replaces this transcendence with the idea of an *oikonomia*, conceived as an immanent ordering—domestic and not political in a strict sense—of both divine and human life. Political philosophy and the modern theory of sovereignty derive from the first paradigm; modern biopolitics up to the current triumph of economy and government over every other aspect of social life derive from the second paradigm" (*The Kingdom and the Glory*, 1). Cf. Esposito, *Two*, 136–42, 203–9.

57. Esposito, *Two*, 208.

58. *Ibid.*, 209.

59. On Jewish messianism, see the studies in Scholem, *The Messianic Idea in Judaism*.

60. "Everyone is born in freedom," Spinoza writes. "If, according to nature, all men were bound by divine law, or if the divine law were a law by nature, it would've been superfluous for God to enter into a contract with men and to bind them by an agreement and an oath. So we

must grant, without qualification, that divine law began when, in an explicit agreement, men promised to obey him in everything. By this they, as it were, surrendered their natural freedom, and transferred their right to God, as we've said happens in the civil state" (TTP 16.55–56).

61. It bears emphasizing that some variants of Jewish messianism admit the possibility that the Messiah can return an infinite number of times, in contrast to Christian conceptions in which the Messiah gives history a linear form and returns only once, at history's end. On this point, see Strauss, "How to Begin to Study *The Guide of the Perplexed.*"

Chapter Five

1. See, for example, Azmanova, *The Scandal of Reason*; Garsten, *Saving Persuasion*; Geuss, *Politics and the Imagination*; Kompridis, *Critique and Disclosure*; Zerilli, *A Democratic Theory of Judgment.*

2. Zerilli, "Value Pluralism," 9; Garsten, *Saving Persuasion*, 185; Vatter, "The Idea of Public Reason and the Reason of the State," 262.

3. Weidenfeld, "Comportment, not Cognition," 233.

4. On the problem of "pure" politics, see Chambers, *The Lessons of Rancière*, 38–64.

5. For a similar definition of jurisprudence, but developed in a Deleuzian vein, see Lefebvre, *The Image of Law*, 53–59.

6. Moreau, *Spinoza: l'expérience et l'éternité*, 453, 465.

7. This subversion of the late medieval idea of public reason is a point of continuity between Spinoza and Kant. See Vatter, "The Idea of Public Reason," for a brief genealogy of this idea.

8. Deleuze, *Spinoza: Practical Philosophy*, 56.

9. *Ibid.*

10. Spinoza's discussion of "common notions" in the *Ethics* has become a key resource for several contemporary theoretical accounts of the formation of new political subjectivities. See Ruddick, "The Politics of Affect"; Hardt and Negri, *Empire* and *Multitude* and *Commonwealth*; Gatens and Lloyd, *Collective Imaginings.* Much of the contemporary interest in this specific area of Spinoza's thought is indebted to Deleuze's path-breaking (if controversial) reading of the common notions as containing the elements of a practical wisdom of empowerment, a reading that Deleuze first develops in his 1968 and 1970 books on Spinoza. See Deleuze, *Spinoza: Practical Philosophy*; Deleuze, *Expressionism in Philosophy*. Balibar's *Spinoza and Politics* and Negri's *The Savage Anomaly* represent other pioneering efforts to read the common notions in this "practical" vein. Their interpretations could be viewed as attempts to make more explicit than Deleuze's reading the political implications of the common notions.

11. Deleuze contends that "Spinoza's common notions are biological, rather than physical or mathematical, ideas" (*Expressionism in Philosophy*, 278). For an elaboration of that claim, see Armstrong, "Some Reflections on Deleuze's Spinoza," 50–56. For a criticism of Deleuze's biological reading of common notions and a defense of their physical character, see Connelly, *Spinoza, Right and Absolute Freedom*, 202–6.

12. Finnegan, *Barbarian Days*, 18.

13. Ibid., 75–76.

14. Ibid., 335.

15. See Ruddick, "The Politics of Affect," 30.

16. What also comes through in Finnegan's memoir is the Spinozist point that, even with a sophisticated causal understanding of waves, a surfer does not stop imagining them spontaneously from the point of view of the imagination, or in terms of what I have called the morality play: "When you are absorbed in surfing [waves], they seem alive. They each have personalities,

distinct and intricate, and quickly changing moods, to which you must react in the most intuitive, almost intimate way—too many people have likened riding waves to making love. And yet waves are of course not alive, not sentient, and the lover you reach to embrace may turn murderous without warning. It's nothing personal. That self-disemboweling death wave on the inside bar is *not* bloody-minded. Thinking so is just reflex anthropomorphism. Wave love is a one-way street" (291).

17. Reiss, *Mirages of the Selfe*, 2; original emphasis.

18. Cf. Esposito's reading of Spinoza as part of a broadly Averroistic tradition in *Two*, chap. 3; and Vatter, "Community, Life, and Subjectivity in Italian Biopolitics."

19. For in-depth examinations of *acquiescentia* in Spinoza's thought, see, for example, Carlisle, "Spinoza's *Aquiescentia*"; Cooper, *Secular Powers*, chap. 3; and Bove, "*Hilaritas* and *Acquiescentia in se ipso.*"

20. Smith, *Spinoza, Liberalism, and the Question of Jewish Identity*, 180.

21. Smith, *Spinoza's Book of Life*, 181.

22. Cited in Levinson, "A Motion and a Spirit: Romancing Spinoza."

23. Spinoza refers here to two earlier definitions: "*Acquiescentia in se ipso* is a joy born of the fact that a man considers himself and his power of acting" (E III def aff 25); and "Glory is a joy accompanied by the idea of some action of ours which we imagine that others praise" (E III def aff 30). Cf. Maimonides' definition of glory, *Guide of the Perplexed*, I, 64.

24. See Agamben, *The Kingdom and the Glory*, chap. 8.

25. *Ibid.*, 234.

26. For a recent argument that democracy, for Spinoza, is the political expression of his "intuitive science," see Del Lucchese, *Conflict, Power, and Multitude in Machiavelli and Spinoza*, 147–66.

27. Cf. Rancière, *Dissensus*, 28.

28. For an illuminating account of the polysemy of justice in Spinoza, see Campos, "Spinoza on Justice."

29. I owe the framing of this point to Stephen Connelly.

30. See Taylor, *From #BlackLivesMatter to Black Liberation.*

31. Havercroft and Owen, "Soul-Blindness, Police Orders and Black Lives," 754.

32. For the platform, see https://policy.m4bl.org/platform. On the significance of the M4BL platform, Keeanga-Yamahtta Taylor notes: "The Movement for Black Lives Platform is an important milestone in the movement. It demonstrates in action how police violence and abuse is only one aspect of state-sanctioned violence in the lives of black and brown people. We have to understand police brutality and murder within the context of an overall assault on the neighborhoods and communities that we live in. Where other public policies have failed—in terms of creating well-resourced schools, good jobs with benefits, decent housing and well-funded hospitals—policing has become the public policy of last resort. The police are used to attend to the products of this inequality, and in the process we have to understand the ways they actually stoke crime and reinforce and deepen poverty. The movement platform gets all of this and then discusses what alternatives could look like. It's an incredibly important document. This document is not concerned with getting cozy with those in power. It is principled and powerful. It's a document that won't get you an invitation to the White House. But it's a document that says, 'We don't want an invitation, we want liberation'" (Denvir, "Scholar Keeanga-Yamahtta Taylor on the 'Exciting' Movement for Black Lives Platform").

33. The judgment that black lives "matter" is, from the theoretical perspective developed in this book, both a juridico-political declaration and an affirmative biopolitical assertion of agency by people routinely and systematically turned into things.

Coda

1. See Deleuze's 1968 work, *Différence et Répétition*, 208, and the 1994 English translation, *Difference and Repetition*, 158.

2. Graeber, *The Democracy Project*, 230.

3. Hardt and Negri, *Commonwealth*, 307.

4. Ostrom, "Crossing the Great Divide." As Jeremy Gilbert elaborates, the idea of coproduction "recognises that services are not merely 'delivered' by 'producers' to 'users' (or 'customers') . . . , instead recognising that service outcomes are the product of collaborative and creative relationships between professionals and members of the wider public. From this perspective, the health of a patient or the education of a student are outcomes which must be *co-produced* by all participants in the process, which by definition cannot be made to follow a preordained path, or be modeled as a retail transaction, without the productivity of that process being vastly impaired. This is an idea which should entail the creation of institutional practices and decision-making procedures which involve all participants in the management of a service in ongoing dialogue and real decision making, and there are many examples of such institutions working in practice around the world—from the movement in the United Kingdom to create effective school councils, and to defend local democratic control of education policy, to the success of 'Nurse-Family Partnership' programmes in the United States" (*Common Ground*, 169).

5. See, for example, Pettit, *On the People's Terms*, chap. 5.

6. Vatter, *The Republic of the Living*, 4–5. See also Prozorov, "Conclusion," for a related argument in favor of reintegrating the study of biopolitics and the study of political "ideologies" such as socialism, Nazism, liberalism—and by extension, republicanism.

7. On elective affinity as a concept of emergence, see McKinnon, "Elective Affinities of the Protestant Ethic." For a discussion of the relationship, theoretical and practical, between public things and the commons (and shared space), see Honig, *Public Things*, 85–97.

8. On the notion of a "useable archive," see Ross and Goswami, "The Meaning of the Paris Commune."

9. Ross, *Communal Luxury*.

10. Citton, *The Ecology of Attention*.

11. See Lordon, *Willing Slaves of Capital*, 126–34. Despite what the English translation of the title suggests, Lordon rejects the notion of voluntary servitude in favor of an idea of passionate servitude (derived from Spinoza) that centers on the capture and complicity of desire. The French title is *Capitalisme, désir et servitude: Marx et Spinoza*.

Bibliography

Agamben, Giorgio. *The Coming Community*. Translated by Michael Hardt. Minneapolis: University of Minnesota Press, 1993.

———. *Means without End: Notes on Politics*. Minneapolis: University of Minnesota Press, 2000.

———. *The Kingdom and the Glory: For a Theological Genealogy of Economy and Government*. Stanford, CA: Stanford University Press, 2011.

———. *The Omnibus Homo Sacer*. Stanford, CA: Stanford University Press, 2017.

Alfarabi. *Philosophy of Plato and Aristotle*. Translated by Muhsin Mahdi. Ithaca, NY: Cornell University Press, 2002.

Amendola, Adalgiso. "The Law of the Living: Material for Hypothesizing the Biojuridical." *Law, Culture and the Humanities* 8, no. 1 (2012): 102–18.

Arendt, Hannah. *Lectures on Kant's Political Philosophy*. Edited by Ronald Beiner. Chicago: University of Chicago Press, 1992.

———. *Between Past and Future*. New York: Penguin, 2006.

Armstrong, Aurelia. "Some Reflections on Deleuze's Spinoza: Composition and Agency." In *Deleuze and Philosophy: The Difference Engineer*. Edited by Keith Ansell Pearson. London: Routledge, 1997.

Atlan, Henri. "Immanent Causality: A Spinozist Viewpoint on Evolution and the Theory of Action." In *Selected Writings*. Edited and with an Introduction by Stefanos Geroulanos and Todd Meyers. New York: Fordham University Press, 2011.

Azmanova, Albena. *The Scandal of Reason: A Critical Theory of Political Judgment*. New York: Columbia University Press, 2012.

Balibar, Étienne. "Spinoza, the Anti-Orwell: The Fear of the Masses." In *Masses, Classes, Ideas: Studies on Politics and Philosophy before and after Marx*, 3–37. London: Routledge, 1994.

———. "*Jus, Pactum, Lex*: On the Constitution of the Subject in the *Theologico-Political Treatise*." In *The New Spinoza*. Edited by Warren Montag and Ted Stolze, 171–205. Minneapolis: University of Minnesota Press, 1997.

———. *Spinoza: From Individuality to Transindividuality*. Delft: Eburon, 1997.

———. *Spinoza and Politics*. Translated by Peter Snowdon. London: Verso, 2008.

Barclay, John M. G. *Pauline Churches and Diaspora Jews*. London: Coronet, 2011.

Beiner, Ronald. *Civil Religion: A Dialogue in the History of Political Philosophy.* Cambridge: Cambridge University Press, 2011.

———. "Three Versions of the Politics of Conscience." *San Diego Law Review* 47, no. 4 (2010): 1107–1124.

Belaeif, Gail. *Spinoza's Philosophy of Law.* The Hague: Mouton, 1971.

Benjamin, Walter. "Critique of Violence." In *Reflections: Essays, Aphorisms, Autobiographical Writings.* Translated by Edmund Jephcott. New York: Schocken, 1986.

Bordoli, Roberto. "*Fundamenta fidei.*" In *The Bloomsbury Companion to Spinoza.* Edited by Wiep van Bunge et al. London: Bloomsbury, 2014. Kindle edition.

Bove, Laurent. "'Bêtes ou automates': la différence anthropologique dans la politique spinoziste." In *Lectures contemporaines de Spinoza*, edited by Claude Cohen-Boulakia, Pierre-François Moreau, and Mireille Delbraccio. Paris: Presses de l'Université Paris-Sorbonne, 2012.

———. *La stratégie du conatus: affirmation et résistance chez Spinoza.* Paris: J. Vrin, 1996.

———. "*Hilaritas* and *Acquiescentia in se ipso.*" In *Spinoza on Reason and the "Free Man."* Edited by Yirmiyahu Yovel. New York: Little Room Press, 2004.

Brown, Wendy. *Walled States, Waning Sovereignty.* Brooklyn, NY: Zone Books, 2010.

Brunkhorst, Hauke. "All Nightmares Back: Dependency and Independency Theories, Religion, Capitalism, and Global Society." In *Crediting God: Sovereignty and Religion in the Age of Global Capitalism.* Edited by Miguel Vatter, 142–59. New York: Fordham University Press, 2011.

———. *Critical Theory of Legal Revolutions.* London: Bloomsbury, 2014.

Buber, Martin. *Kingship of God.* Translated by Richard Scheimann. Amherst, NY: Humanity Books, 1990.

Butler, Judith. *Frames of War: When Is Life Grievable?* London: Verso, 2010.

Caffentzis, George. "Commons." In *Keywords for Radicals: The Contested Vocabulary of Late Capitalist Struggle.* Edited by Kelly Fritsch, Clare O'Connor, and A. K. Thompson. Oakland: AK Press, 2016.

Campos, Andre Santos. *Spinoza's Revolutions in Natural Law.* Basingstoke: Palgrave Macmillan, 2012.

———. "Introduction." In *Spinoza and Law.* Edited by Andre Santos Campos. Farnham: Ashgate, 2015.

———. "Spinoza on Justice: Understanding the *Suum Cuique.*" *Epoché* 21, no. 1 (2016): 127–43.

Canguilhem, Georges. *The Normal and the Pathological.* Translated by Carolyn R. Fawcett. New York: Zone Books, 1991.

———. *A Vital Rationalist: Selected Writings from Georges Canguilhem.* Translated by Arthur Goldhammer. New York: Zone Books, 2000.

Carlisle, Clare. "Spinoza's *Acquiescentia.*" *Journal of the History of Philosophy* 55, no. 2 (2017): 209–36.

Casarino, Cesare. "Surplus Common." In Cesare Casarino and Antonio Negri. *In Praise of the Common: A Conversation on Philosophy and Politics.* Minneapolis: University of Minnesota Press, 2008.

Chambers, Samuel A. *The Lessons of Rancière.* Oxford: Oxford University Press, 2013.

Citton, Yves. *The Ecology of Attention.* London: Polity, 2017.

Clemens, Justin. "Spinoza's Ass." In *Spinoza Now.* Edited by Dimitris Vardoulakis. Minneapolis: University of Minnesota Press, 2011.

Cohen, Ed. *A Body Worth Defending: Immunity, Biopolitics, and the Apotheosis of the Human Body.* Durham, NC: Duke University Press, 2009.

Cohen, Jean, and Cécile Laborde, eds. *Religion, Secularism, and Constitutional Democracy*. New York: Columbia University Press, 2016.

Connelly, Stephen. *Spinoza, Right and Absolute Freedom*. Abingdon: Birkbeck Law Press, 2015.

Constans, Lucius Antistius. *Du Droit des Ecclésiastiques*. Translated by V. Butori. Caen: Université de Caen, 1991.

Cooper, Julie E. *Secular Powers: Humility in Modern Political Thought*. Chicago: University of Chicago Press, 2013.

———. "Reevaluating Spinoza's Legacy for Jewish Political Thought." *Journal of Politics* 79, no. 2 (2017): 473–84.

Cristofolini, Paolo. "*Esse sui juris* and Political Science." In *Spinoza and Law*. Edited by Andre Santos Campos. Farnham: Ashgate, 2015.

Curley, Edwin. "Kissinger, Spinoza, and Genghis Khan." In *The Cambridge Companion to Spinoza*. Edited by Don Garrett. Cambridge: Cambridge University Press, 1995.

Dean, Jodi. *The Communist Horizon*. London: Verso, 2012.

Del Lucchese, Filippo. "Sedition and Modernity: Division as Politics and Conflict as Freedom in Machiavelli and Spinoza." *Borderlands* 6, no. 3 (2007).

———. *Conflict, Power, and Multitude in Machiavelli and Spinoza*. London and New York: Continuum. 2009.

———. "Spinoza and Constituent Power." *Contemporary Political Theory* 15, no. 2 (2016): 182–204.

Deleuze, Gilles. *Différence et répetition*. Paris: Presses universitaires de France, 1968.

———. *Spinoza: Practical Philosophy*. Translated by Robert Hurley. San Francisco: City Lights Books, 1988.

———. *Expressionism in Philosophy: Spinoza*. Translated by Martin Joughin. New York: Zone Books, 1992.

———. *Difference and Repetition*. Translated by Paul Patton. New York: Columbia University Press, 1994.

Den Uyl, Douglas J. *Power, State and Freedom: An Interpretation of Spinoza's Political Philosophy*. Assen, Netherlands: Van Gorcum, 1983.

Denvir, Daniel. "Scholar Keeanga-Yamahtta Taylor on the 'Exciting' Movement for Black Lives Platform," *Salon*, August 24, 2016. http://www.salon.com/2016/08/24/scholar-keeanga-yamahtta-taylor-on-the-exciting-movement-for-black-lives-platform/

Derrida, Jacques. "Force of Law: the Mystical Foundation of Authority." In *Deconstruction and the Possibility of Justice*. Edited by Drucilla Cornell et al. London: Routledge, 1992.

———. *Rogues: Two Essays on Reason*. Translated by Pascale-Anne Brault and Michael Naas. Stanford, CA: Stanford University Press, 2005.

Dobbs-Weinstein, Idit. "The Power of Prejudice and the Force of Law: Spinoza's Critique of Religion and Its Heirs." *Epoché, A Journal for the History of Philosophy* 7, no. 1 (2002): 51–70.

———. *Spinoza's Critique of Religion and Its Heirs*. Cambridge: Cambridge University Press, 2015.

Douglas, Alexander. "The Affects." In *Spinoza: Basic Concepts*. Edited by Andre Santos Campos. Exeter, UK: Imprint Academic, 2015. Kindle edition.

Douzinas, Costas, and Slavoj Žižek, eds. *The Idea of Communism*. London: Verso, 2016.

Esposito, Roberto. *Bíos: Biopolitics and Philosophy*. Translated by Timothy Campbell. Stanford, CA: Stanford University Press, 2009.

———. *Immunitas*. Translated by Zakiya Hanifa. London: Polity Press, 2011.

———. *Terms of the Political.* Translated by Rhiannon Noel Welch. New York: Fordham University Press, 2012.

———. *The Third Person.* Translated by Zakiya Hanifa. London: Polity Press, 2012.

———. *Two: The Machine of Political Theology and the Place of Thought.* Translated by Zakiya Hanifa. New York: Fordham University Press, 2015.

Esposito, Roberto, and Timothy Campbell, "Interview." *Diacritics* 36, no. 2 (2006): 49–56.

Finnegan, William. *Barbarian Days: A Surfing Life.* New York: Penguin, 2015.

Flatto, David C. "Theocracy and the Rule of Law: A Novel Josephan Doctrine and Its Modern Misconceptions." *Dine Israel* 28 (2011): 5–30.

Fleming, Peter. *The Mythology of Work: How Capitalism Persists Despite Itself.* London: Pluto Press, 2015.

Foucault, Michel. "The Political Technology of Individuals." In *Power: Essential Works of Foucault, 1954–1984, Volume 3.* Edited by James D. Faubion. New York: New Press, 2002.

———. *Society Must Be Defended: Lectures at the Collège de France, 1975–76.* London: Picador, 2003.

———. *Security, Territory, Population: Lectures at the Collège de France, 1977–1978.* London: Picador, 2009.

Frijhoff, Willem, and Marijke Spies, eds. *Dutch Culture in a European Perspective, Volume 1. 1650: Hard-Won Unity.* Basingstoke: Palgrave Macmillan, 2004.

Garsten, Bryan. *Saving Persuasion: A Defense of Rhetoric and Judgment.* Cambridge, MA: Harvard University Press, 2009.

Garver, Eugene. "Spinoza on Constitutional Interpretation." *Law, Culture and the Humanities* 6, no. 2 (2010): 274–95.

Gatens, Moira, and Genevieve Lloyd. *Collective Imaginings: Spinoza, Past and Present.* London: Routledge, 1999.

Geuss, Raymond. *Politics and the Imagination.* Princeton, NJ: Princeton University Press, 2009.

Gilbert, Jeremy. *Common Ground: Democracy and Collectivity in an Age of Individualism.* London: Pluto Press, 2014.

Girard, René. "Mimesis and Violence." In *The Girard Reader.* Edited by James G. Williams. New York: Crossroad Herder, 1996.

———. "Triangular Desire." In *The Girard Reader.* Edited by James G. Williams. New York: Crossroad Herder, 1996.

Goldenbaum, Ursula. "Sovereignty and Obedience." In *The Oxford Handbook of Philosophy in Early Modern Europe.* Edited by Desmond M. Clarke and Catherine Wilson. Oxford: Oxford University Press, 2011.

Graeber, David. *The Democracy Project: A History, a Crisis, a Movement.* New York: Spiegel and Grau, 2013.

Grotius, Hugo. *The Freedom of the Seas; or, The Right Which Belongs to the Dutch to Take Part in the East Indian Trade.* Translated by Ralph Van Deman Magoffin. Oxford: Oxford University Press, 1916.

———. *De Iure Praedae.* Oxford: Clarendon Press, 1950.

Guattari, Félix. *The Three Ecologies.* Translated by Ian Pindar and Paul Sutton. London: Bloomsbury, 2008.

Habermas, Jürgen. *The Inclusion of the Other.* Edited by Ciaran Cronin and Pablo De Greiff. Cambridge, MA: MIT Press, 2000.

Hammill, Graham. *The Mosaic Constitution: Political Theology and Imagination from Machiavelli to Milton.* Chicago: University of Chicago Press, 2012.

Hardin, Garrett. "The Tragedy of the Commons." *Science* 162, no. 3859 (1968): 1243–48.

Hardt, Michael. "The Common in Communism." In *The Idea of Communism*. Edited by Costas Douzinas and Slavoj Žižek, 131–44. London: Verso, 2010.

Hardt, Michael, and Antonio Negri. *Empire*. Cambridge, MA: Harvard University Press, 2000.

———. *Multitude: War and Democracy in the Age of Empire*. New York: Penguin, 2004.

———. *Commonwealth*. Cambridge, MA: Belknap Press of Harvard University Press, 2009.

———. *Declaration*. New York: Argo-Navis, 2012.

Harvey, David. *Rebel Cities: From the Right to the City to the Urban Revolution*. London: Verso, 2013.

Harvey, David, Michael Hardt, and Antonio Negri. "Commonwealth: An Exchange." *Artforum* 48, no. 3 (2009): 210–21.

Havercroft, Jonathan, and David Owen. "Soul-Blindness, Police Orders and Black Lives Matter: Wittgenstein, Cavell, and Rancière." *Political Theory* 44, no. 6 (2016): 739–63.

Hobbes, Thomas. *Man and Citizen (De Homine* and *De Cive)*. Edited by Bernard Gert. Indianapolis: Hackett, 1991.

———. *Leviathan*. Edited by Richard Tuck. Cambridge: Cambridge University Press, 1996.

Holmes, Stephen. "Constitutions and Constitutionalism." In *The Oxford Handbook of Comparative Constitutional Law*. Edited by Michel Rosenfeld and András Sajó, 189–216. Oxford: Oxford University Press, 2012.

Honig, Bonnie. *Public Things: Democracy in Disrepair*. New York: Fordham University Press, 2017.

Horkheimer, Max, and Theodor Adorno. *Dialectic of Enlightenment*. Translated by Edmund Jephcott. Stanford, CA: Stanford University Press, 2007.

Hunter, Ian. *Rival Enlightenments: Civil and Metaphysical Philosophy in Early Modern Germany*. Cambridge: Cambridge University Press, 2001.

Israel, Jonathan. *Radical Enlightenment: Philosophy and the Making of Modernity, 1650–1750*. Oxford: Oxford University Press, 2001.

———. *Enlightenment Contested: Philosophy, Modernity, and the Emancipation of Man, 1670–1752*. Oxford: Oxford University Press, 2006.

———. "Introduction." In Benedictus de Spinoza, *Theological-Political Treatise*. Edited by Jonathan Israel and translated by Michael Silverthorne and Jonathan Israel. Cambridge: Cambridge University Press, 2007.

———. *A Revolution of the Mind: Radical Enlightenment and the Intellectual Origins of Modern Democracy*. Princeton, NJ: Princeton University Press, 2009.

Israël, Nicolas. *Spinoza: Le temps de la vigilance*. Paris: Payot, 2001.

James, Susan. "Law and Sovereignty in Spinoza's Politics." In *Feminist Interpretations of Benedict Spinoza*. Edited by Moira Gatens, 211–28. University Park: Pennsylvania State University Press, 2009.

———. *Spinoza on Philosophy, Religion, and Politics: The Theologico-Political Treatise*. Oxford: Oxford University Press, 2012.

Jaquet, Chantal. *Spinoza ou la prudence*. Paris: Quintette, 2004.

———. *Les transclasses ou la non-reproduction*. Paris: Presses universitaires de France, 2014.

Klein, Naomi. *This Changes Everything: Capitalism vs. the Climate*. New York: Simon & Schuster, 2015.

Koekkoek, René. "Spinoza's Conception of Political Liberty and the Dutch Republic, 1650–1677." Master's thesis, Universiteit Utrecht, 2010.

Kompridis, Nikolas. *Critique and Disclosure: Critical Theory between Past and Future*. Cambridge, MA: MIT Press, 2011.

Koselleck, Reinhart. *Critique and Crisis: Enlightenment and the Pathogenesis of Modern Society.* Cambridge, MA: MIT Press, 1998.

Laborde, Cécile. *Critical Republicanism: The Hijab Controversy and Political Philosophy.* Oxford: Oxford University Press, 2008.

———. "Liberal Neutrality, Religion, and the Good." In *Religion, Secularism, and Constitutional Democracy.* Edited by Jean Cohen and Cécile Laborde, 249–72. New York: Columbia University Press, 2016.

Lærke, Mogens. "Jus Circa Sacra: Elements of Theological Politics in 17th-Century Rationalism: From Hobbes and Spinoza to Leibniz." *Distinktion: Scandinavian Journal of Social Theory* 6, no. 1 (2005): 41–64.

———. *Leibniz lecteur de Spinoza: La genèse d'une opposition complèxe.* Paris: Honoré Champion, 2008.

Lagioia, Nicola. "Writing Is an Act of Pride: A Conversation with Elena Ferrante." *The New Yorker,* May 19, 2016. http://www.newyorker.com/books/page-turner/writing-is-an-act-of-pride-a-conversation-with-elena-ferrante.

Lagrée, Jacqueline. *La raison ardente: Religion naturelle et raison au XVIIe siècle.* Paris: Vrin, 1991.

———. "Irrationality with or without Reason: An Analysis of Chapter XV of the *Tractatus Theologico-Politicus.*" In *The Books of Nature and Scripture.* Edited by James E. Force and Richard Popkin, 25–38. Dordrecht: Kluwer, 1994.

———. *Spinoza et le débat réligieux: Lectures du* Traité théologico-politique. Rennes: Presses universitaires de Rennes, 2004.

Laursen, John Christian. "Spinoza on Toleration: Arming the State and Reining in the Magistrate." In *Difference and Dissent: Theories of Tolerance in Medieval and Early Modern Europe.* Edited by John Christian Laursen and Cary J. Nederman. New York: Rowman & Littlefield, 1996.

Lazzeri, Christian. *Droit, pouvoir et liberté: Spinoza critique de Hobbes.* Paris: Presses universitaires de France, 1998.

LeBlanc, Guillaume, and Pascal Sévérac. "Spinoza et la normativité du *conatus.* Lecture canguilhemienne." In *Spinoza et la norme.* Edited by Jacqueline Lagrée. Besançon: Presses universitaires de Besançon, 1998.

Lefebvre, Alexandre. *The Image of Law: Deleuze, Bergson, Spinoza.* Stanford, CA: Stanford University Press, 2008.

Leibniz, G. W. "The Controversy of Controversies." In *G. W. Leibniz: The Art of Controversies.* Edited by M. Dascal et al., 7–24. Dordrecht: Springer, 2006.

Lemke, Thomas. *Biopolitics: An Advanced Introduction.* New York: NYU Press, 2011.

Lemm, Vanessa. "Nietzsche, *Einverleibung* and the Politics of Immunity." *International Journal of Philosophical Studies* 21, no. 1 (2013): 3–19.

Levene, Nancy K. *Spinoza's Revelation: Religion, Democracy, and Reason.* Cambridge: Cambridge University Press, 2004.

Levinson, Marjorie. "A Motion and a Spirit: Romancing Spinoza." *Studies in Romanticism* 46, no. 4 (2007): 367–408.

Locke, John. *Second Treatise of Government.* Edited by C. B. Macpherson. Indianapolis: Hackett, 1980.

Lordon, Frédéric. *Willing Slaves of Capital: Spinoza and Marx on Desire.* London: Verso, 2014.

Loughlin, Martin. *The Idea of Public Law.* Oxford: Oxford University Press, 2004.

———. "What Is Constitutionalisation?" In *The Twilight of Constitutionalism?* Edited by Petra Dobner and Martin Loughlin, 47–72. Oxford: Oxford University Press, 2011.

———. "The Concept of Constituent Power." *European Journal of Political Theory* 13, no. 2 (2014): 218–37.

Macherey, Pierre. *Introduction à l'Ethique de Spinoza: La deuxième partie, La réalité mentale.* Paris: Presses universitaires de France, 1997.

Machiavelli, Niccolo. *Discourses on Livy.* Translated by Harvey Mansfield and Nathan Tarcov. Chicago: University of Chicago Press, 1998.

Maimonides, Moses. *The Guide of the Perplexed.* Translated by Shlomo Pines, edited by Leo Strauss. Chicago: University of Chicago Press, 1963.

Markell, Patchen. "The Moment Has Passed: Power after Arendt." In *Radical Futures Past: Untimely Political Theory.* Edited by Rom Coles, Mark Reinhardt, and George Shulman, 114–43. Lexington: University of Kentucky Press, 2014.

Martel, James. "Division Is Common." *South Atlantic Quarterly* 113, no. 4 (2014): 701–11.

Matheron, Alexandre. *Individu et communauté chez Spinoza.* Paris: Les Éditions de Minuit, 1969.

———. "The Theoretical Function of Democracy in Spinoza and Hobbes." In *The New Spinoza.* Edited by Warren Montag and Ted Stolze, 207–18. Minneapolis: University of Minnesota Press, 1997.

McIlwain, Charles Howard. *Constitutionalism: Ancient and Modern.* Indianapolis: Liberty Fund Inc., 2010.

McKinnon, Andrew M. "Elective Affinities of the Protestant Ethic: Weber and the Chemistry of Capitalism." *Sociological Theory* 28, no. 1 (2010): 108–26.

Meador, Daniel John. *Habeas Corpus and Magna Carta.* Charlottesville: University Press of Virginia, 1966.

Melamed, Abraham. *The Philosopher-King in Medieval and Renaissance Jewish Political Thought.* Edited by Lenn E. Goodman. Albany: State University of New York Press, 2003.

Mills, Catherine. "Biopolitics and Human Reproduction." In *The Routledge Handbook of Biopolitics.* Edited by Sergei Prozorov and Simona Rentea. Abingdon: Routledge, 2017. Kindle edition.

Mitchell, W. J. T. "Image, Space, Revolution: The Arts of Occupation." In *Occupy: Three Inquiries in Disobedience.* Edited by W. J. T. Mitchell, Bernard E. Harcourt, and Michael Taussig. Chicago: University of Chicago Press, 2013.

Montag, Warren. *Bodies, Masses, Power: Spinoza and His Contemporaries.* London: Verso, 1999.

Moreau, Pierre-François. *Spinoza: l'expérience et l'éternité.* Paris: Presses universitaires de France, 1994.

———. "Introduction." In Spinoza, *Traité Théologico-Politique.* Edited by Fokke Akkerman, Jacqueline Lagrée, and Pierre-François Moreau. Paris: Presses universitaires de France, 1999.

———. "The Necessary Incompleteness of the Republic," *Graduate Faculty Philosophy Faculty Journal* 23, no. 2 (2002): 145–53.

———. *Spinoza et le spinozisme.* Paris: Presses universitaires de France, 2003.

———. "La place de la politique dans l'*Éthique*." In *Spinoza: État et religion.* Lyon: ENS Éditions, 2005.

———. "Spinoza et le *jus circa sacra*." In *Spinoza: État et religion.* Lyon: ENS Éditions, 2005.

———. "La duperie de soi." In *Problèmes du Spinozisme.* Paris: J. Vrin, 2006.

———. "Le jugement." In *Problèmes du Spinozisme.* Paris: J. Vrin, 2006.

———. "Imitation of the Affects and Interhuman Relations." In *Spinoza's Ethics: A Collective Commentary*. Edited by Michael Hampe, Ursula Renz, and Robert Schnepf, 167–78. Leiden: Brill, 2011.

Morfino, Vittorio. *Plural Temporality: Transindividuality and the Aleatory between Spinoza and Althusser*. Chicago: Haymarket Books, 2015.

Morvan, Myriam. "Admiration dans le Spinozisme et fascination dans la psychanalyse." In *Spinoza et la psychanalyse*. Paris: Hermann, 2012.

Muhle, Maria. "A Genealogy of Biopolitics: The Notion of Life in Canguilhem and Foucault." In *The Government of Life: Foucault, Biopolitics, and Neoliberalism*. Edited by Vanessa Lemm and Miguel Vatter, 77–97. New York: Fordham University Press, 2014.

Nadler, Steven. *Spinoza: A Life*. Cambridge: Cambridge University Press, 2001.

———. "Spinoza's Theory of Divine Providence: Rationalist Solutions, Jewish Sources." *Mededelingen vanwege Het Spinozahuis 87*. Budel, Netherlands: Damon, 2005.

———. *A Book Forged in Hell: Spinoza's Scandalous Treatise and the Birth of the Secular Age*. Princeton, NJ: Princeton University Press, 2011.

———. "On Spinoza's 'Free Man.'" *Journal of the American Philosophical Association* 1, no. 1 (2015): 103–20.

Negri, Antonio. *The Savage Anomaly: The Power of Spinoza's Metaphysics and Politics*. Translated by Michael Hardt. Minneapolis: University of Minnesota Press, 2003.

———. *The Subversive Spinoza: (Un)contemporary Variations*. Edited by Timothy S. Murphy. Manchester: Manchester University Press, 2004.

———. *Empire and Beyond*. London: Polity Press, 2008.

———. *Spinoza for Our Time: Politics and Postmodernity*. Translated by William McCuaig. New York: Columbia University Press, 2013.

Nelson, Eric. *The Hebrew Republic: Jewish Sources and the Transformation of European Political Thought*. Cambridge, MA: Harvard University Press, 2011.

Oakeshott, Michael. *On History and Other Essays*. Totowa: Barnes & Noble, 1983.

Ochoa Espejo, Paulina. *The Time of Popular Sovereignty: Process and the Democratic State*. University Park: Pennsylvania State University Press, 2011.

Ostrom, Elinor. *Governing the Commons: The Evolution of Institutions for Collective Action*. Cambridge: Cambridge University Press, 1990.

———. "Crossing the Great Divide: Coproduction, Synergy and Development." *World Development* 24, no. 6 (1996): 1073–1087.

Ovid. *Amores*. Translated by Grant Showerman. Cambridge, MA: Harvard University Press, 1977.

Pettit, Philip. *Republicanism: A Theory of Freedom and Government*. Oxford: Clarendon Press, 1997.

———. *On the People's Terms: A Republican Theory and Model of Democracy*. Cambridge: Cambridge University Press, 2013.

Popkin, Richard. *Spinoza*. London: Oneworld, 2013. Kindle edition.

Prozorov, Sergei. "Conclusion: Whither Biopolitics? Current Tendencies and Directions of Future Research." In *The Routledge Handbook of Biopolitics*. Edited by Sergei Prozorov and Simona Rentea. Abingdon: Routledge, 2017. Kindle edition.

Purdy, Jedidiah. "What Trump's Rise Means for Democracy." *Dissent*, May 4, 2016. https://www.dissentmagazine.org/online_articles/andrew-sullivan-trump-concern-trolling-for-democracy.

Rancière, Jacques. *Disagreement: Politics and Philosophy*. Translated by Julie Rose. Minneapolis: University of Minnesota Press, 2004.

———. *Hatred of Democracy*. Translated by Steven Corcoran. London: Verso, 2009.

———. *Dissensus: On Politics and Aesthetics*. Edited and translated by Steven Corcoran. London and New York: Continuum, 2010.

———. "The Thinking of Dissensus: Politics and Aesthetics." In *Reading Rancière*. Edited by Paul Bowman and Richard Stamp. London: Bloomsbury, 2011. Kindle edition.

———. "Occupation." *Political Concepts: A Critical Lexicon* 3, no. 5 (2016). https://www.politicalconcepts.org/occupation-jacques-ranciere/

Rawls, John. *Political Liberalism*. New York: Columbia University Press, 2005.

Read, Jason. *The Politics of Transindividuality*. London: Brill, 2015.

Reiss, Timothy J. *Mirages of the Selfe*. Stanford, CA: Stanford University Press, 2002.

Rosanvallon, Pierre. *Counter-Democracy: Politics in an Age of Distrust*. Translated by Arthur Goldhammer. Cambridge: Cambridge University Press, 2008.

Rosenthal, Michael. "Why Spinoza Chose the Hebrews: The Exemplary Function of Prophecy in the *Theological-Political Treatise*." In *Jewish Themes in Spinoza's Philosophy*. Edited by Heidi M. Ravven and Lenn E. Goodman, 225–60. Albany: State University of New York Press, 2002.

Ross, Kristin. *Communal Luxury: The Political Imaginary of the Paris Commune*. London: Verso, 2015.

Ross, Kristin, and Manu Goswami. "The Meaning of the Paris Commune." *Jacobin*, May 4, 2015. https://www.jacobinmag.com/2015/05/kristin-ross-communal-luxury-paris-commune/

Rousseau, Jean-Jacques. *The Social Contract*. Translated by Maurice Cranston. London: Penguin, 1968.

Ruddick, Susan. "The Politics of Affect: Spinoza in the Work of Negri and Deleuze." *Theory, Culture and Society* 27, no. 4 (2010): 21–45.

Rutherford, Donald. "Spinoza's Conception of Law: Metaphysics and Ethics." In *Spinoza's Theological-Political Treatise: A Critical Guide*. Edited by Yitzhak Y. Melamed and Michael A. Rosenthal, 143–67. Cambridge: Cambridge University Press, 2010.

Santner, Eric. *The Royal Remains: The People's Two Bodies and the Endgames of Sovereignty*. Chicago: University of Chicago Press, 2011.

Schmitt, Carl. *The Leviathan in the State Theory of Thomas Hobbes*. Chicago: University of Chicago Press, 2008.

Scholem, Gershom. *The Messianic Idea in Judaism*. New York: Schocken Books, 1971.

Sharp, Hasana. *Spinoza and the Politics of Renaturalization*. Chicago: University of Chicago Press, 2011.

———. "Eve's Perfection: Spinoza on Sexual (In)Equality," *Journal of the History of Philosophy* 50, no. 4 (2012): 559–80.

Silk, Mark. "Numa Pompilius and the Idea of Civil Religion in the West." *Journal of the American Academy of Religion* 72, no. 4 (2004): 863–96.

Simondon, Gilbert. *L'individuation psychique et collective*. Paris: Flammarion, 2007.

Skinner, Quentin. *Liberty before Liberalism*. Cambridge: Cambridge University Press, 1997.

———. "A Genealogy of the Modern State." *Proceedings of the British Academy* 162 (2009): 325–70.

Smith, Jason E. "Preface: The Multitude and the Moving Train." In Vittorio Morfino, *Plural Temporality: Transindividuality and the Aleatory between Spinoza and Althusser*. Chicago: Haymarket Books, 2015.

Smith, Steven B. *Spinoza, Liberalism, and the Question of Jewish Identity*. New Haven, CT: Yale University Press, 1997.

———. *Spinoza's Book of Life: Freedom and Redemption in the* Ethics. New Haven, CT: Yale University Press, 2003.

Steinberg, Justin D. "Spinoza on Being *Sui Iuris* and the Republican Conception of Liberty," *History of European Ideas* 34, no. 3 (2008): 239–49.

———. "Spinoza's Political Philosophy." In *The Stanford Encyclopedia.* Edited by Edward N. Zalta, Spring 2009 Edition.

———. "Following a *Recta Ratio Vivendi*: The Practical Utility of Spinoza's Dictates of Reason." In *Essays on Spinoza's Ethical Theory.* Edited by Matthew J. Kisner and Andrew Youpa, 178–96. Cambridge: Cambridge University Press, 2014.

Stewart, Michael A. "*Libertas Philosophandi*: From Natural to Speculative Philosophy." *Australian Journal of Politics* 40 (1994): 29–46.

Strauss, Leo. "How to Begin to Study *The Guide of the Perplexed.*" In *The Guide of the Perplexed.* Edited by Shlomo Pines, xi-lvi. Chicago: University of Chicago Press, 1963.

———. *Philosophy and Law. Contributions to the Understanding of Maimonides and His Predecessors.* Albany: State University of New York Press, 1995.

———. *Spinoza's Critique of Religion.* Translated by E. M. Sinclair. Chicago: University of Chicago Press, 1997.

Sullivan, Andrew. "Democracies End When They Are Too Democratic." *New York Magazine,* May 1, 2016. http://nymag.com/daily/intelligencer/2016/04/america-tyranny-donald-trump.html.

Syros, Vasileios. "Founders and Kings versus Orators: Medieval and Early Modern Views on the Origins of Social Life." *Viator* 42, no. 1 (2011): 383–408.

Taek-Gwang Lee, Alex and Slavoj Žižek, eds. *The Idea of Communism 3: The Seoul Conference.* London: Verso, 2016.

Taylor, Keeanga-Yamahtta. *From #BlackLivesMatter to Black Liberation.* Chicago: Haymarket Books, 2016.

Te Brake, Wayne. *Shaping History: Ordinary People in European Politics, 1500–1700.* Berkeley: University of California Press, 1998.

Terence. *Phormio, or the Scheming Parasite.* Edited by Henry Thomas Riley. New York: Harper & Brothers, 1874. http://www.perseus.tufts.edu/hopper/text?doc=Perseus%3atext%3a1999.02.0117.

Trigano, Shmuel. "The Politics of the Ban of Representation." In *Crediting God: Sovereignty and Religion in the Age of Global Capitalism.* Edited by Miguel Vatter, 67–82. New York: Fordham University Press, 2011.

Urbinati, Nadia. *Democracy Disfigured: Opinion, Truth, and the People.* Cambridge, MA: Harvard University Press, 2014.

Van Bunge, Wiep. "Philosophy." In *Dutch Culture in a European Perspective, Volume 1. 1650: Hard-Won Unity.* Edited by Willem Frijhoff and Marijke Spies. Basingstoke: Palgrave Macmillan, 2004.

———. *Spinoza Past and Present: Essays on Spinoza, Spinozism, and Spinoza Scholarship.* Leiden: Brill, 2012.

Van Gelderen, Martin. "Arminian Trouble: Calvinist Debates on Freedom." In *Freedom and the Construction of Europe, Volume 1: Religious and Constitutional Liberties.* Cambridge: Cambridge University Press, 2013.

Vardoulakis, Dimitris. *Sovereignty and Its Other: Toward the Dejustification of Violence.* New York: Fordham University Press, 2013.

Vatter, Miguel. "Legality and Resistance: Arendt and Negri on Constituent Power." In *The Philosophy of Antonio Negri: Volume 2*. Edited by Timothy S. Murphy and Abdul-Karim Mustapha, 52–84. London: Pluto Press, 2007.

———. "The Idea of Public Reason and the Reason of the State: Schmitt and Rawls on the Political." *Political Theory* 36, no. 2 (2008): 239–71.

———. "Biopolitics: From Surplus Value to Surplus Life." *Theory and Event* 12, no. 2 (2009).

———, ed. *Crediting God: Sovereignty and Religion in the Age of Global Capitalism*. New York: Fordham University Press, 2011.

———. *Machiavelli's The Prince*. London: Bloomsbury, 2013.

———. *Between Form and Event: Machiavelli's Theory of Political Freedom*. New York: Fordham University Press, 2014.

———. "Republics Are a Species of State: Machiavelli and the Genealogy of the Modern State." *Social Research* 81, no. 1 (2014): 217–41.

———. *The Republic of the Living: Biopolitics and the Critique of Civil Society*. New York: Fordham University Press, 2014.

———. "Law and Life beyond Incorporation: Agamben, Highest Poverty and the Papal Legal Revolution." In *Agamben and Radical Politics*. Edited by Daniel McLoughlin. Edinburgh: Edinburgh University Press, 2016.

———. "Community, Life, and Subjectivity in Italian Biopolitics." In *The Routledge Handbook of Biopolitics*. Edited by Sergei Prozorov and Simona Rentea. Abingdon: Routledge, 2017. Kindle edition.

———. "Machiavelli, 'Ancient Theology' and the Problem of Civil Religion." In *Machiavelli on Liberty and Conflict*. Edited by David C. Johnston, Nadia Urbinati, and Camila Vergara. Chicago: University of Chicago Press, 2017.

Wark, McKenzie. "How to Occupy an Abstraction." In *Telesthesia: Communication, Culture and Class*. London: Polity Press, 2012.

Weidenfeld, Matthew. "Comportment, not Cognition: Contributions to a Phenomenology of Judgment." *Contemporary Political Theory* 10, no. 2 (2011): 232–54.

Williams, Caroline. "'Subjectivity without the Subject': Thinking beyond the Subject with / through Spinoza." In *Spinoza beyond Philosophy*. Edited by Beth Lord, 11–27. Edinburgh: Edinburgh University Press, 2012.

Wirszubski, Chaim. *Libertas as a Political Idea at Rome during the Late Republic and Early Principate*. Cambridge: Cambridge University Press, 1950.

Wootton, David, ed. *Republicanism, Liberty, and Commercial Society, 1649–1776*. Stanford, CA: Stanford University Press, 1994.

Zerilli, Linda. "Value Pluralism and the Problem of Judgment: Farewell to Public Reason." *Political Theory* 40, no. 1 (2012): 6–31.

———. "Judgment." In *The Encyclopedia of Political Thought*. Edited by Michael T. Gibbons. Oxford: Blackwell, 2015.

———. *A Democratic Theory of Judgment*. Chicago: University of Chicago Press, 2016.

Žižek, Slavoj, ed. *The Idea of Communism 2: The New York Conference*. London: Verso, 2013.

Index